GUIDE TO CIVIL WAR BOOKS

An Annotated Selection of Modern Works on the War Between the States

Domenica M. Barbuto
Martha Kreisel

D1602125

American Library Association
Chicago and London
1996

The paper used in this publication meets the minimum requirements of American National Standard for Information Sciences—Permanence of Paper for Printed Library Materials, ANSI Z39.48-1992.⊚

Cover designed by Richmond A. Jones

Text designed by Dianne M. Rooney

Composed by Publishing Services, Inc. in Sabon and Gills Sans on Xyvision/L330

Printed on 50-pound Glatfelter B-06, a pH-neutral stock, and bound in 10-point C1S cover stock by McNaughton & Gunn Lithographers, Inc.

Illustrations on pages 166 and 183 courtesy of U.S. Army Military History Institute, Carlisle Barracks, Penn. Cover and all other text illustrations from *Ready-to-Use Authentic Civil War Illustrations,* selected and arranged by Carol Belanger Grafton (Dover, 1995) and *Civil War Etchings,* edited by William Forrest Dawson (Dover, 1994).

Library of Congress Cataloging-in-Publication Data

Barbuto, Domenica M., 1951–
    Guide to Civil War books : an annotated selection of modern works on the War Between the States / Domenica M. Barbuto, Martha Kreisel.
        p.   cm.
    Includes index.
    ISBN 0-8389-0672-9 (acid-free paper)
    1. United States—History—Civil War, 1861–1865—Bibliography. I. Kreisel, Martha, 1948– . II. Title.
    Z1242.B18   1996
    [E468]
    016.9737—dc20   95-40623

Printed in the United States of America.

00 99 98 97 96   5 4 3 2 1

CONTENTS

Contents

CITATION SOURCES

ALI	American Literature
AMQ	American Quarterly
AHR	American Historical Review
APS	American Political Science Review
CHO	Choice
CRL	College and Research Libraries
CWH	Civil War History
CWT	Civil War Times Illustrated
FHQ	Florida Historical Quarterly
GHQ	Georgia Historical Quarterly
HIS	Historian
HRN	History Reviews of New Books
JAH	Journal of American History
JAS	Journal of American Studies
JEH	Journal of Economic History
JMH	Journal of Military History
JMI	Journal of Mississippi History
JSH	Journal of Social History
JSO	Journal of Southern History
LAH	Louisiana History
LAT	Los Angeles Times Book Review
LIJ	Library Journal
MIA	Military Affairs
MIR	Military History

NCH	North Carolina Historical Review
NCL	Nineteenth Century Literature
NYR	New York Review of Books
NYT	New York Times Book Review
PUW	Publishers Weekly
RAH	Reviews in American History
RKH	Register of the Kentucky Historical Society
RSR	Reference Services Review
SCH	South Carolina Historical Magazine
SHR	Southern History Review
THQ	Tennessee Historical Quarterly
VMH	Virginia Magazine of History and Biography
VQR	Virginia Quarterly Review
WVH	West Virginia History

PREFACE

Guide to Civil War Books will be of interest to Civil War enthusiasts as well as to students, teachers, and librarians. The book will be a help in locating information about a specific person, battle, or campaign, as well as social or political conditions during the Civil War period. Teachers and librarians will find it useful when developing assignments or guiding students to sources for their research.

This resource guide brings together books of general interest about the Civil War published during the past twenty years. The selected works address all issues of the war, including causes of the conflict, secession, battles and campaigns, race and slavery, biographies and personal narratives, and Reconstruction. In selecting among thousands of possible titles, the authors consulted resources such as bibliographies and subject-specific indexes, both print and computerized, such as *America History and Life*.

Unlike other Civil War bibliographies, this work not only supplies basic bibliographic information about the selected titles, but also lists sources of printed reviews, providing a valuable source of information for those evaluating the relative merits of books. With few exceptions, the selection of reviews includes citations to scholarly review media. The review citation provides the name of the periodical, the volume number, the date of publication, and the page or pages where the review may be found. The publication titles are cited by three-letter abbreviations, a list of which precedes this preface.

The guide is arranged by subject, and within each subject category the materials are arranged alphabetically. Each entry is numbered and includes a brief annotation. In addition to relating the scope of the book, where appropriate, the annotation provides information about special features, such as maps or tables, and about supplementary material in appendixes.

There are three indexes: author-editor, subject, and title. The numbers listed in the indexes correspond to the numbers assigned to the entries.

We wish to thank our colleagues in the Joan and Donald E. Axinn Library for their interest, encouragement, and support during this project, particularly Elena Cevallos, Charles Secter, and Janet Wagner. The staff of the Axinn Library Interlibrary Loan Department, Maureen Brown, Maureen Hough, and Sonia McCarron, was, as always, especially helpful in assisting us in securing materials. Special thanks to Frances and Attilia Barbuto, Sara Elizabeth Kreisel, and Amanda and Ken Kaplan.

Much has been written on the Civil War. The authors hope that this book will help users quickly locate the recent literature best suited to specific projects and interests.

Art and the War

001 *The Civil War Sketchbook of Charles Ellery Stedman, Surgeon, United States Navy.* Biography and commentary by Jim Dan Hill. San Rafael, Calif.: Presidio Press, 1976. xvi, 218 pp. : ill. Includes index and references.

ISBN: 0-891-41001-5   LC: 76-004164

An astute observer and an artist of some ability, Dr. Charles Ellery Stedman served aboard the blockader *Huron* on patrol along the coasts of Georgia and South Carolina, on the monitor *Nahant* during the battle of Charleston Harbor, and on the supply ship *Circassian* operating in the Gulf of Mexico. Stedman was a narrative artist who had a sharp eye for significant, human-interest details. His caricatures are laden with the "substance of history." Serving aboard ship during this extraordinary period in naval history---the transition from sail to steam and from wood to metals—Stedman was able to portray the impact of this transition on the daily lives of Civil War sailors. In addition to the caricatures of men aboard ship, some wonderful sketches of ships in battle are also included. The drawings were made in 1865 from sketches taken during the war and from memory. They were compiled into an album in 1884 for the State of Massachusetts Commandery, Military Order of the Loyal Legion of the United States. The captions originally used by Dr. Stedman have been retained in their original form to preserve the original intent of the artist. A glossary of naval terms is included. Jim Dan Hill, a Navy enlisted man—merchant sailor, and a member of the Secretary of the Navy's Advisory Committee on Naval History—was uniquely qualified to prepare the commentary that accompanies the Stedman drawings. Hill uses contemporary sources, such as letters from Stedman, to fit the drawings into a proper historical sequence. He discusses Stedman's early life and the background of the action Stedman saw, the capabilities of the ships that Stedman served on, and the laws and customs of the Navy.

Reviewed in: JAH   64 (Sept. 77) 442

002   Neely, Mark E., Jr., Harold Holzer, and Gabor S. Boritt. *The Confederate Image: Prints of the Lost Cause*. Chapel Hill, N.C.: University of North Carolina Press, 1987. xiv, 257 pp. : ill., photographs. Includes index and bibliography.

ISBN: 0-8078-1742-2   LC: 86-30797

This work examines the popular lithographs and engravings that were produced during and after the Civil War. These works of art, which were highly valued by Southerners, helped revive and sustain the Southern identity after the collapse of the Confederacy. A major portion of the book is devoted to an examination of portraits of the "Immortal Three"—Robert E. Lee, Thomas "Stonewall" Jackson, and Jefferson Davis—the subjects of the majority of the prints produced at the time. Many of the prints that are reproduced in this volume are familiar to present-day readers. They come from Currier and Ives collections and from the *Southern Illustrated News,* which produced most of the wartime engravings of Confederate military heroes. Most of the reproductions, however, are of rare engravings from private collections. The introduction is a discussion of one of the most famous lithographs of the period, *The Burial of Latane*. Each chapter begins with an essay that provides a perspective for the highlighted works of art. A useful bibliography and index of illustrations are included.

Reviewed in: GHQ   72 (Fall 88) 561–562
                JAH   75 (Sept. 88) 623–624
                JSO   55 (Feb. 89) 131–133
                NCH   65 (Jan. 88) 104–105
                THQ   47 (Winter 88) 237–238
                VMH   96 (Apr. 88) 232–233

003   Sweet, Timothy. *Traces of War: Poetry, Photography, and the Crisis of the Union*. Baltimore, Md.: Johns Hopkins University Press, 1990. x, 240 pp. : ill. Includes index and bibliography.

ISBN: 0-8018-395-99   LC: 89-38436

Focusing on five texts, Sweet examines how poetry and photography could reconstruct and legitimatize the Union, "sanitizing" its horrors. The book is not for the casual reader; it requires close reading. The texts that are examined are Walt Whitman's *Drum-Taps* (1865) and *Sequel to Drum-Taps* (1865–1866), Alexander Gardner's *Photographic Sketch Book of the Civil War* (1866), George Barnard's *Photographic Views of Sherman's Campaign* (1866), and Herman Melville's *Battle-Pieces* (1866). One must read this book carefully for its larger meaning. According to Sweet, Whitman, Gardner, and Barnard sought the tradition of the pastoral and the picturesque to restore the nation and heal the wounds of war. Sweet sees Melville as critical of the naturalizing of war and as one whose poetry set forth images of chaos and disruption. Whitman and others distanced themselves from the war, prompting Sweet's inquiry into the literature of the period. Sweet notes the romanticization of war in the poetry as contrasting with the representation in the photographs and private diaries and journals of the men who saw war firsthand. Sweet explores the interconnection between the artistic and the political.

Reviewed in: AMQ   43 (Sept. 91) 510–517

004   Wood, Peter H., and Karen C. C. Dalton. *Winslow Homer's Images of Blacks: The Civil War and Reconstruction Years.* Austin, Tex.: University of Texas Press, 1988. 144 pp. : ill., photographs.

ISBN: 0-292-7904-3   LC: 88-26629

During the war, Winslow Homer periodically visited the Union Army encampments in Virginia, often sketching and painting the blacks who were there. Over time, Homer's depiction of blacks in his works became increasingly sympathetic until eventually they were portrayed as citizens of significance. Eventually, Homer began to portray women and children in his works. This book is the catalog for an exhibition that was arranged in 1989 and displayed in Richmond, Raleigh, and Houston. In addition to forty-one works by Homer, Wood and Dalton have included works by other artists to help place Homer and his work in context. The text is supplemented with a chronology of Winslow Homer.

Reviewed in: JSO   56 (Aug. 90) 544–546
                  VMH   97 (July 89) 404

Assassination of Abraham Lincoln

005 Hanchett, William. *The Lincoln Murder Conspiracies*. Urbana, Ill.: University of Illinois Press, 1983. 303 pp. : ill., photographs. Includes index, bibliography, and references.

ISBN: 0-252-01046-9   LC: 83-1065

Hanchett begins with a brief overview of recent books about Lincoln's death. He attempts to put the assassination in focus by relating it to the bitter disputes that were responsible for it: secession, fighting, political arrests, emancipation, and the tactics of total war. Hanchett also traces the formulation and influence of various interpretations of the assassination and speculates on how these have altered our perception of what happened. He contends that the assassination was sensationalized because Booth was not captured alive and never had the opportunity to tell his own story.

Reviewed in: AHR   89 (Dec. 84) 1395
                JAS   19 (Aug. 85) 292

006 Turner, Thomas Reed. *Beware the People Weeping: Public Opinion and the Assassination of Abraham Lincoln*. Baton Rouge, La.: Louisiana State University Press, 1982. xvi, 265 pp. : ill. Includes index and references.

ISBN: 0-8071-7722-6   LC: 81-14252

There have been many conspiracy theories regarding the death of Abraham Lincoln. Some believed it was the Confederates, including Jefferson Davis, or Andrew Johnson or Northerners or even Lincoln's secretary of war, Edwin M. Stanton. Turner tries to place these changes in the historical context and public opinion of 1865 rather than with the guide of hindsight. Turner goes further, contending that it would not have been illogical for the Confederates to plan the assassination, nor would the execution of Mary Surratt have been inappropriate for the times. Numerous photographs and prints of the supposed conspirators are included. Turner states that he was more concerned with understanding the events as they actually happened than trying to interpret them. He reexamines the newspapers, letters, and sermons that dealt with the assassination and the conspiracy trials, as well as the transcripts of the trial itself, to test the validity of the conspiracy theories in view of contemporary events.

Reviewed in:	AHR	88 (Oct. 83) 1070
	CHO	20 (Oct. 82) 341
	JAS	18 (Apr. 84) 115
	JSO	48 (Nov. 82) 587
	LIJ	107 (Apr. 82) 728

007 Weichmann, Louis J. *A True History of the Assassination of Abraham Lincoln and the Conspiracy of 1865.* Edited by Floyd E. Risvold. New York: Alfred A. Knopf, 1975. xxxii, xvi, 492 pp. : ill., photographs. Includes index and references.

ISBN: 0-394-49319-2   LC: 74-21278

Louis Weichmann, a twenty-three-year-old clerk in the War Department, was a boarder in Mary Surratt's house during the time that John Wilkes Booth and his coconspirators were meeting in the house to plan the assassination of Abraham Lincoln. Weichmann and John M. Lloyd were the government's two principal witnesses during the trial. Weichmann knew many of the participants personally; and although much of his testimony was circumstantial, he proved to be a reliable witness. After the trial, Weichmann left Washington, D.C., to work in the Philadelphia Customshouse. In 1886 he moved to Anderson, Indiana, where he opened a stenographic school. It was while he was in Indiana that Weichmann wrote his vivid account of the conspiracy that led to Lincoln's death, in part to prove that he had been telling the truth during the earlier trials. Weichmann's account is significant because it is the only one kept by a participant who was intimately associated with the conspirators.

Reviewed in:	CHO	12 (Feb. 76) 1624
	JAH	63 (June 76) 137
	JSO	42 (May 76) 288–289
	RKH	74 (July 76) 247–248
	VQR	52 (Winter 76) 18

5

Battles and Campaigns

008   Adams, Michael C. *Our Masters the Rebels: A Speculation on Union Military Failure in the East, 1861–1865.* Cambridge, Mass.: Harvard University Press, 1978. x, 256 pp. Includes index and references.

ISBN: 0-7837-2213-3   LC: 78-017107

Adams carefully considers the many traditional explanations for the military result of the Civil War and the reasons for the difference in operation of the Eastern and Western theaters. Fostered by stereotypes and upheld by Northern perceptions, the Northerners with their industrial background perceived themselves as inferior to the genteel Southerners. The author compares the North—wealthier, more industrialized, and possessing the better of the transportation systems—to the South, which chose "to fight a conventional war in the face of a stronger opponent." Adams reassesses the thought that Union victory was merely the result of numerical advantage, however, and considers alternative explanations and connections among culture, perceptions, combat. Further, he sees the well-bred and professional Northerner, in a true crisis, as lacking sufficient "faith in democracy and industrial capitalism." Adams's main contribution lies not in the well-known arguments but in the connections between culture and combat. He reminds the reader that Civil War military history must be studied in the wider circle of currents that made up nineteenth-century America.

Reviewed in:	AHR	84 (Dec. 79) 1479
	HIS	42 (May 80) 514
	JAH	66 (Dec. 79) 658
	JAS	5 (Aug. 81) 281–282
	JSO	46 (Feb. 80) 118
	RAH	8 (March 80) 63

009 Bergeron, Arthur W., Jr. *Confederate Mobile.* Jackson, Miss.: University Press of Mississippi, 1991. xii, 271 pp. : ill., photographs, maps. Includes index, bibliography, and references.

ISBN: 0-87805-512-6   LC: 91-15776

This work offers a descriptive account of the role of the port of Mobile, Alabama, in the Confederacy's military strategy. Mobile was an important link in the South's transportation and supply networks, especially following the fall of New Orleans. After 1862 Mobile functioned as the only rail link between the states of Alabama and Mississippi, supplying agricultural and manufactured goods in both the Eastern and Western theaters of war. Mobile also served as the principle base of operations for Confederate blockade runners in the southeastern Gulf region. Aware of the city's strategic importance, Confederate leaders carefully fortified Mobile against Union attacks. Most of this book is concerned with the construction of this defensive system, which included two forts—Morgan and Gaines. Bergeron claims that the fortifications surrounding Mobile ultimately proved so formidable that Union commanders hesitated to attack the city. The author provides limited coverage of the experiences of the city's population, which was forced to endure food shortages, among other hardships, notable because of the popular protests against them organized by the women of Mobile.

Reviewed in: CHO   29 (Apr. 92) 1287

JSO   59 (May 93) 377

010 Castel, Albert E. *Decision in the West: The Atlanta Campaign of 1864.* Maps by Laura Kriegstrom Poracsky. Lawrence, Kans.: University Press of Kansas, 1992. xvi, 665 pp. Includes index and references.

ISBN: 0-7006-0562-2   LC: 92-10882

Castel's treatment of the Atlanta campaign, not explored so fully since the nineteenth century, is written in the present tense, conveying the feeling of the battles and the campaigns as the commanders may have experienced them. The Atlanta campaign was a large and decisive operation—its outcome, according to Castel, decided as much by the generals' flaws as their capabilities. The appendixes include short essays: "Sherman and Stoneman," "Sherman, Stanley, Thomas, and the Second Battle of Jonesboro" (showing how faulty their memories were when writing their memoirs), and "McClellan and the War—If McClellan Had Replaced Lincoln as President."

Reviewed in: CHO   30 (Feb. 93) 1015

HIS   55 (Summer 93) 781

NYT   (March 14, 93) 10

011   *The Civil War Battlefield Guide.* Edited by Frances H. Kennedy. Boston: Houghton Mifflin, 1990. xv, 317 pp.

ISBN: 0-395-52282-X/0-395-5283-X(paper)   LC: 89-029619

With the increased need for concern over battlefield preservation, the Conservation Fund produced this guide to some sixty-five Civil War battlefields and campaigns. In one of the best primers on the battles of the Civil War, the individual field maps are drawn on modern-day U.S. geological-topographical maps with troops' movements clearly color keyed. The maps for the seven campaigns are reproductions of Library of Congress originals. In addition to the maps, detailed descriptions of the battles and campaigns by outstanding Civil War historians are provided. This volume also includes a comprehensive list of Civil War battles indicating the name of the site, the state it is located in, and the current management of the area (for example, the National Park Service or state park). Also included are a list of twenty-two Civil War battlefields that have been totally or partially lost forever, tables of combat strengths and casualties by battle for Union and Confederate forces, and a statistical comparison of dead and wounded troops in American service in nine wars. Several additional essays enhance the work: "Mapping the Civil War" (procedures used during the war by both Union and Confederate forces), "Preserving the Battlefields," "The Gettysburg Address," "Hallowed Ground" (with a plea for the preservation, and not the commercialization, of the fields in which so much blood was spilled as a historical legacy belonging to all Americans), "The Staff Ride and Civil War Battlefields" (the Staff Ride, a long-standing army tradition, through which a thoughtful and structured revisit of the battlefields helps connect today's officers to military history), and "'Making Free,' African Americans and the Civil War" (includes photographs of seven of the sixteen black soldiers and four black sailors who were Medal of Honor winners). A glossary of terms is appended, as are brief biographical sketches of the authors.

Reviewed in: CWH   37 (Jan. 91) 185–186

GHQ   75 (Spring 91) 164–165

012 Cooling, Benjamin Franklin. *Forts Henry and Donelson: The Key to the Confederate Heartland.* Knoxville, Tenn.: University of Tennessee Press, 1987. xiv, 354 pp. : ill., photographs, maps. Includes index and bibliography.

ISBN: 0-8704-953-80   LC: 87-5910

Historians have named the area comprising Tennessee, north-central Alabama, north-central Georgia, and northeastern Mississippi the "Heartland." The twin river forts, Henry and Donelson, on the Tennessee and Cumberland Rivers, were vital components in the Confederacy's attempt to maintain control of the Southern Heartland region. This narrative traces the role of the river from economic trade route to military access way for the Northern invasion of the South. Cooling, a former park historian at Fort Donelson, has written a definitive account of the battle for control of these strategic forts, which resulted in the first significant Union victory of the war in the winter of 1861–1862. Although the focus of the book is the surrender at Fort Donelson in February 1862, the scope of the narrative is broader than a simple campaign history. Cooling uses newspaper accounts, diaries, letters, contemporary drawings, and a variety of secondary sources to describe the socioeconomics of the region, the health conditions and medical care available to the combatants, and the reaction of civilians

Drummer boys

to the war. An added dimension to the narrative is the author's consideration of the psychological effects of winter combat. Cooling presents a detailed account of the rise of the Union "brown-water navy," which included ironclad ships and mortar rafts, and its combined operations with General Ulysses S. Grant's infantry. He contends that the Henry-Donelson campaign was an opportunity missed by the Confederacy to shatter the yet-untried Grant. Cooling believes that Grant triumphed because of his organized professionalism, which stood in stark contrast to the Confederacy's segmented leadership. The text is supplemented with clear maps.

Reviewed in:	AHR	94 (June 89) 851–852
	CWH	34 (Dec. 88) 357–358
	CWT	27 (Sept. 88) 12–14
	HRN	17 (Spring 89) 103–104
	JAH	75 (Dec. 88) 960–961
	JSO	56 (Feb. 90) 129

013 Cozzens, Peter. *No Better Place to Die: The Battle of Stones River.* Urbana, Ill.: University of Illinois Press, 1990. 281 pp. : ill., maps. Includes bibliography.

ISBN: 0-252-06229-9   LC: 89-30577

Using letters, dairies, memoirs, and battlefield communications, Cozzens lets the men of Stones River speak for themselves. He recounts, in this battle chronicle, the movements of the battle and the performance of individual regiments. The large-scale action never captured the attention of the public, nor did either side achieve a decisive victory, but the battle did cost each side more than a quarter of its forces. This overview presents the differences between General Braxton Bragg's and General William S. Rosecrans's tactics. It presents Cozzens's belief that this battle was a cause of much infighting in the Southern command, which gave the North a victory at a crucial time. A list of the opposing forces in the battle of Stones River is appended.

Reviewed in:	CWH	36 (Dec. 90) 343–344
	HRN	19 (Fall 90) 7–8
	JAH	77 (Dec. 90) 1034–1035
	JSO	57 (Aug. 91) 525–526
	NCH	68 (April 91) 191–192

014   Cozzens, Peter. *This Terrible Sound: The Battle of Chickamauga.* Urbana, Ill.: University of Illinois Press, 1992. xii, 675 pp. : ill., maps. Includes index and references.

ISBN: 0-252-01703-X   LC: 92-725

In the northwest corner of Georgia, just south of Chattanooga, General William S. Rosencrans and the Army of the Cumberland fought two days of bloody combat against General Braxton Bragg and the Army of Tennessee in September of 1863. One of the costliest of battles in terms of casualties, it is described by Cozzens in detail that gives the reader the feel of the battle—full of savage fighting and heroism, of missed opportunities and tactical blunders. Bragg failed to follow up and retake Chattanooga, and Rosencrans had given a wrong order to a subordinate. Detailed maps of the battle are drawn to specific times, and the list of opposing forces in the Chickamauga campaign is included.

Reviewed in:	CHO	30 (April 93) 1376
	HIS	55 (Summer 93) 783
	HRN	221 (Fall 93) 10
	NYT	(Nov. 29, 92) 27

015   Davis, William C. *The Battle at Bull Run: A History of the First Major Campaign of the Civil War.* Baton Rouge, La.: Louisiana State University Press, 1977. xiii, 298 pp. : ill., photographs, maps. Includes index and references.

ISBN: 0-385-12261-6   LC: 76-42322

This is the first significantly detailed study in modern historiography of the First Battle of Bull Run. Davis uses manuscripts, regimental histories, government reports, letters, diaries, and memoirs to provide detailed accounts of the tactics and movements of both sides. He also focuses on the officers involved in the fighting by examining their backgrounds, identifying unusual characteristics, and providing critical appraisals of their leadership capabilities. Davis includes maps detailing the battle at different times during the day on July 21.

Reviewed in:	CHO	15 (March 78) 136
	CWT	17 (Aug. 78) 49–50
	GHQ	65 (Summer 81) 164–165
	LIJ	102 (July 77) 1493
	NCH	55 (Winter 78) 85
	VMH	86 (April 78) 207–208

016 Davis, William C. *The Battle of New Market*. New York: Doubleday, 1975. 249 pp. : ill., photographs, maps. Includes index,
bibliography, references, and appendixes.

ISBN: 0-385-09789-1   LC: 74-18788

This is the definitive account of the battle of New Market (May
15, 1864) and the campaign that led up to it. The farm community of
New Market had little military significance. It is memorable for two
reasons: First, as a result of the battle, Franz Sigel, who had repeatedly
demonstrated an incapacity for high command, was dismissed. The
participation of the corps of cadets of the Virginia Military Institute
marks the second significant aspect of New Market. There were 222
members in the corps, mostly boys in their teens. Of this number, 57
were killed or wounded in a charge on Captain Albert von Kleiser's
battery during the climax of the battle. Davis uses a wide range of
manuscript sources to tell the story of how the Confederate forces,
outnumbered four to one, managed to defeat their Union foes. The
text is supplemented by clear maps and two appendixes, one detailing
the strength of each command and the other listing the casualties of
each unit.

Reviewed in: AHR   81 (June 76) 668

CWT   15 (Dec. 76) 47

JAH   62 (March 76) 1003–1004

JSO   42 (Feb. 76) 127–128

NCH   53 (Winter 76) 98–99

017 Davis, William C. *Duel between the First Ironclads*. New York:
Doubleday, 1975. x, 201 pp. : ill., photographs. Includes index
and bibliography.

ISBN: 0-385-09868-5   LC: 75-11071

Davis has written a full-scale history of the first two modern
armored warships, the *Merrimack* and the *Monitor*, in this brief, comprehensive volume. After tracing the history of ironclad warships, he
focuses on the design, construction, and operation of the vessels. Davis
details how the CSS *Virginia* was fashioned out of the *Merrimack*'s
scuttled hull and machinery after the latter was sunk by Union forces
attempting to destroy the Norfolk, Virginia navy yard. There is a discussion of the men who designed and captained the two ships and a
description of the 1862 battle of Hampton Roads.

Reviewed in: CWT   15 (Jan. 77) 49–50

GHQ   65 (Summer 81) 164–165
JSO   42 (Aug. 76) 435–436
MIR   56 (April 76) 105–106

018   Fellman, Michael. *Inside War: The Guerrilla Conflict in Missouri during the American Civil War*. New York: Oxford University Press, 1988. xx, 331 pp. : ill., maps, photographs, tables. Includes index and references.

ISBN: 0-19505-198-X   LC: 88-22690

Fellman claims that Missouri was the site of widespread, prolonged, and destructive guerilla fighting. To illustrate, he uses letters, diaries, military reports, court-martial transcripts, and newspaper accounts to examine the physical, emotional, and moral experiences of the people of Missouri during the war. Fellman claims that neither Union nor Confederate military authorities could control the fighting in Missouri and that therefore the guerilla struggle was worse there than in any other state. In fact, each side developed an ambivalent attitude about guerilla fighters—abhorring their methods but at the same time applauding the damage they wrought. As a result of this "muddled" official policy, soldiers in the field often engaged in illegal or unethical behavior and then issued false reports to cover up their actions. The book begins with an analysis of the society and the ideology of prewar Missouri, including a discussion of the state's demographics, economics, and politics. The second half of the book examines the physical and psychological impacts of guerilla warfare on the civilian population. According to Fellman, women were often the most severely affected members of the community. Although they were frequently the victims of guerilla violence, many women also served as informants, suppliers, and at times fighters. Fellman includes graphic accounts of the guerrillas' tactics, which included robbery, arson, torture, and murder. There is also a discussion of how the postwar myth of the "noble" guerilla fighter arose.

Reviewed in: AHR   96 (April 91) 611–612
CWH   36 (June 90) 187–188
GHQ   74 (Fall 90) 526–528
HRN   18 (Winter 90) 58
RAH   17 (Dec. 89) 559–565

019   Frank, Joseph Allan, and George A. Reaves. *"Seeing the Elephant": Raw Recruits at the Battle of Shiloh*. New York: Green-

wood Press, 1989. 215 pp. : ill., photographs, maps. Includes index and bibliography.

ISBN: 0-313-26692-1   LC: 88-34823

The battle of Shiloh was fought on April 6 and 7, 1862. It was the largest battle in the Western theater in which raw recruits participated. The authors identify Shiloh as the "archetypical soldiers' battle, because the generals lost command and control early in the engagement." Their objective is to understand how the raw recruits' morale and combat behavior were affected by various morale factors during each stage of the campaign. These factors include tactical preparation, political attitudes, logistics, leadership, espirit de corps, comradeship, and officer competence. The authors have used diaries, letters, reminiscences, and letters to the editor of 450 men who fought at Shiloh, to measure troop morale. Their study suggests which motivating factors were most important at different times during the campaign.

Reviewed in: AHR   96 (Feb. 91) 764

CWH   36 (Dec. 90) 351–352

HIS   53 (Winter 91) 363–364

JAH   77 (Dec. 90) 1033

020 Furgurson, Ernest B. *Chancellorsville, 1863: The Souls of the Brave.* New York: Alfred A. Knopf, 1992. xv, 405 pp. : ill., maps. Includes index and references.

ISBN: 0-394-58301-9   LC: 91-047059

Chancellorsville, one of the most decisive campaigns of the war, was not a single battle, according to Furgurson, but a series of battles that were the subject of the classic work *The Campaign of Chancellorsville* by John Bigelow, Jr. It is the unnamed battle forever placed in our memory by Stephen Crane's *The Red Badge of Courage.* Historians have researched this conflict, which was so completely dominated by Robert E. Lee's overtaking of the highly superior forces of General Joseph Hooker, but Furgurson's goal was to uncover first-person accounts from letters, diaries, and memoirs to make the tactical studies more human in scope. It is said to be the "last splendid victory of the cavalier over modernity." It was also the battle in which General Thomas "Stonewall" Jackson was mortally wounded by friendly fire.

Reviewed in: LIJ   117 (Oct. 15, 92) 81

NYT   (Jan. 24, 93) 18

PUW   239 (Sept. 14, 92) 96

RAH   21 (Sept. 93) 424

021   Glatthaar, Joseph T. *The March to the Sea and Beyond: Sherman's Troops in the Savannah and Carolinas Campaigns.* New York: New York University Press, 1985. xvi, 318 pp. : ill., photographs, maps. Includes index, bibliography, references, and appendixes.

ISBN: 0-8147-3001-9   LC: 84-29496

Glatthaar presents a dramatic account of General William Tecumseh Sherman's devastating sweep through the South from a new perspective, through the eyes of the common soldier. The significant insight the author contributes is his emphasis on the veteran character of Sherman's army. Glatthaar estimates that almost 80 percent of the men under Sherman's command had enlisted in 1861 or 1862. Most had received training in the Western theater, which meant that they were accustomed to prolonged campaigns waged under difficult circumstances. By 1864 their years of service in the army had significantly altered their outlook so that they had developed a "clear understanding of whom and for what they were fighting." Glatthaar writes from the viewpoint of the common soldier. Using diaries, local documents, and photographs to highlight individual soldier's characters and experience, he relates the duties and hardships of the march, camp life, and the confusion and chance encounters on the battlefield. The text is supple-

Waiting for dinner

mented with three appendixes: one presents the composition of Sherman's army, the second includes comparative medical statistics for the United States Army and for Sherman's army, and the third lists voting statistics in the 1867 presidential election for the men who served in Sherman's army.

Reviewed in: AHR   91 (April 86) 469

CHO   23 (Dec. 85) 658

JAH   72 (March 86) 963

LIJ   110 (June 15, 85) 61

022   Gramm, Kent. *Gettysburg: A Meditation on War and Values.*
Bloomington, Ind.: Indiana University Press, 1994. 270 pp. : ill.,
map. Includes index and references.

ISBN: 0-253-32621-5   LC: 93-19551

It has been said of Gramm's "meditation" that he has added to
the "enduring cultural conversation Americans carry on with the
dynamic places of memory." His thesis is that we have forgotten the
enormity of death, the courage, and the sense of duty that compelled
men to go forward in battle on the deceptively peaceful landscape of
the Gettysburg battlefield. Gramm identifies the need for lending some
contemporary meaning to the tragedy—the ideals the North fought
and died for, and the ensuing years of racism as the result of enormous
industrial expansion. To Gramm the concluding irony is that whereas
at Gettysburg patriots of both sides fought for freedom, convinced
that freedom demands justice, that very justice has been lost by "corporate greed" and "political cowardice."

Reviewed in: JMH   58 (July 94) 564

023   Hattaway, Herman, and Archer Jones. *How the North Won: A
Military History of the Civil War.* Urbana, Ill.: University of
Illinois Press, 1983. xii, 762 pp. : ill., maps. Includes index, bib-
liography, and appendixes.

ISBN: 0-252-06210-8   LC: 81-16332

This is an examination of the military history of the war from the
perspective of higher commanders, emphasizing strategy and logistics
over tactics. It is intended to provide for those unacquainted with military history a general account of the conduct, management, and support of the war. Hattaway and Jones go beyond most strategic studies
to include logistical, industrial, economic, political, and organizational influences on military policy. They claim that an important reason the North won was that it had a superior management system.
Those responsible for the Union war effort realized the importance of
setting goals. The authors' examination of Ulysses S. Grant's management and planning techniques and his use of resources is especially
noteworthy. Two useful appendixes—"An Introduction to the Study of
Military Operations" and "Mobilization and Combat Effectiveness"—
analyze combat efficiency in twenty-six battles.

Reviewed in: GHQ   67 (Fall 83) 397–398
                  HRN   11 (Aug. 83) 197–198

JAH   70 (Dec. 83) 675–676

JSO   49 (Nov. 83) 627

024 Hearn, Chester G. *Mobile Bay and the Mobile Campaign: The Last Great Battles of the Civil War.* Jefferson, N.C.: McFarland, 1993. viii, 264 pp. : ill., photographs. Includes index, bibliography, references, and appendixes.

ISBN: 0-89950-820-0   LC: 92-50891

The Anaconda Plan—which called for the occupation of the Mississippi River and the blockading of all Southern ports from Norfolk, Virginia, to Galveston, Texas—was developed by General Winfield Scott. Scott believed that closing the Southern ports was the most effective way to prevent war materiels from reaching the Confederacy. Union Secretary of the Navy Gideon Welles opposed Scott's plan, claiming that it acknowledged the Confederate States of America as a political entity. Hearn relates the story of the two-year-long discussion between Admiral David G. Farragut and Welles over the need to attack and occupy the forts protecting Mobile Bay. He also describes the combined naval and military operation to capture Mobile. The text is supplemented with maps and two appendixes.

Reviewed in: CHO   31 (Sept. 93) 202

HRN   21 (Spring 93) 100

025 Hennessy, John J. *Return to Bull Run: The Campaign and Battle of Second Manassas.* New York: Simon & Schuster, 1993. xiv, 607 pp. : ill., photographs, maps. Includes index, bibliography, references, and appendixes.

ISBN: 0-671-79368-3   LC: 92-1580

Hennessy provides the first thorough study of an often-overlooked, though significant, battle that was fought on August 29–30, 1862, thirteen months after the First Battle of Bull Run. This campaign included two other significant battles: the battle of Groveton, fought just before, and the battle of Chantilly (or Ox Hill), fought just afterward. According to Hennessy, the story of this Confederate victory has never been fully told because it was overshadowed by significant surrounding events such as Robert E. Lee's repulse of George B. McClellan from Richmond and the battle of Antietam. The author provides the strategic and political background for the Second Battle of Bull Run and offers clear assessments of the commanders on both sides. He contends that this battle was important because, among other things, it established Lee's reputation as a field commander and opened the way for the Confederacy's forces to move into Maryland. The text is supplemented with especially useful maps.

Reviewed in: CHO   30 (March 93) 7228

HRN   21 (Summer 93) 150–151

LIJ   117 (Oct. 1, 93) 103

RAH   21 (Sept. 93) 424

026   Hewitt, Lawrence Lee. *Port Hudson: Confederate Bastion on the Mississippi.* Baton Rouge, La.: Louisiana State University Press, 1987. xvi, 221 pp. : ill., maps, photographs. Includes index, bibliography, and appendixes.

ISBN: 0-8071-1351-4   LC: 87-3198

Hewitt recounts the story of Port Hudson, the last Confederate stronghold on the Mississippi, located twenty-five miles upriver from Baton Rouge. The Confederate Army occupied the town in 1862, constructing a bastion stronger than Vicksburg. These two Confederate strongholds denied Union troops access to a large portion of the Mississippi and at the same time protected the vital Red River supply line between western Louisiana and the Southern Heartland. Hewitt emphasizes the strategic importance of the town and examines the effect

A moment's rest

that the struggle for control of Port Hudson had on the course of the war. Early in 1863 Union commanders Admiral David G. Farragut and Major General Nathaniel P. Banks first attempted to starve out the Confederates by gaining control of the mouth of the Red River in a combined naval and army operation. When this failed, Banks called for a direct assault on May 27, 1863. This initial attack was also unsuccessful. Compelled to secure a fresh source of manpower to reinforce his troops, Banks called in black regiments to assist in the ensuing siege, which lasted for forty-three days. This marked the first time that black soldiers in the regular United States Army participated in a major assault. Hewitt maintains that newspaper coverage of the black troops' charge on Port Hudson helped to convince the federal government to accept black soldiers in the Union Army. Union troops were able to capture Port Hudson only after Vicksburg had fallen. Although Hewitt writes at length about many aspects of garrison life, he is primarily concerned with the strategies developed and implemented by both the North and the South during the course of what was the longest genuine siege in American military history.

Reviewed in: AHR   95 (April 90) 589

CWH   34 (Sept. 88) 275–276

GHQ   72 (Winter 88) 748–750

JAH   75 (Dec. 88) 961

JSO   55 (May 89) 333–334

027   Hughes, Nathaniel Cheairs, Jr. *The Battle of Belmont: Grant Strikes South.* Chapel Hill, N.C.: University of North Carolina Press, 1991. xvii, 310 pp. : ill., photographs, maps. Includes index, bibliography, and references.

ISBN: 0-8078-1968-9   LC: 90-26401

This is the first book-length study of the battle of Belmont, the first battle in the Western theater and the first in which Ulysses S. Grant fought. Using diaries, letters, official documents, and contemporary newspaper accounts, Hughes provides a detailed retracing of battle-field movements and exposes weaknesses on both sides. Belmont—a bloody, day-long encounter on November 7, 1861—set a pattern for later confrontations with the use of Yankee timberclad ships and of the infantry at the staging area in Cairo, Illinois. Although the Southern troops under the command of Gideon J. Pillow enjoyed the dual advantage of position and superior numbers, Grant drove the Confederates out of Belmont, only to be routed himself by Confederate reinforcements led by Leonidas Polk. During the fighting Grant lost 20 percent of his troops, but Hughes claims that his determination during the engagement helped establish his reputation as an "audacious fighting general."

Reviewed in: NCH   69 (April 92) 232–233

028   Krick, Robert K. *Stonewall Jackson at Cedar Mountain.* Chapel Hill, N.C.: University of North Carolina Press, 1990. 472 pp. : ill., photographs, maps. Includes references.

ISBN: 0-8078-1887-9   LC: 89-36158

Krick, chief historian of the National Military Park, offers a detailed, minute-by-minute, tactical study of this single battle. The narration focuses on Thomas "Stonewall" Jackson's conduct and sets the scene of battle with quotes from Krick's extensive sources and his own insight and information on the fate of the participants. Appendixes deal with the military aftermath, the organization of the two armies, the history of the battlefield since the war, and the casualties of the battle.

Reviewed in: CWH   36 (Dec. 90) 344–346
CWT   29 (Oct. 90) 12
JAH   78 (June 91) 340
JMH   55 (April 91) 255–256
JSO   57 (Nov. 91) 748–749
VMH   99 (Jan. 91) 101–102

029 MacDonald, John. *Great Battles of the Civil War.* Foreword by John Keegan. New York: Collier Books, 1992. 200 pp. Includes index and references.

ISBN: 0-02-577300-3   LC: 90-39626

Illustrated partly in color, this book by a British military historian examines seventeen battles of the Civil War from First Bull Run in 1861 to the final surrender at Appomattox in April 1865. The battles are described and examined in detail and augmented by computer-enhanced maps of the battle landscape. Charts, diagrams, photographs, and biographical sketches are also included. An added feature is the inclusion of the names and addresses of Civil War parks, a gazetteer, details on directions to the parks, available tours, and places of interest in the park vicinity.

Reviewed in: HRN   17 (Winter 89) 51
NCH   66 (April 89) 254–255

030 McDonough, James Lee. *Chattanooga—A Death Grip on the Confederacy.* Knoxville, Tenn.: University of Tennessee Press, 1984. 298 pp. : ill., photographs and maps. Includes bibliography.

ISBN: 0-87049-125-2/0-87049-630-1(paper)   LC: 83-23582

McDonough reconstructs the events of the campaign, the tactical errors of Braxton Bragg, the replacement of William S. Rosecrans by General Ulysses S. Grant, and the nullification of the Southern victory at Chickamauga by this battle. An appendix includes the organizational charts of the Union and Confederate armies in the Chattanooga campaign.

Reviewed in: HIS   50 (Feb. 88) 289

MIA   52 (April 88) 102

031   McDonough, James Lee. *Shiloh: In Hell before Night*. Knoxville, Tenn.: University of Tennessee Press, 1977. xii, 260 pp. : ill., photographs, maps. Includes index, bibliography, references, and appendixes.

ISBN: 0-87049-199-7   LC: 76-18864

This is a well-researched study of the battle of Shiloh, one of the bloodiest and most exhausting confrontations of the war. Almost one hundred thousand combatants and several of the most important commanders on both sides were involved—Ulysses S. Grant, William Tecumseh Sherman, Albert S. Johnston, Pierre Beauregard, Braxton Bragg, and Nathan Bedford Forrest. Up to this time, Shiloh was the largest battle of the war, the largest in American history. The two-day-long encounter at Shiloh was an important battle in a significant campaign in the struggle to gain control of the Mississippi Valley. According to McDonough, Shiloh kept alive Grant's reputation as a winner while at the same time damaging Beauregard's standing. The text is supplemented with excellent maps and two appendixes that present the organization of the Confederate and Union armies.

Reviewed in: CHO   15 (May 78) 462

HRN   6 (March 78) 95–96

JAH   65 (Sept. 78) 475

LIJ   102 (Sept. 15, 77) 1846

032   McDonough, James Lee. *Stones River—Bloody Winter in Tennessee*. Knoxville, Tenn.: University of Tennessee Press, 1980. 271 pp. : ill., photographs, and maps. Includes bibliography.

ISBN: 0-87049-301-9   LC: 80-11580

It is McDonough's intent to show the importance of this Union victory for the control of Middle Tennessee's farms and railroads. It was a victory that both sides needed, and some twenty-four thousand men became casualties of the battle. The narration blends the emotional reactions of the participants with the study of the battle. The appendix includes the organization of the Confederate and Union armies in this battle.

Reviewed in:	AHR	87 (Feb. 82) 260
	CWH	28 (March 82) 89–90
	FHQ	60 (Jan. 82) 385–388
	JAH	68 (Sept. 81) 392
	JSO	47 (Nov. 81) 615–616
	MIR	61 (Oct. 81) 86–87

033 McDonough, James Lee, and James Pickett Jones. *"War So Terrible": Sherman and Atlanta.* New York: W. W. Norton, 1987. xx, 385 pp. : ill., photographs, maps. Includes index and bibliography.

ISBN: 0-3930-2497-0   LC: 87-18766

This book describes and analyzes Sherman's 1865 Atlanta campaign, which the authors consider one of the most significant confrontations of the Civil War. McDonough and Jones contend that the Atlanta campaign was a decisive element in the Union effort to bring down the Confederacy. They follow the events of the campaign closely, focusing on the contrasts between the opposing military principals— William Tecumseh Sherman, whose main strength they identify as his ability to grasp the significance of the totality of war, and Joseph E. Johnston, who they believe was seriously hampered by a "lack of aggressive strategy." Much of this study is based on information contained in unpublished manuscript sources. The text is supplemented with clear, detailed maps and with photographs. Readers should find the "Critical Bibliography"—which includes citations for manuscripts, memoirs, unit histories, and published letters and diaries—to be especially useful. The epilogue details Margaret Mitchell's research for her version of the Atlanta campaign in preparation for writing *Gone with the Wind.*

Reviewed in:	AHR	94 (June 89) 850–851
	CWT	27 (March 88) 8
	HRN	16 (Summer 88) 150
	JAH	75 (Dec. 88) 958
	JSO	55 (May 89) 337–338
	MIR	68 (Dec. 88) 98

034 Matter, William D. *If It Takes All Summer: The Battle of Spotsylvania.* Chapel Hill, N.C.: University of North Carolina Press, 1988. x, 455 pp. : ill. Includes bibliography and index.

ISBN: 0-8078-1781-3   LC: 87-31950

Working with the physical setting of the battle and print sources, Matter has provided clear maps, portraits of the sites of the battle. The focus of this book is on the bloody conflict near the village of Spotsylvania Court House. It is an account of the military tactics between May 7 and May 21, 1864. He describes the difficulty the Union forces had with unfamiliar terrain and a complicated command structure, and analyzes the battle and its implications for the Virginia campaign. The ferocity of the battle is exemplified by the anecdote Matter retells concerning the large oak tree whose trunk was severed by Union musket balls.

Reviewed in:	CWH	35 (Sept. 89) 262–263
	JAH	76 (Dec. 89) 940–942
	JSO	56 (May 90) 359
	NCH	66 (April 89) 253–254
	THQ	48 (Winter 89) 249
	VMH	96 (April 90) 321–322

035 Muench, David. *Landscapes of Battle: The Civil War.* Photographs by David Muench, text by Michael B. Ballard. Jackson, Miss.: University Press of Mississippi, 1988. 141 pp. : ill., photographs. Includes bibliography.

ISBN: 0-878-05365-4   LC: 88-14345

The lush photographs, augmented by commentary on the battles that had scarred the landscape, do not evoke the horrors of the battles but rather give testimony to the silence and solemnity of these now-sacred fields. With the commentary and photographs there are also simplified maps of the battles and contemporary Civil War photographs of the area.

Reviewed in: JSH 55 (Aug. 89) 535

036 Nulty, William H. *Confederate Florida: The Road to Olustee.* Tuscaloosa, Ala.: University of Alabama Press, 1990. 273 pp. : ill. Includes references.

ISBN: 0-8173-0473-8/0-8173-0748-6(paper)   LC: 89-33849

The secession of Florida from the Union proved not to be important to the Confederacy for its military uses, the state's long coastline proving too difficult to protect. Although it was a source of raids and occupation by the North, it also provided the South with much-needed troops and supplies. This victory near Olustee allowed Florida to remain part of the Confederacy and leave the supply routes open. Using personal accounts, regimental histories, combat correspondence, and official dispatches, Nulty details the military and economic impact of this limited but bloody defeat for the Union.

Reviewed in:	CWH	37 (June 91) 177–179
	FHQ	69 (Jan. 91) 363–365
	JAH	78 (June 91) 337
	JSO	58 (Feb. 92) 145–146
	LAH	32 (Spring 91) 220–222
	NCH	68 (April 91) 192–193

037   Pfanz, Harry W. *Gettysburg: The Second Day.* Chapel Hill, N.C.: University of North Carolina Press, 1987. xx, 601 pp. : ill., photographs, maps. Includes index, bibliography, and appendix.

ISBN: 0-8078-1749-X   LC: 87-5965

Written by a former historian at Gettysburg National Military Park, this book is a definitive account of the fighting that took place during three hours late in the afternoon of July 2, 1863, the second day of the battle of Gettysburg. To tell the story of the assault by the Army of Northern Virginia against the left and center of the Army of the Potomac, Pfanz draws on his extensive personal knowledge of the battlefield itself as well as on many previously uncited sources, including regimental histories, diaries, personal papers, and newspaper files. Pfanz begins by describing the preparations for the day's fighting, both Union and Confederate. He introduces the men and the units involved in the encounter, examines the development of tactical plans, and analyzes the strategies of the opposing commanders, Robert E. Lee and George G. Meade. The emphasis of the book is on the fighting itself. The author's analysis of the decisions and events that took place during the hard-fought campaign is supplemented with thirteen superbly detailed maps. The appendix presents the "order of battle" reproduced from the United States War Department records.

Reviewed in:	CWH	34 (Dec. 88) 355–357
	FHQ	67 (Jan. 89) 378–380
	JAH	75 (Dec. 88) 955–956
	NCH	66 (Jan. 89) 117–118

038 Priest, John M. *Antietam: The Soldiers' Battle*. Shippensburg, Pa.: White Mane Publishing Co., 1989. xxiv, 437 pp. : ill., photographs, and maps. Includes index.

ISBN: 0-942597-09-5   LC: 89-5557

This book is intended to enhance the reader's understanding of the Civil War soldier, not to analyze battle movements. Incorporating a broad selection of primary and secondary sources—including personal reminiscences, diaries and letters, regimental histories, and contemporary periodical accounts—Priest offers a vivid, detailed narrative of the experiences of a number of individuals who fought at the battle of Antietam in September 1862. He weaves anecdotes and vignettes into an intimate hour-by-hour account of what some historians have described as the bloodiest twelve hours of war in America's history. What emerges is a series of insightful portraits of some of the individuals who made up Robert E. Lee's Army of Northern Virginia and George B. McClellan's Army of the Potomac. The text is supplemented with seventy-two detailed maps.

Reviewed in: HRN   18 (Spring 90) 102
                 JAH   77 (Sept. 90) 679
                 JMH   54 (Jan. 90) 91–92
                 JSO   57 (Feb. 91) 124–135

039 Robertson, William Glenn. *Back Door to Richmond: The Bermuda Hundred Campaign, April–June 1864*. Newark, Del.: University of Delaware Press, 1987. 284 pp. : ill., photographs, maps. Includes index, bibliography, and appendixes.

ISBN: 0-87413-303-3   LC: 85-41048

The Bermuda Hundred campaign was a subsidiary operation of Ulysses S. Grant's 1864 spring offensive. The Army of the James, a Union force of more than forty thousand men under the command of Major General Benjamin F. Butler, was supposed to establish a base on the Bermuda Hundred Peninsula at the confluence of the James and Appomattox Rivers. Butler's next tasks were to destroy Confederate rail lines, turn back reinforcements intended to aid the Army of Northern Virginia, and if possible to capture Richmond before meeting up with the Army of the Potomac. Instead, Butler's forces were defeated by General Pierre Beauregard's army at Drewry's Bluff, south of Richmond, and driven back to their base, where they remained, as Ulysses S. Grant described them, like "a bottle strongly corked." Robertson reassesses the Union defeat and enhances the military analysis with soldiers' letters to impart a feeling of what it was actually like to participate in a field campaign. The text is supplemented with fifteen explicit maps and two appendixes, which list the composition of Butler's and Beauregard's armies.

Reviewed in: AHR   94 (April 89) 524–525

                  CWH   34 (June 88) 176–178

                  CWT   28 (March 89) 10

                  JAH   75 (June 88) 269–270

                  JSO   54 (Nov. 88) 672–673

                  MIR   66 (Nov. 88) 88

040 Sears, Stephen W. *Landscape Turned Red: The Battle of Antietam.* New Haven, Conn.: Ticknor & Fields, 1983. xii, 431 pp. : ill., photographs, maps. Includes index, bibliography, references, and appendixes.

ISBN: 0-89919-172-X   LC: 82-19519

The battle of Antietam was fought on September 17, 1862, near Antietam Creek in Maryland. Sears focuses on the lives of the men in the ranks while providing a discussion of a broad spectrum of events—

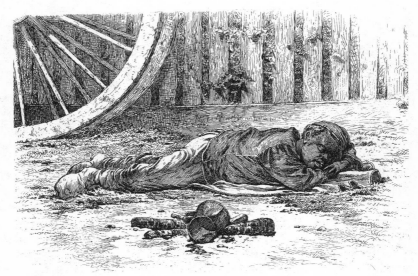

A good soldier could sleep anywhere.

military, political, social, and diplomatic. The first half of the book sets the stage for the battle and provides detailed accounts of other confrontations leading up 'to Antietam. Sears draws upon previously unpublished materials to relay the actual events and the impressions of the participants. Two men who fought at Antietam, Colonel Ezra A. Carman of the Thirteenth New Jersey and Major John M. Gould of the Tenth Maine, surveyed thousands of Antietam veterans, both Union and Confederate, and compiled their recollections. The text is supplemented by excellent maps.

Reviewed in: CHO   21 (Oct. 83) 344

HIS   47 (Aug. 85) 594

LIJ   108 (May 15, 83) 1001

NYT   (Aug. 7, 83) 3

RAH   14 (Sept. 86) 368

041   Sears, Stephen W. *To the Gates of Richmond: The Peninsula Campaign.* New York: Ticknor & Fields, 1992. xii, 468 pp. Includes references.

ISBN: 0-89919-790-6   LC: 92-006923

In perhaps the best study of the Peninsula campaign, Sears conveys the texture of the war as experienced by the soldiers and the officers of this campaign waged in April through July 1862 on the peninsula east of Richmond. The Peninsula campaign was the first advance launched by Union General George B. McClellan and the first time as field commander for the Southern General Robert E. Lee. It was also important for the beginning of the partnership between Lee and Thomas "Stonewall" Jackson. There have been partisan studies of the campaign, but Sears has provided the literary bridge between the events and the individuals on both sides. Many quotes from men of both armies let the participants tell their own story. It is military history at its best. The thorough research provides information on governmental concerns, complete accounts of the battle of Seven Pines, McClellan's vendetta with Secretary of War Edwin M. Stanton, and Jackson's movement from the Shenandoah Valley. The appendixes include a listing of the participants of the armies of Yorktown, Seven Pines and the Seven Days. Enhanced by photographs and drawings, the book contains several drawings and sketches by Winslow Homer and Alfred Waud. It also includes clear maps showing Union and Confederate brigades. This campaign that changed the course of the war has found an important narrator and interpreter in Stephen W. Sears.

Reviewed in: CHO   30 (March 3, 93) 1230
LIJ   117 (July 92) 1034
NYT   (Jan. 24, 93) 184

042   Shea, William L. *Pea Ridge: Civil War Campaign in the West.* Chapel Hill, N.C.: University of North Carolina Press, 1992. xiii, 417 pp. Includes references.

ISBN: 0-807-82042-3   LC: 92-004465

Numerous maps and illustrations of both period and contemporary photographs enhance this discussion of what may have been the most important Trans-Mississippi operation—which occurred in northwestern Alabama, west of the Mississippi, in March 1862—and of its impact on the course of events in the West. The Union victory here may have ended any serious chance for the Confederacy to gain control of Missouri. Military tactics from company to battery level are also part of the investigation of the battlefield. An essay, "The Legacy of Pea Ridge," ends the book. It discusses the folk stories, songs, popular literature, poetry, and films that have grown up around Pea Ridge. Also included is the order of battle for the campaign.

Reviewed in: AHR   98 (Dec. 93) 1686
CHO   30 (March 93) 1230
HRN   22 (Spring 94) 115
JAH   81 (June 94) 284
JMH   57 (July 93) 5554
JSO   60 (May 94) 405

043   Sommers, Richard J. *Richmond Redeemed: The Siege at Petersburg.* New York: Doubleday, 1981. xxii, 670 pp. : ill., photographs, maps. Includes index, bibliography, references, and appendixes.

ISBN: 0-385-15626-X   LC: 79-7843

Twenty miles south of Richmond, Petersburg was the town through which all Confederate rail lines except one passed to supply Richmond. The Union Army's siege of Petersburg began in mid-June 1864 and lasted for 9½ months. It was a decisive campaign that all but destroyed the Army of Northern Virginia. Sommers's narrative concentrates on the fighting that took place during the early autumn of 1864. His principal focus is providing an in-depth analysis of Ulysses S.

Grant's so-called "fifth offensive," especially the opening battles of Chaffen's Bluff and Poplar Spring. Sommers assesses the strategies and tactics of the siege and describes the course of the operation in detail. He contends that military history is valuable because it illuminates the human experience. In this study he places the Petersburg-Richmond campaign into the larger framework of the war. His narrative includes discussions of weaponry, military technology, camp life, and life on the march, as well as accounts of the fighting from the point of view of the common soldier. Sommers consulted more than one hundred manuscript depositories and libraries. His text is supplemented with twenty-two excellent maps and more than eighty photographs.

Reviewed in: AHR   86 (Oct. 81) 929–930

CWH   27 (Dec. 81) 370–371

JAH   68 (Dec. 81) 678–679

JSO   47 (Nov. 81) 616–617

MIR   62 (Sept. 82) 88–89

VMH   89 (July 81) 376–377

044 *Struggle for the Shenandoah: Essays on the 1864 Valley Campaign.* Edited by Gary W. Gallagher. Kent, Ohio: Kent State University Press, 1991. x, 137 pp. : ill., maps, photographs. Includes index and references.

ISBN: 0-873-38429-6/0-873-38430-X(paper)   LC: 90-47368

The five essays in this volume are revised papers from the 1989 Mont Alto Conference on the Civil War. They are concerned with military operations in the Shenandoah Valley during 1864, a campaign that Gallagher believes "exceeded in scale and importance" the 1862 operations in the valley. Gallagher establishes the geography of the area, discusses its logistical and strategic importance to both the North and the South, and presents a summary of the campaign. The other contributors examine the efforts of the commanders involved. Jeffrey D. Wert focuses on Confederate commander Jubal Early and concludes that his reputation suffered when he failed to defeat Union commander Philip H. Sheridan in the Shenandoah. Robert K. Krick concludes that most of Early's problems were caused by failures on the part of his cavalry and that there was little he could do to correct the situation. A. Wilson Greene focuses on Sheridan and examines the reasons he was appointed to oppose Early and the strategy Grant developed for him. Finally, Dennis E. Frye considers the impact that guerilla leader John S. Mosby had on the Shenandoah campaign.

Reviewed in: FHQ   70 (April 92) 513–514

GHQ   76 (Spring 92) 169–171

HIS   54 (Aug. 91) 153–154

JAH   78 (March 92) 1458

LAH   33 (Spring 92) 215–218

NCH   68 (Oct. 91) 468

045 Svenson, Peter. *Battlefield: Farming a Civil War Battleground.* Boston: Faber & Faber, 1992. ix, 246 pp. Includes references.

ISBN: 0-571-19798-1   LC: 92-30036

When Svenson and his family bought a small farm in the community of Cross Keys in the Shenandoah, he was soon to find out that they had bought more than a forty-acre wheat farm; they had also purchased bloodied and hallowed ground. On the morning of June 8, 1862, the armies commanded by Isaac R. Trimble repulsed the attack by the Union commander John C. Fremont, and 972 men were wounded or dying casualties of war. It was here that Svenson had planned to start his life over in the privacy of rural Virginia, build a house, refurbish an old barn, and teach himself to farm hay. As his life and labors on the farm unfold before us, so does his telling of the battle, as if superimposed on the landscape. The field reports and firsthand accounts of the battle are intertwined with Svenson's own war against pesticides and the weather, and his deep respect and feeling of responsiblity for the area's past. Svenson has included a compilation of battle reports, including dispatches between Lincoln and Fremont, as well as a listing of the forces involved.

Reviewed in: LAT   (March 20, 94) 9

PUW   241 (July 21, 94) 250

046 Sword, Wiley. *Shiloh: Bloody April.* New York: William Morrow & Co., 1974. xv, 519 pp. Includes bibliography.

ISBN: 0-688-002-714   LC: 74-007455

Shiloh, often considered a draw but in fact a pivotal battle of the Civil War, is here represented as a major reversal for the Confederacy. This incredible surprise attack allowed the Confederacy nearly to inflict a major disaster upon the North. Shiloh was a major battle that cost the lives of Confederate General Albert S. Johnston and four thousand others. According to author Sword, the loss of Johnston, may have been the most decisive of all the important events at Shiloh, if for no other reason than that the commanders who succeeded Johnston in the command of the Army of the Mississippi were lacking in ability. Included in the appendixes are the order of battle for the battle of Shiloh, April 6–7, 1862; and the numbers and losses of the Union Army of Tennessee, the Union Army of the Ohio, and the Confederate Army of Mississippi. The worth of the book is enhanced by the inclusion of a noteworthy foreword by military historian S. L. A. Marshall and excellent maps and portraits of the major individuals.

Reviewed in: AHR   81 (April 76) 450

CWT   14 (Oct. 75) 47–48

JSO   41 (March 75) 264–265

MIA   39 (April 75) 93

MIR   55 (Feb. 75) 102–103

047   Tanner, Robert G. *Stonewall in the Valley: Thomas J. "Stonewall" Jackson's Shenandoah Valley Campaign, Spring, 1862.* Garden City, N.Y.: Doubleday, 1976. xix, 436 pp. : ill., photographs, maps. Includes index, bibliography, references, and appendixes.

ISBN: 0-385-12148-2   LC: 76-3002

Davis presents an account of Thomas "Stonewall" Jackson's campaign in the Shenandoah Valley in the spring of 1862. Writing from the Southern point of view, he discusses the strategy and tactics employed in the valley and their effect on forces operating in other theaters of battle. Taking advantage of Northern errors, Jackson's outnumbered army defeated several significantly larger Union forces. The appendixes present "Jackson's Plans and Marches, May 24, 1862," and the "Valley Army Tables of Organization, January–June 1862." The text is enhanced by useful maps.

Reviewed in: CWT   16 (April 77) 48

GHQ   61 (Summer 77) 204–205

MIA   42 (Feb. 78) 56

MIR   57 (June 77) 110

048   Trudeau, Noah Andre. *Bloody Roads South: The Wilderness to Cold Harbor, May–June 1864.* Boston: Little, Brown and Company, 1989. viii, 354 pp. : ill., maps. Includes index and bibliography.

ISBN: 0-316-85326-7   LC: 89-32817

Trudeau describes this as an "informal history" of the Wilderness (or Overland) Campaign, which took place between May 5 and June 12, 1864, and included some of the most savage and relentless fighting of the war. The battles in this campaign were the only ones to pit Ulysses S. Grant, the North's best general in command of the Union's least successful army, against Robert E. Lee, the South's best general in command of the Confederacy's most successful army. Trudeau presents a series of vignettes from the perspective of the men in the ranks, using their published letters and diaries as well as unit histories to tell their stories. The text is supplemented with twenty-one original field sketches, tables, lists of casualties (54,259 for the North, 31,763 for the South), and a list of the organization of the Union and Confederate forces.

Reviewed in:	CWH	36 (Sept. 90) 286–287
	CWT	28 (Feb. 90) 10, 67
	FHQ	69 (April 91) 505–507
	JSO	57 (May 91) 336–337

049 Woodworth, Steven E. *Jefferson Davis and His Generals: The Failure of Confederate Command in the West.* Lawrence, Kans.: University Press of Kansas, 1990. xv, 380 pp. Includes references.

ISBN: 0-700-6046-18   LC: 89-028668

Woodworth concentrates his analysis not on all of the Confederate generals but on the major issues for the Confederate leadership in the West. One of the questions that is asked is how Jefferson Davis's superior preparation as a West Point graduate with extensive military experience helped him in the role he was to play in the Confederacy. Woodworth sees Davis's talents being tested in the theater in the West and seeks to provide an in-depth study of the relationship between the personality of Davis and those of his commanders. In a revised view of Davis as a strong and resourceful military leader, Woodworth views Davis as having weaknesses and making mistakes that may have cost the Confederacy the final victory. In Woodworth's analysis some of the weaknesses may have included placing too much faith in the advice of his Western generals, his insistence on keeping the resources of the trans-Mississippi department separated from the rest of the Confederacy, and his intervention in the tactics of the Western theater. Also offered are revisionist analyses of General Albert Sidney Johnston and

Braxton Bragg, and of the prewar bishop Leonidas Polk, a strong personal friend of Davis, whom Woodworth argues bears a large measure of blame for Confederate defeat in the West and therefore that of the war. Portraits and maps are also included.

Reviewed in: AHR   96 (Oct. 91) 1296
                 CHO   28 (Nov. 90) 554
                 JSO   58 (May 92) 355
                 LIJ   115 (July 90) 106

Bibliographies

050 *The Civil War in the North: A Selective Bibliography.* Edited by Eugene C. Murdock. New York: Garland Publishing, Inc., 1987. xx, 764 pp. Includes indexes.

ISBN: 0-8240-8941-3   LC: 86-19582

This bibliography provides comprehensive coverage of a broad range of topics, including government, the Army, the Navy, Lincoln, biographies and personal accounts, the arts, minorities, and special topics such as religion, intellectual matters, and the Constitution. There are citations to books, essays, articles, diaries, memoirs, speeches, music, novels, poetry, drama, biographies, official documents, newspapers, and unpublished doctoral dissertations arranged within each category.

Reviewed in: CWH   34 (Dec. 88) 361–362
                 JAH   75 (March 89) 1406

051 Cole, Garold. *Civil War Eyewitnesses: An Annotated Bibliography of Books and Articles, 1955–1986.* Foreword by James I.

Robertson, Jr. Columbia, S.C.: University of South Carolina Press, 1988. viii, 351 pp. Includes index.

ISBN: 0-872-4954-50   LC: 87-34273

Civil War Eyewitnesses updates and supplements many of the older Civil War bibliographies and the work by Eugene G. Murdock, *The Civil War in the North*. Almost fourteen hundred entries are compiled from personal narratives, diaries, letters from soldiers' memoirs, and are divided into North and South sections. Entries are annotated, with dates, identification by rank and civilian occupation of the writer, and descriptions of military engagements or the places from which the documents were written. Many direct quotations are included to give the reader the sense of the writer's style. The detailed index provides access to both titles and subjects.

Reviewed in: CHO   26 (Oct. 88) 286

JAH   76 (March 90) 1370

052   Freemon, Frank R. *Microbes and Minie Balls: An Annotated Bibliography of Civil War Medicine*. Rutherford, N.J.: Fairleigh Dickinson University Press, 1993. 253 pp. : ill., photographs. Includes index.

ISBN: 0-8386-3484-2   LC: 92-52706

The American Civil War took place during a period of transition between two medical world views. The old view emphasized the sick person who could be restored to life by correcting an imbalance. The new view held that disease existed outside the person and could be treated by a specific remedy. Freemon believes that the story of the war is incomplete without a consideration of its medical aspects. His introduction presents a brief, concise history of the development of medical practice in the United States, emphasizing the differences between the North and the South. This bibliography identifies approximately six hundred citations to primary and secondary sources, including books, pamphlets, government reports, and contemporary journal articles. Reports by soldiers and officers who were wounded or hospitalized present the viewpoint of those who received medical care. Freemon offers a unique perspective on the war while clarifying the prevailing attitudes and practices of dealing with health emergencies in wartime.

Reviewed in: CHO   30 (July 93) 1749

CRL   54 (Sept. 93) 434

Biographies

053   Ballard, Michael B. *Pemberton: A Biography.* Jackson, Miss.: University Press of Mississippi, 1991. xiii, 250 pp. : ill., photographs, maps. Includes index and references.

ISBN: 0-87805-511-8   LC: 91-19760

John Glifford Pemberton was a complex, contradictory individual best remembered as the Confederate general who surrendered the Confederate stronghold at Vicksburg to Ulysses S. Grant, signaling the end of the South's control of the Mississippi. Most historians have been critical of Pemberton's performance at Vicksburg. Ballard agrees with this analysis, pointing out that Pemberton might have made a more positive contribution had his abilities been put to better use. He believes that if Pemberton had been assigned to an administrative or staff command he would have made a significant contribution to the cause of the Confederate States of America. In March 1862 Pemberton assumed command of Confederate defenses in South Carolina and Georgia. A significant portion of the book is devoted to the general's service on the southern Atlantic coast between November 1861 and September 1862. Although he is critical of Pemberton's role at Vicksburg, Ballard considers him a victim of the war.

Reviewed in: CHO 29 (May 92) 1455

054   Blakey, Arch Fredric. *General John H. Winder, C.S.A.* Gainesville, Fla.: University of Florida Press, 1990. xvi, 275 pp. : ill. Includes index and references.

ISBN: 0-813-0099-79   LC: 90-34655

Confederate Brigadier General John Henry Winder served as the provost marshal of Richmond and the commander of the Andersonville Prison. This is the first comprehensive biography that covers Winder's family background, his years in West Point, his business ventures, and most importantly the years between 1861 and 1865. Resigning his commission in 1861 from the Union Army, Winder is seen by Blakey as an officer trying to honor the ethics of a career army officer with the execution of his duty to command Richmond, Virginia, and to oversee all of the Union prisoners of war east of the Mississippi. The civilians of Richmond considered him to be a "power-crazed czar," and Northerners labeled him the "beast" of Andersonville Prison. Blakey tries to reexamine the evidence and balance the facts with the image that has been reinforced through the years. This study of military ethics and the consequences of Winder's failures are, for Blakey, a glimpse into why the Confederacy failed. Winder and the Confederacy were caught in a situation that could not be controlled. Included is a list of Confederate military prisons.

Reviewed in:	HRN	20 (Winter 92) 77
	JAH	78 (Dec. 91) 1093
	JSO	58 (Aug. 92) 543

055   Blight, David N. *Frederick Douglass' Civil War: Keeping Faith in Jubilee*. Baton Rouge, La.: Louisiana State University Press, 1989. xv, 270 pp. Includes index, bibliography, and references.

ISBN: 0-807-11463-4   LC: 88-29200

Blight presents an intellectual biography of Frederick Douglass, the fugitive slave who became a symbol of his age. According to Blight, Douglass viewed the Civil War within a spiritual framework. For him, the conflict was an "apocalyptic power" that forever altered the African American experience. Blight builds his narrative around the assumption that the war was central to both the history of the United States and to the experience of black men and women. Douglass is viewed as a participant in the "midst of crisis" who sought to observe and to advocate, and who became the most influential black leader of the nineteenth century.

Reviewed in:	AHR	95 (Dec. 90) 1633–1634
	CWH	36 (Dec. 90) 358–359
	GHQ	74 (Spring 90) 172–174
	JSO	57 (Feb. 91) 117–118
	NCH	67 (April 90) 273
	RAH	18 (March 90) 55–63

056   Bowers, John. *Stonewall Jackson: Portrait of a Soldier.* New York: William Morrow & Co., 1989. 367 pp. : ill., photographs, maps. Includes index.

ISBN: 0-688-05747-0
LC: 88-37918

Bowers uses diaries, letters, memoirs, and eyewitness accounts to examine the sometimes-puzzling character of Thomas "Stonewall" Jackson. The author recounts Jackson's childhood on his uncle's farm and his early career at West Point. Bowers also discusses Jackson's military service during the Mexican War. The main focus of this biography is Jackson's Civil War service, and Bowers portrays the general as a stern yet tender-hearted leader. The text of this fully rounded portrait is supplemented by maps.

General Thomas J. ("Stonewall") Jackson

Reviewed in: GHQ   74 (Fall 90) 530–531
                LIJ   114 (May 15, 89) 74
                NYT   (Sept. 10, 89) 34

057   Brandt, Nat. *The Man Who Tried to Burn New York.* Syracuse, N.Y.: Syracuse University Press, 1986. xiv, 292 pp. : ill. Includes index and bibliography.

ISBN: 0-815-6020-73   LC: 86-5833

Brandt writes about a little-known Confederate plot to burn down New York City conjured up in Canada, where Confederate agents were sent to cultivate Copperhead sentiment, spoil Abraham Lincoln's reelection bid in 1864, and free Confederate prisoners. On November 25, 1864, a small group of Confederate spies tried to burn some New York City hotels. The devices failed, resulting only in smoke and short-lived panic. Brandt centers his narrative on Robert Cobb Kennedy, the only spy to be captured and executed. Biographical material on Kennedy is provided, and the proceedings of his trial and sentencing are examined. The depiction of the Canadian operations and the attempted plan to burn New York City gives readers a well-researched look into Confederate covert operations.

> *Reviewed in:*   HRN   15 (Jan. 87) 69
>
> JSO   54 (Feb. 88) 122–123
>
> LIJ   111 (Aug. 86) 145

058 Breeden, James O. *Joseph Jones, M.D.: Scientist of the Old South.* Lexington, Ky.: University Press of Kentucky, 1975. xiii, 293 pp. : ill., photographs, tables. Includes index, bibliography, and references.

ISBN: 0-8131-1296-6   LC: 73-80462

Breeden recounts and interprets the career of Joseph Jones of Georgia, one of only a handful of Southerners who achieved prominence in science and medicine. Jones was educated at the University of Pennsylvania. He returned to the South to teach and study Southern diseases, especially fevers. As a Civil War surgeon, Jones conducted exhaustive studies of Confederate medical problems. He visited hospitals, military prisons, and troop encampments to conduct studies on tetanus, gangrene, typhoid fever, malaria, and smallpox. Jones conducted postmortem examinations in Andersonville Prison and wrote a report on the prison that was subsequently used to convict the prison commandant. Following the war Jones settled in New Orleans, where he became an authority on public health.

> *Reviewed in:*   CHO   12 (Nov. 75) 1192
>
> JAH   63 (June 76) 115
>
> HIS   39 (Feb. 77) 372–373

059 Connelly, Thomas Lawrence. *The Marble Man: Robert E. Lee and His Image in American Society.* New York: Alfred A. Knopf, 1977. xv, 249 pp. : ill., photographs. Includes index, bibliography, and references.

ISBN: 0-394-47179-2   LC: 76-41778

Connelly has written a psychobiography of General Robert E. Lee and a study of the efforts of a number of influential Confederates to canonize Lee in the years following the war. He claims that the Virginians, such as Jubal Early, who dominated the Richmond-based Southern Historical Society during the years following Lee's death protected the general's reputation by depicting him as an "unsurpassed soldier of serene moral greatness." Connelly asserts that Early and his followers created the "Virginia Pattern" in Civil War historiography, which exalted Lee and all things Virginian at the expense of other generals and locales. Although he recognizes Lee's merit, Connelly believes that the cultivated image of Lee has transformed him into a symbol so that he is no longer understandable as a human being.

Reviewed in: AHR   82 (Dec. 77) 1333

CWH   23 (Sept. 77) 261–263

CWT   17 (June 78) 49–50

JAH   65 (June 78) 173–174

JSO   44 (Feb. 78) 127–128

VMH   86 (Jan. 78) 120–121

060 Cornish, Dudley Taylor. *Lincoln's Lee: The Life of Samuel Phillips Lee, United States Navy, 1812–1897.* Lawrence, Kans.: University Press of Kansas, 1986. 245 pp. : ill., photographs, maps. Includes bibliography.

ISBN: 0-700-60296-8   LC: 86-4083

Samuel Phillips Lee, cousin of Robert E. Lee, remained loyal to the Union and served conclusively in the Union blockade of the South. He had command of the two largest squadrons in the Union navy, although only competent and not extraordinary in the execution of his duties. His family heritage, political connections, and social standing made him highly visible at the time, yet he remains a somewhat obscure but important person in the history of the United States Navy.

Reviewed in: AHR   92 (Oct. 87) 1030

JAH   74 (June 87) 182

JSO   53 (Nov. 87) 662

061 Coryell, Janet L. *Neither Heroine nor Fool: Anna Ella Carroll of Maryland.* Kent, Ohio: Kent State University Press, 1990. 177 pp. : ill. Includes index and references.

ISBN: 0-873-3840-59   LC: 89-24403

Anna Ella Carroll's life was full of contradictions. Much of what we know of her is legend yet the reality is as interesting as her reputation. She was a Southern woman who, as a pamphlet writer for the Know-Nothing Party, supported Lincoln's actions at the beginning of the Civil War. Carroll was well educated and outspoken at a time when women were not expected to exert influence. Coryell has used military records, correspondence, and newspaper accounts to deny Carroll's claim to be "Lincoln's secret weapon," but does give her the recognition due for her place in history and as a political writer.

Reviewed in: AHR   96 (June 91) 954

CWH   37 (June 91) 157–158

JAH   78 (June 91) 333–334

JSO   58 (Feb. 92) 149–151

NCH   67 (Oct. 90) 478–479

062 Davis, William C. *Breckinridge: Statesman, Soldier, Symbol.* Baton Rouge, La.: Louisiana State University Press, 1974. xxii, 687 pp. : ill., photographs. Includes index and bibliography.

ISBN: 0-807-1006-84   LC: 73-077658

Davis sees John C. Breckinridge as a moderate having devotion to his country's welfare as he saw it. Rising in military command by trial and error, Breckinridge was an untrained civilian who contributed significantly to the Confederate cause as a general. In Davis's opinion he should have been appointed Jefferson Davis's secretary of war as early as 1861. Davis traces the career of Breckinridge from pre–Civil War Democratic politician to Confederate military leader and Southerner in exile after Appomattox. The three parts of the book come together to provide readers with a full study of this man who grew in stature from an uninfluential politician to a symbol for thousands of former Confederates who left the South. This work gives new importance to a man who served as a congressman, vice-president, and senator before serving with the Confederacy as a general and the South's last secretary of war. This is more than a biography; it is also the story of Kentucky in the Civil War.

Reviewed in: AHR   81 (Dec. 76) 1252–1253

CWH   21 (March 75) 82–84

FHQ   54 (Oct. 75) 229–230

GHQ   59 (Spring 75) 78–79

HRN   3 (Jan. 75) 56

JAH   62 (Dec. 75) 699–701

063 Davis, William C. *Jefferson Davis: The Man and His Hour.* New York: HarperCollins Publishers, 1991. xv, 784 pp. : ill., photographs. Includes index and references.

ISBN: 0-06-016706-8   LC: 90-56352

The author uses papers, diaries, and memoirs of Jefferson Davis's associates, as well as new materials recently released from Davis's own papers, to present a vivid picture of a multifaceted man. Loved by his close friends for his personal courage, intense loyalty, and eloquence, Jefferson Davis was just as strongly disliked by informal acquaintances for his obstinacy, vanity, excessive sensitivity to criticism, and unwillingness to delegate responsibility. After an examination of Davis's life as a student at Transylvania University and West Point, his tenure as a successful planter, and his career as a senator, secretary of war, and congressman, the author devotes approximately one-half of this book to his subject's years as president of the Confederate States of America. According to the author, Davis's personal weaknesses were magnified by the pressures of the war, and as a result many historians have come to believe he was unqualified for the job. However, the author believes that the blame is not entirely Jefferson Davis's because he had little talent to draw from in the Confederate leadership, especially within the ranks of the military.

Reviewed in: AHR   97 (Dec. 92) 1597

JAH   79 (Dec. 92) 1178

JSO   59 (Aug. 93) 554

064   Delany, Norman C. *John McIntosh Kell of the Raider Alabama.* Tuscaloosa, Ala.: University of Alabama Press, 1973. 270 pp. : ill., photograph. Includes index, bibliography, and references.

ISBN: 0-8173-5106-X   LC: 72-7349

This definitive life of John McIntosh Kell is primarily concerned with Kell's naval career (1841–1865), which included service during the California phase of the Mexican War and participation in Admiral Matthew Perry's expedition to Japan. A midshipman in 1841, Kell attained the rank of lieutenant by 1855 and was first officer under Captain Raphael Semmes aboard the CSS *Sumter* in 1861. When Semmes assumed command of the *Alabama*, Kell once again served as his second in command. The *Alabama* was the most successful of the Confederate raiders, and Delany focuses on Kell's contribution to its success. He presents a detailed account of the encounter between the *Alabama* and the *Kearsarge* off Cherbourg. Following the war Kell returned to work on his family's farm, but he was never very successful. He attained a level of economic sufficiency when he was appointed adjutant-general of Georgia in 1886. Kell's major literary work was an autobiographical account titled *Recollections of a Naval Life* (1900), in which, as an ardent Confederate partisan, he defended the actions of Captain Semmes and had high praise for the crew of the *Alabama*.

Reviewed in:	AHR	79 (Oct. 74) 1265
	HRN	1 (May–June 73) 160
	JAH	60 (March 74) 1132
	RKH	72 (Jan. 74) 55–56

065 D'Entremont, John. *Southern Emancipator: Moncure Conway, the American Years, 1832–1865*. New York: Oxford University Press, 1987. xiii, 282 pp. : ill., photographs. Includes index and references.

ISBN: 0-195-04264-6   LC: 86-23756

This book is the first of a projected two-volume study of the life of Moncure Conway—transcendentalist, Unitarian, and radical abolitionist. D'Entremont begins with a discussion of Conway's questioning and ultimate rejection of his aristocratic Virginia heritage. This is followed by an examination of the evolution of Conway's career as a social reformer and religious radical beginning with his education, first at the Methodist Dickinson College in Pennsylvania and later at Harvard Divinity School. The author discusses Conway's ministries at the Washington, D.C., Unitarian Church and at the more radical First Congregational Church in Cincinnati. Conway viewed the conflict between the North and the South in very personal terms. Although he wanted to see the end of slavery, he could not accept the violence of war, and so in 1863 he chose expatriation in England to escape the conflict that was "killing his spirit." The end of the war and the abolition of slavery signaled an end to Conway's preoccupation with American society. By the late 1860s he considered himself a "citizen of the world" and had established himself in London's South Place Chapel. This book includes a bibliography of works by Conway.

Reviewed in:	AHR	94 (April 89) 521–522
	CWH	35 (March 89) 74–75
	GHQ	72 (Spring 88) 151–152
	JAH	75 (Sept. 88) 617–618
	JSO	55 (Feb. 89) 122–123
	VMH	96 (April 88) 231–232

066   Eaton, Clement. *Jefferson Davis*. New York: Free Press, 1977. xii, 334 pp. : ill., photographs. Includes index and references.

ISBN: 0-02-908700-7   LC: 77-2512

Eaton presents a balanced, measured treatment of Jefferson Davis's life. This biography reflects the history of important national events during the 1840s and through the 1860s. Eaton states that despite Davis's long career in public service, he remains a sphinx, his austere manner effectively masking his inner self. Many of Davis's personal papers relating to his early life were burned when Union troops overran his plantation, Brierfield, in 1862. Eaton relies on public documents, extant personal papers, and secondary sources to tell the story of a self-contained, reserved man. His analysis emphasizes Davis's leadership qualities. Eaton claims that the stress of the war brought out weaknesses in Davis's character and exposed him as a very sensitive individual with an unconquerable pride.

> *Reviewed in:*   CHO   15 (March 78) 136
>
> HRN   6 (March 78) 96
>
> LIJ   102 (Oct. 1, 77) 2054

067   Eckert, Ralph Lowell. *John Brown Gordon: Soldier, Southerner, American*. Baton Rouge, La.: Louisiana State University Press, 1989. xvii, 367 pp. : ill., photographs, maps. Includes index and bibliography.

ISBN: 0-807-1145-53   LC: 88-30339

John Brown Gordon of Georgia, known as "Gallant" Gordon and the "hero of Appomattox," began his public career at the age of twenty-nine, when he led a volunteer company that became part of the Sixth Alabama Infantry Regiment. Wounded five times at Sharpsburg, he rose quickly through the ranks to become a corps commander and to serve with distinction in the Army of Northern Virginia. Eckert's definitive study examines Gordon's military career and his contributions to the Confederate cause, as well as his more significant postwar career as a politician and businessman. He stresses the seemingly contradictory nature of Gordon's life in this account: a devout Christian, he was also a devoted Klansman; a living embodiment of the Lost Cause, he was an untiring advocate of postwar nationalism. After the war, Gordon served as governor of Georgia for one term and as a U.S. senator for two terms. As a senator he worked to remove federal troops from the South and to restore harmony between the two sections of the nation. At the same time, he celebrated the memory of antebellum society and the Confederacy, and in his political dealings sought terms favorable to white Southerners. Eventually, Gordon resigned his Senate seat to work for the railroad. Held in high esteem by many Southerners, Gordon was almost reviled by many others as a betrayer of the South and the Democratic party. His family home was destroyed by fire in 1899, and almost no personal papers survive. Eckert has consulted a variety of manuscript and archival sources—as well as official publications, reports, and records—to reconstruct the life of the man whom he considers one of the most significant figures in Southern and American history during the last half of the nineteenth century.

Reviewed in:	AHR	95 (Dec. 90) 1634–1635
	CWH	36 (June 90) 184–185
	FHQ	70 (July 91) 91–93
	GHQ	76 (Winter 90) 651–665
	JAH	77 (Sept. 90) 676–677
	JSO	57 (May 91) 331–332

068 Fehrenbacher, Don E. *Lincoln in Text and Context: Collected Essays.* Stanford, Calif.: Stanford University Press, 1987. 364 pp. Includes index and references.

ISBN: 0-8047-1329-4   LC: 86-14346

This is a collection of nineteen generally high-quality essays by Fehrenbacher that first appeared as articles, conference papers, and lectures over the course of thirty-three years beginning in 1953. The first two parts of the book are arranged chronologically. Part 1 presents contrasting views on a variety of topics, beginning with the Mexican War up to the election of 1860. Part 2 is concerned with the war years and includes essays on Abraham Lincoln and his attitudes toward a number of issues such as race, the Constitution, and a strategy for reconstruction. The essays in part 3 of the collection focus on images of Lincoln that various historians have presented in their writings and chronicles the changing image of Lincoln in American historiography.

Reviewed in: HRN 16 (Spring 88) 116–117

069 Grayson, George Washington. *A Creek Warrior for the Confederacy: The Autobiography of Chief G. W. Grayson.* Edited with an introduction by W. David Baird. Norman, Okla.: University

of Oklahoma Press, 1988. xvii, 181 pp. Includes index and bibliography.

ISBN: 0-806-1210-33   LC: 87-27617

A volume in the Civilization of the American Indian series, Grayson breathes life into historical facts. The reader is offered a first-hand account of events as they unfolded for the participant. Born in 1843, George Washington Grayson was a tribal *métis*, or mixed-blood, Creek whose parents had European ancestors. His family epitomized the split within the Creek Nation: his father's family lived among the Upper Creeks and identified with the Conservative Red Sticks, whereas his maternal relations were Lower Creeks and supported the progressive McIntosh party. His life, typical of that of the majority of *métis* in the Indian territory, was disrupted by the Civil War. Attached to the armies of the Confederate states, Grayson was a participant in almost all of the significant engagements that took place in Indian territory and rose to the rank of captain. By all accounts Grayson's autobiography is a remarkable, almost-unique, document: an eyewitness account of the most significant Civil War action in Indian territory. A detailed narrative of multiple campaigns, Grayson viewed the events from the perspective of a Creek Indian warrior in the service of the Confederate States of America. This intensely personal document is also unique for the glimpse it offers into the corporate life of the Creek Indians and its observations on the political and social factionalism that divided the tribe both before and after the war. Baird, as editor, has described himself as being faithful to the intent of the text while retaining as much as possible of it in an uncompromised form. He cross-references the places in the narrative that fit in the chronological and historical framework. Events, people and places, and circumstances have been identified, all of which add to this valuable account from the perspective of a Native American participant in America's bloodiest hours. Photographs are included.

> *Reviewed in:*   CHO   26 (Dec. 88) 700
>   JSO   55 (Nov. 89) 726

070   Hallock, Judith Lee. *Braxton Bragg and Confederate Defeat.* Vol. 2. Tuscaloosa, Ala.: University of Alabama Press, 1991. xii, 298 pp. : ill., photograph, maps. Includes index and bibliography.

ISBN: 0-8173-0543-2   LC: 91-3554

Hallock's examination of Braxton Bragg's life takes up where Grady McWhiney's account ends (see entry 078). Displaying an impressive command of primary and secondary sources, the author examines what she considers the most interesting portion of Bragg's career—January 1863 to May 1865. During this period Bragg faced first William S. Rosencrans and then Ulysses S. Grant in important campaigns in the Western theater. Hallock concentrates on Braxton Bragg's stormy relationships with his peers and his subordinates. She relates the story of how Bragg was relieved of his field command following the battle of Missionary Ridge in 1863 and how he went on to serve as a military advisor to Jefferson Davis until the end of the war.

Reviewed in: JAH   79 (Dec. 92) 1186

071 Hattaway, Herman. *General Stephen D. Lee.* Jackson, Miss.: University Press of Mississippi, 1976. xii, 293 pp. : ill. Includes index and bibliography.

ISBN: 0-878-05071-X   LC: 75-042612

To Hattaway, General Stephen D. Lee has been one of the forgotten men of history. Having resigned his commission in February 1861 after graduating from West Point, he made his mark as an officer in the Confederacy. A competent and often-brilliant commander, he was praised by superiors and opponents and revered by Mississippians. Fighting as a professional soldier to preserve the old way of life, and then helping to lead and shape the new social order in the South, Lee held every rank from captain to general—eventually, after the war, becoming a college president.

Reviewed in: CWH   23 (June 77) 179–181

JAH   64 (June 77) 161–162

JSO   43 (May 77) 300–301

LAH   19 (Summer 78) 362–363

072 Jordan, David M. *Winfield Scott Hancock: A Soldier's Life.* Bloomington, Ind.: Indiana University Press, 1988. xii, 393 pp. : ill., photographs. Includes index, bibliography, and references.

ISBN: 0-253-36580-5   LC: 87-46091

Jordan has written a well-researched account of the military career of Winfield Scott Hancock, who was educated at West Point and saw military service in Mexico and the West. In 1861 he was appointed brigadier general of a unit of Union volunteers. Hancock had a particular skill for exploiting battlefield opportunities and was universally recognized as one of the Union's best generals. He was involved in the fighting at Chancellorsville and Gettysburg, and in the Wilderness and the Spotsylvania campaigns. Hancock remained a professional soldier after the war and went west to subdue the Native American uprisings. He was appointed commander of the Fifth Military District by Andrew Johnson and relocated to New Orleans. Hancock, politically active after the war, was the nominee of the Democratic party in the presidential election of 1880.

Reviewed in: AHR   95 (June 90) 909

CHO   26 (April 89) 1392

HIS   52 (Aug. 90) 669

HRN   18 (Fall 89) 38

JAH   76 (Dec. 89) 940

073 Lash, Jeffrey N. *Destroyer of the Iron Horse: General Joseph E. Johnston and Confederate Rail Transport, 1861–1865.* Kent, Ohio: Kent State University Press, 1991. viii, 228 pp. : ill., photographs, map. Includes index, bibliography, and references.

ISBN: 0-873-38423-7   LC: 90-5372

This study breaks new ground for a reexamination of General Joseph E. Johnston and his abilities. It examines what Lash considers "serious deficiencies in logistical command" on the part of several high-ranking Confederate officers, including Johnston. According to Lash, many Southern commanders were ignorant of, and indifferent to, the fundamental mechanical aspects of railroad technology. They never subsequently developed an awareness of the potentially decisive military applications of mechanized transportation. Lash argues that Johnston, who served as a federal quartermaster general before the war, should have realized the strategic importance of rail transportation, especially in the South, where provisions and men had to be moved long distances. Lash questions Johnston's reputation as a strategist and logistician, and claims that his failure to make effective use of the railroads in the South irreparably damaged the Confederate war effort. Beloved by his troops, Johnston feuded with the Confederate high command, particularly Jefferson Davis, throughout the war. According to Lash, Johnston never really understood Confederate railroad policy; nor did he effectively coordinate transportation operations among the Confederate high command, the war department, and Southern railway officials. Lash concludes that although Johnston did eventually realize the logistical importance of the railroad, he seldom used it effectively in major campaigns.

Reviewed in: JAH 78 (March 92) 1454–1455
JSO 58 (Nov. 92) 729–730
CHO 29 (Oct. 91) 342

074 Longacre, Edward G. *The Man behind the Guns: A Biography of General Henry Jackson Hunt, Chief of Artillery, Army of the Potomac.* South Brunswick, N.J.: A. S. Barnes and Co., 1977. 294 pp., ill., photographs. Includes index, bibliography, and references.

ISBN: 0-498-01656-0   LC: 76-10885

This is the first full-length study of the life and career of Henry Jackson Hunt, who graduated from West Point in 1839 as an artillery specialist and went on to earn a reputation as the foremost authority of his time on the art and science of gunnery. Hunt slowly advanced through the ranks of the regular army at a time when the artillery, unlike the infantry or the cavalry, was not operated as an independent command. He saw combat duty during the Mexican War. When the Civil War began, Hunt was an experienced major, and he soon assumed command of artillery in the Army of the Potomac with responsibility for overall direction and maintenance. Eventually he rose to the temporary wartime rank of brigadier general. The zenith of Hunt's career was at Gettysburg on July 3, 1863, where his 270 strategically placed cannon shattered Pickett's Charge. Hunt provided a valuable service to the Union cause. Longacre maintains that because his artillery experience was so highly valued, he was never able to assume other duties and thus forfeited rank, recognition, and pay. Hunt was a master artillerist who transformed the disorganized federal artillery corps into the most effective service arm of the Army. An outspoken Democrat, Hunt antagonized many people during the war as well as while serving in a variety of administrative posts in the South during Reconstruction. In addition to his active military service, Hunt wrote articles, pamphlets, and papers on historical and technological subjects. He retired in 1883 having achieved the rank of colonel. At the time of his death six years later, Hunt was acknowledged by his peers as a fine tactician and military theorist as well as an able administrator and skillful field commander.

Reviewed in: AHR 83 (June 78) 810
CHO 14 (Jan. 78) 1562
JAH 65 (Sept. 78) 476
LIJ 103 (Jan. 15, 78) 157

075 Losson, Christopher. *Tennessee's Forgotten Warriors: Frank Cheatham and His Confederate Division.* Knoxville, Tenn.: University of Tennessee Press, 1989. xvi, 352 pp.

ISBN: 0-870-49615-8   LC: 89-33944

This is the first full-length biography of Benjamin Franklin Cheatham, and Losson provides a favorable but balanced account. More than just a biography, it is also an account of his command, and because of this represents a significant contribution to the understanding of the Army of Tennessee. Losson pursues a dual approach in this book. The first focuses on Cheatham and provides a useful portrait of him as a brigade, division, and corps commander. The second concentrates on Cheatham's command and discusses the unit's involvement in battles such as Shiloh and Stones River, and the Georgia and Tennessee campaigns.

Reviewed in:	CWH	37 (March 91) 67–69
	CWT	29 (Jan.–Feb. 91) 10
	GHQ	75 (Summer 91) 444–445
	JAH	77 (March 91) 1369
	JSO	57 (Nov. 91) 747–748
	THQ	49 (Winter 90) 257–258

076 McFeely, William S. *Grant: A Biography.* New York: W. W. Norton, 1981. xiii, 592 pp. : ill., photographs. Includes index, bibliography, and references.

ISBN: 0-393-01372-3   LC: 80-25279

According to William McFeely, Ulysses S. Grant and his wife, Julia, never thought of themselves as "ordinary." They always believed that Grant was destined to be "a man of consequence." This is why McFeely chose to write about Grant, whose life story McFeely saw as the "quest of an ordinary American man in the mid-nineteenth century to make his mark." Before reenlisting in the Army, Grant had failed as a peacetime army officer, a farmer, a businessman, and a store clerk. The war made all the difference for Grant. A keen observer, he grasped the nature of the conflict, and although he spoke little, issued his orders surely and confidently. McFeely claims that eventually killing became the "core" of Grant's life and that after the war he had difficulty returning to civilian life. It was his need for public adulation that prompted Grant to seek the presidency. He had no program for the country—only a need to find some substitute for the intense experience of the war. According to McFeely, Grant was a common man who, having achieved a measure of fame, was unable, or unwilling, to associate once again with common men. Unfortunately, Grant's military achievements did not successfully transfer into the political sphere. This book gives considerable attention to a discussion of the fact that during Grant's presidency many opportunities for the reconstruction of the South were not pursued.

Reviewed in: AHR   87 (Oct. 82) 1166–1167
                  CWH   27 (Dec. 81) 362–366
                  CWT   20 (Oct. 81) 49
                  HRN   9 (Sept. 81) 225
                  MIR   61 (Dec. 81) 84–85
                  RAH   9 (Dec. 81) 507–509

Drying the wash

077   McMurry, Richard M. *John Bell Hood and the War for Southern Independence.* Lexington, Ky.: University Press of Kentucky, 1982. 239 pp. : ill., maps. Includes index and bibliography.

ISBN: 0-813-1145-78   LC: 82-040175

John Bell Hood was the controversial general who lost Atlanta to General William Tecumseh Sherman and led the Army of Tennessee to total destruction. McMurry examines Hood in light not of biased memoirs but of an expansion of more-recent critical analyses. Hood's reverence for Robert E. Lee's tactics in 1862 did not serve his command at the end of the war; his recklessness and bravery advanced him to full general beyond his capabilities. McMurry examines the influences on Hood together with his achievements and failures as a product of the insular society of the Old South.

Reviewed in: HIS   47 (Feb. 85) 291

078   McWhiney, Grady. *Braxton Bragg and Confederate Defeat.* Vol. 1. Tuscaloosa, Ala.: University of Alabama Press, 1991. xiv, 421 pp. : ill., photograph.

ISBN: 0-8173-0545-9   LC: 69-19856

Braxton Bragg was a Mexican War hero and one of the most distinguished soldiers to join the Confederacy, yet within two years he had become the Confederacy's most discredited commander. McWhiney is primarily concerned with Bragg's development as a soldier. He claims that Bragg's West Point training and his Mexican War experiences instilled in him a propensity for offensive tactics that, by the time of the Civil War, were rendered impractical by the introduction of the rifle. According to McWhiney, Bragg failed to learn from his mistakes on the battlefield. Although he was an organizer and a disciplinarian capable of praiseworthy strategic maneuvers, Bragg was a poor tactician, who frequently ignored intelligence reports and was ultimately judged unsuitable for field command. See entry 070.

Reviewed in: JSO   59 (May 93) 381

079   Marszalek, John F. *Sherman: A Soldier's Passion for Order.* New York: Free Press, 1993. xvi, 635 pp. : ill., photographs, maps. Includes index, bibliography, and references.

ISBN: 0-02-920135-7   LC: 92-24533

Marszalek employs a psychological approach in recounting William Tecumseh Sherman's military career and his relationship with his wife and children. The author claims that events surrounding the death of Sherman's father and his own subsequent adoption by a wealthy neighbor, Thomas Ewing, imbued Sherman with an overriding need to achieve order in his life. In fact, according to Marszalek, Sherman believed that "order was necessary to success in life." Sherman is portrayed as an uncompromising conservative with a powerful ego who never doubted his own opinion and only deferred to Ulysses S. Grant out of loyalty. The author considers Sherman one of the great military leaders of the war. He discusses Sherman's reliance on a tactic that had been taught at West Point for many years—namely, that troop movement rather than pitched battle was the key to victory—and he points out that the general's new twist on this old maxim was a psychological assault on the will of the Southern people. Although he acknowledges that Sherman's controversial methods were destructive, Marszalek considers them an attempt to restore order. For Sherman, the restoration of the Union was the ultimate symbol of order. Marszalek contends that Sherman's peacetime career was not so glorious as his combat record and that, because he did not understand postwar politics, Sherman often spoke without thinking and incurred the wrath of many politicians.

Reviewed in:	CHO	30 (May 93) 1537
	HRN	22 (Winter 94) 67
	JAH	81 (June 94) 281
	JSO	60 (May 94) 414
	LIJ	117 (Nov. 1, 92) 6

080 Martin, Samuel J. *The Road to Glory: Confederate General Richard S. Ewell.* Indianapolis, Ind.: Guild Press of Indiana, 1991. iv, 432 pp. : ill., photographs, maps. Includes bibliography and references.

ISBN: 1-878208-07-1/1-878208-08-X(paper)   LC: 91-058045

Richard Stoddard Ewell, known as "Old Bald Head" to his contemporaries, was a key participant in most of the battles fought by the Army of Northern Virginia, beginning with the First Battle of Bull Run. Ewell was a talented soldier who had a distinguished and controversial career. He lost his leg in 1862 during the battle of Groveton; the following year he succeeded Thomas "Stonewall" Jackson as the commander of the Second Corps. Martin uses Ewell's private and official correspondence in his discussion of the general's career and personality. He also examines the psychological and physical effects on Ewell of the amputation, as well as Ewell's relationships with other Confederate military leaders such as Robert E. Lee, Jackson, Jubal Early, and A. P. Hill. The text is supplemented with excellent maps.

Reviewed in: JSO   58 (May 92) 356

081 Marvel, William. *Burnside.* Chapel Hill, N.C.: University of North Carolina Press, 1991. xii, 541 pp. : ill., photographs, maps. Includes index, bibliography, and references.

ISBN: 0-8078-1983-2   LC: 91-8419

Marvel presents a detailed account of the military career of Ambrose Everett Burnside, best remembered as one of several Union generals who mismanaged the Army of the Potomac between 1861 and 1864. Burnside led the Union Army to defeat at Fredericksburg in 1862 and had no better luck as a corps commander during the Battle of The Crater at Petersburg in 1864, after which he was relieved of his command. Burnside resigned from the Army on the day Abraham Lincoln was killed. Indecisive, slow, and unlucky, he never commanded the respect and loyalty of his fellow officers; nor did he publicly defend himself against his critics. Although he captured Knoxville in 1863, his relatively small successes were overshadowed by his failure and defeat in more-significant engagements. Marvel scrupulously details Burnside's failures in battle and is frank about his personal failings. Nevertheless, he challenges the traditional evaluation of Burnside as a nice man who failed miserably as a general. Marvel attempts to redeem Burnside's reputation by arguing that, whatever the general's personal failures, the collective dysfunctional behavior of the Union Army's general staff was more responsible for Burnside's failure than was Burnside himself. Marvel's account is especially valuable because it examines military operations in some of the war's lesser-known theaters in North Carolina and in the border states.

Reviewed in: JAH   20 (Sept. 92) 668–669

                   LIJ   116 (Oct. 15, 91) 96

082 Morris, Roy. *Sheridan: The Life and Wars of General Phil Sheridan.* New York: Crown Publishers, 1992. x, 464 pp. : ill., maps. Includes index and references.

ISBN: 0-517-5807-05   LC: 91-43304

Not a physically attractive man, Philip H. Sheridan had the personal attributes necessary for a wartime commander and became one of the most important Union generals in the Civil War. Morris discusses Sheridan's battles and shows the connection between his success on the battlefield and that in the political arena. Stones River, Chickamauga, and the Shenandoah Valley campaign, are all important parts of this work as they were of Sheridan's career. Morris brings out Sheridan's assertiveness, combativeness, and armywide reputation for having the best scouts through the war years. The author continues into Sheridan's Reconstruction assignments and campaigns against the Native Americans in the trans-Mississippi West.

> *Reviewed in:*   LIJ   117 (March 1, 92) 102
>
> NYT   (July 5, 92) 1
>
> PUW   239 (March 30, 92) 95

083 Muhlenfeld, Elisabeth. *Mary Boykin Chesnut: A Biography.* Baton Rouge, La.: Louisiana State University Press, 1981. xv, 271 pp. : ill., photographs. Includes index and bibliography.

ISBN: 0-8071-0852-9   LC: 80-26610

This book uses Mary Boykin Miller Chesnut's autobiographical writings, her papers, and those of her family to tell the life story of a woman whose drawing room became a social center for prominent Confederate political and military figures. Chesnut was the daughter of a United States senator from South Carolina who married James Chesnut, the son of a wealthy South Carolina planter. James later served as an aide to both General Pierre Beauregard and to Jefferson Davis. During the war Chesnut kept a journal, much of which was eventually published under the title *A Diary from Dixie.* After the war she wrote and translated novels and revised her war-years journals for publication. Muhlenfeld focuses on the last twenty years of Chesnut's life, a time when she helped her family repay debts incurred during the war and reestablished a sense of order in her life. Muhlenfeld considers Chesnut's "an extremely complex and emotional personality, an active and wide-ranging intelligence that could easily grasp large political, psychological and moral issues."

> *Reviewed in:*   AHR   91 (April 86) 468
>
> HIS   45 (May 83) 423
>
> JAH   68 (March 82) 939
>
> JAS   17 (April 83) 117

JSO   47 (Nov. 81) 585

RAH   10 (March 82) 54

084   Neely, Mark E., Jr. *The Last Best Hope of Earth: Abraham Lincoln and the Promise of America.* Cambridge, Mass.: Harvard University Press, 1993. viii, 214 pp. : ill., photographs. Includes index and references.

ISBN: 0-674-51125-5   LC: 93-22863

Neely presents an insightful, brief biography of Abraham Lincoln, concentrating on his years as president. He begins by discussing Lincoln's Western background; his grasp of politics, race, and economics; and his concept of nation. This is followed by a series of chronologically arranged topical essays. One essay focuses on Lincoln's role as the war president and the ways in which he exercised his constitutional powers. Another examines his emancipation policy, focusing on the military justification for freeing the slaves. There are essays about conscription, desertion, and public opinion. The final essay analyzes the major theories that have been put forth to explain the assassination.

Reviewed in: CHO   31 (March 94) 1209

LIJ   118 (Sept. 1, 93) 194

PUW   240 (Sept. 20, 93) 58

NYT   (June 12, 94) 17

085   Nolan, Alan T. *Lee Considered: General Robert E. Lee and Civil War History.* Chapel Hill, N.C.: University of North Carolina Press, 1991. xii, 231 pp. : ill., photographs. Includes index, bibliography, references, and appendixes.

ISBN: 0-8078-1956-5   LC: 90-48296

Nolan believes that Robert E. Lee was a great man. In this biography he attacks what he calls the "Lee tradition." He begins this study with an analysis of several previously published biographies of Lee and examines various elements of the Lee legend. Nolan believes that Lee was a tactically effective but strategically limited general who prolonged the bloodshed of the war by ordering relentless offensives. The text is supplemented by three appendixes. One of them is an analysis of an army commander's authority to surrender, which Nolan has included to evaluate Lee's conduct when he surrendered.

Reviewed in: JAH   19 (June 92) 280

JAS   27 (April 93) 113

JSO   59 (Feb. 93) 142

RAH   21 (Sept. 93) 415

086 Parks, Joseph Howard. *Joseph E. Brown of Georgia.* Baton
Rouge, La.: Louisiana State University Press, 1977. x, 612 pp. :
ill., photographs. Includes index, bibliography, and references.

ISBN: 0-8071-0189-3   LC: 74-27192

Parks has written the first comprehensive biography of Joseph E.
Brown, one of the most distinctive and controversial men in Southern
history. This is a balanced account of the life of a strong-willed, capable political leader and competent businessman. The author begins by
tracing Brown's yeoman-farmer roots in South Carolina and Georgia,
and his entry into Georgia state politics. During his career, Brown was
identified as a spokesman for the "plain people" even though he became wealthy as a result of owning land, slaves, and interests in mining operations. Brown was elected governor of Georgia four times,
serving during the secession crisis and the war. He was an ardent supporter of slavery and states' rights, and he persistently resisted the authority of the Confederate central government. In the years following
the war, Brown accepted congressional Reconstruction. He became a
Republican and served as a United States senator from 1880 to 1890.
He also became one of Georgia's leading entrepreneurs, acquiring and
managing a number of railroad, mining, and manufacturing interests.

Reviewed in: AHR   82 (Dec. 77) 1334

CHO   15 (Sept. 78) 943

JAH   65 (June 78) 172

JSO   44 (Feb. 78) 129–131

087 Parrish, T. Michael. *Richard Taylor, Soldier Prince of Dixie.*
Chapel Hill, N.C.: University of North Carolina Press, 1992. xiv,
553 pp. : ill., maps. Includes index and bibliographical references.

ISBN: 0-8078-2032-6   LC: 91-46467

Parrish has consulted Richard Taylor's memoirs and other primary documents to present a full biography of one of the Confederacy's more important personages, and one of its few non-West Point
lieutenant generals. He personified the antebellum South's planter
aristocracy, whose members believed that traditional leadership and
prominence would prevail. Secession and capitalism struck at the
foundation of Taylor's values. He served with distinction in Virginia,

Louisiana, and Mississippi, and Parrish discusses those battles and campaigns in full detail. Although he began to feel that the Southern cause was hopeless, he continued to honor his duty as a soldier.

Reviewed in: CHO   30 (Jan. 93) 872

JAH   80 (Dec. 93) 11004

JSO   60 (Feb. 94) 148

088   Phillips, Christopher. *Damned Yankee: The Life of General Nathaniel Lyon.* Columbia, Mo.: University of Missouri Press, 1990. xiv, 243 pp. : ill. Includes index and bibliography.

ISBN: 0-826-2073-16   LC: 89-20470

Nathaniel Lyon has been called the "savior of Missouri," being the first Union general to fall in battle, while keeping the border state of Missouri from seceding. Beneath the title, however, was an unstable man who, motivated by a sense of duty and a twisted perception of punishment, deliberately provoked a bloody civil conflict in Missouri. Missouri was dragged into a war it had chosen to avoid. Using untapped sources, Phillips goes beyond the biography written by a friend of the Lyon family in 1862 in an attempt to understand why Lyon would recklessly attack when outnumbered, or allow neither individual nor government to impede his search for his place in the world.

Reviewed in: AHQ   50 (Autumn 91) 304–305

JSO   57 (Nov. 91) 746–747

089   Piston, William Garrett. *Lee's Tarnished Lieutenant: James Longstreet and His Place in Southern History.* Athens, Ga.: University of Georgia Press, 1987. xv, 252 pp. : ill., maps, photograph. Includes index and bibliography.

ISBN: 0-8203-0907-9   LC: 86-16025

Piston considers James Longstreet the best corps-level commander of the war. This is not a traditional biography in that it does not chronicle every aspect of Longstreet's life but is primarily concerned with his image and place in history. The first part of the book reappraises Longstreet's contribution to the Confederate war effort. Piston praises him for his willingness to place the Confederacy above personal ambition. The second part of the book examines Longstreet's controversial postwar career as a Republican, which cost him his status as a war hero. Piston also discusses the events that lead to Longstreet's becoming the scapegoat for the Confederate defeat at Gettysburg.

Reviewed in: AHR   94 (June 89) 852–853

HRN   17 (Fall 88) 9

JAH   75 (Dec. 88) 456–457

JSO   55 (May 89) 339

VMH   98 (April 90) 318–319

090 Ramage, James A. *Rebel Raider: The Life of General John Hunt Morgan.* Lexington, Ky.: University Press of Kentucky, 1986. 306 pp. : ill., photographs. Includes bibliography.

ISBN: 0-813-1157-60   LC: 86-001548

John Hunt Morgan, grandson of Kentucky's John Wesley Hunt and grandnephew of John Marshall, was a military amateur who fought with the Kentucky Mounted Volunteers. Ramage tells of Morgan's depression, his disdain of authority and training, and his tactics as an "adventurous partisan." He was slain in Richmond while he and his raiders were being arraigned for bank robbery and looting. His guerilla tactics caught people's imagination but did little to aid the Confederate cause.

Reviewed in: CWH   34 (June 88) 175–176

HIS   54 (Feb. 88) 442–443

JSO   54 (Feb. 88) 120–121

091 *Rank and File: Civil War Essays in Honor of Bell Irvin Wiley.* Edited by James I. Robinson, Jr., and Richard M. McMurry. San Rafael, Calif.: Presidio Press, 1976. 164 pp.

ISBN: 0-891-4101-12   LC: 76-048787

Bell Wiley, distinguished professor of Civil War history, was honored by his graduate students with the publication of these essays including "Bell Irvin Wiley: Uncommon Soldier," "Thomas C. Handman: Arkansas Politician and General," "Rise to Glory: A Speculative Essay on the Early Career of John Bell Hood," "Transatlantic Misunderstanding: William Henry Seward and the Declaration of Paris Negotiation, 1861," "Colonel Cyrus B. Harkie: A Troubled Military," "For the Union as It Was and the Constitution as It Is: A Copperhead Views the Civil War," "Chaplain William E. Wiatt: Soldier of the Cloth," and "The Boys Who Stayed Behind: Northern Industrialists and the Civil War." There is a bibliography of Wiley's works included.

Reviewed in: CWH   24 (March 78) 90–91

MIA   42 (Oct. 78) 163
VMH   86 (April 78) 209–210

092 Royster, Charles. *The Destructive War: William Tecumseh Sherman, Stonewall Jackson, and the Americans.* New York: Alfred A. Knopf, 1991. xii, 523 pp. : ill., photographs, maps. Includes index and references.

ISBN: 0-394-52485-3   LC: 90-26458

Royster examines the concept of violence as a way to understand the conflict and the impact that William Tecumseh Sherman and Thomas "Stonewall" Jackson had on public thinking about the military conduct of the war. The author goes on to show how these two men came to personify the kind of war that both Northerners and Southerners believed was necessary to achieve victory. Royster traces the roots of the conflict's destructive violence to zealots in both camps who were driven by a need to define a national identity and validate their own definition of America. According to Royster, both sides assumed that the war would be horrendous, and this assumption resulted in a willingness to make it so. There is also a discussion of the link between destruction and the attainment of political ends.

Reviewed in: CHO   29 (May 92) 1460
　　　　　　　　LIJ   116 (Sept. 15, 91) 102
　　　　　　　　NYR   38 (Nov. 7, 91) 10
　　　　　　　　NYT   (Nov. 3, 91) 13
　　　　　　　　RAH   20 (Sept. 92) 326

093 Sears, Stephen W. *George B. McClellan: The Young Napoleon.* New York: Ticknor & Fields, 1988. xii, 482 pp. Includes index and bibliography.

ISBN: 0-8991-9264-5   LC: 88-2138

Drawing on primary sources, Sears presents a full portrait of this general of contradictions and controversy. The youngest in his class at West Point, George B. McClellan rose to commander of the Army of the Potomac after becoming the first Union military hero. He missed great war opportunities to rise in stature and continually blamed others for his shortcomings. Believing that the Confederate forces were greater than his and that there were those who conspired to defeat him, he also, according to Sears, believed he was the chosen instrument to save the Union.

Reviewed in: JSO   56 (Feb. 90) 127

CHO   26 (Dec. 88) 704

094 Symonds, Craig L. *Joseph E. Johnston: A Civil War Biography.*
New York: W. W. Norton, 1992. xiv, 450 pp. Includes index and
references.

ISBN: 0-393-03058-X   LC: 91-017899

Joseph E. Johnston was the first in many things. He was the first
graduate of West Point to be promoted to the rank of general in the
regular army and the most senior U.S. Army officer to resign his commission and fight for the Confederacy in 1861. He was considered by
many of his contemporaries to be second only to Robert E. Lee in his
greatness as a field commander during the war; yet he commanded
forces in four battles for the Confederacy, none of which was decisive.
Symonds's overview of the career of this important general claims to
strive for evenhandedness in his quarrels with Jefferson Davis, but it
does defend Johnston against those in the Confederacy who were on
bad terms with Johnston. The author is equally critical, however, of
Johnston.

Reviewed in: AHR   98 (Feb. 93) 2554

CHO   30 (Oct. 92) 3724

HRN   21 (Winter 93) 84

JAH   79 (March 93) 1620

JSO   59 (Aug. 93) 565

095 Taylor, John M. *William Henry Seward: Lincoln's Right Hand.*
New York: HarperCollins Publishers, 1991. xi, 340 pp. Includes
index, bibliography, references, and appendix.

ISBN: 0-06-016307-0   LC: 90-55943

Taylor has produced a well-written, concise biography that
carefully delineates William Henry Seward's character. Taylor believes
that Seward was one of the greatest American secretaries of state because of the way he managed, on more than one occasion, to diffuse
problems that could have led to European intervention on the side of
the Confederacy. A complicated and occasionally devious character,
Seward was a pioneer in prison reform while governor of New York.
He fought to contain expansion of slavery and to bring about its eventual abolition while serving as a United States senator. The appendix
presents a memorandum (dated April 1, 1861) that Seward sent to

Lincoln, which contains the secretary of state's thoughts on the conduct of the war.

Reviewed in: JAH   79 (Sept. 92) 666

096   Thomas, Emory M. *Bold Dragoon: The Life of J. E. B. Stuart.* New York: Harper & Row, 1986. xi, 354 pp. Includes index and bibliography.

ISBN: 0-0601-5566-3   LC: 85-45577

Shrouded in myth, J. E. B. Stuart's image was of the cavalier, a talented but self-absorbed man, a defender of Southern ideals, one who sought to make the most of his life. He became a respected cavalryman; but controlled by his ambition, he lost sight of his own limitations. Thomas follows Stuart's life from his early childhood to his death a year before Appomattox. Using Stuart's letters to understand the man behind the myth, his role in the major battles is also explored as is his distortion of facts in the military records to enhance his reputation. Campaign maps and photographs are also included.

Reviewed in: AHR   93 (April 88) 505

CHO   24 (Dec. 86) 623

JAH   73 (March 87) 1042

JSO   53 (Nov. 87) 673

NYT   (Sept. 21, 86) 46

097   Trulock, Alice Rains. *In the Hands of Providence: Joshua L. Chamberlain and the American Civil War.* Chapel Hill, N.C.: University of North Carolina Press, 1992. xxii, 569 pp. : ill., photographs, maps. Includes index, bibliography, references, and appendix.

ISBN: 0-8078-2020-2   LC: 91-50791

Trulock has written a definitive biography of Joshua L. Chamberlain, placing him within a social, political, and military context. She used official records, contemporary accounts, and memoirs of participants, as well as Chamberlain's own writings. In 1862 Chamberlain left his position as an instructor in logic and natural theology at Bowdin College to accept a commission as a lieutenant colonel in the Twentieth Maine Infantry Regiment. Chamberlain first saw action at Antietam. He was wounded six times during the war. The Twentieth Maine is known for its stalwart defense of Little Round Top during the battle of Gettysburg. It was Chamberlain who ordered the charge that saved Little Round Top, an action that earned him the Congressional Medal of Honor. By the end of the war, Chamberlain had achieved the rank of brigadier general. He was among the Union officers who accepted Lee's surrender at Appomattox. After the war he was elected governor of Maine four times and served as president of Bowdin. Chamberlain wrote and lectured on his war experiences. The appendix presents the "Command Organization of the Fifth Army Corps, Army of the Potomac, Antietam through Appomattox, in conjunction with the army career of Joshua L. Chamberlain."

Reviewed in: LIJ   117 (June 1, 92) 140

NYT   (Sept. 27, 92) 34

JAH   80 (June 93) 276

JSO   59 (May 93) 383

098 Van der Heuvel, Gerry. *Crowns of Thorns and Glory: Mary Todd Lincoln and Varina Howell Davis, the Two First Ladies of the Civil War.* New York: Dutton, 1988. ix, 306 pp. Includes index and bibliography.

ISBN: 0-525-24599-5   LC: 87-30707

Van der Heuvel, a one-time press secretary to a first lady and former White House correspondent, provides balance to the lives of the presidents of the Union and the Confederacy with this biography of their wives. Mary Todd and Varina Howell were both born into Southern families of relative privilege; both married older men, albeit with very different political careers, and suffered the loss of all but one of their children. According to Van der Heuvel, Mary Todd did not do well as the First Lady of the land, and her fragile personality made her the second victim after the shooting at Ford's Theater. Varina Davis, in contrast, did not suffer the same scrutiny of the press and was able to support her husband while he was in prison. She became an accomplished writer of her memoirs, ending her days with honor. Family portraits of both the Lincolns and the Davises enhance the text.

Reviewed in: FHQ   68 (July 89) 106–107

JSH   56 (May 90) 363–364

099 Wakelyn, Jon L. *Biographical Dictionary of the Confederacy.* Westport, Conn.: Greenwood Press, 1977. xii, 601 pp. Includes index, bibliography, and appendixes.

ISBN: 0-8371-6124-X   LC: 72-13870

Captain Joe Hutton of the 12th New York
Volunteers at Culpepper, Virginia

Wakelyn provides concise, informative sketches of the 267 congressmen who served in the Confederate Congress, many of whom have not appeared in any biographical directory before. The introduction provides background on the formation of the Confederate Congress, the apportionment of representatives, and a statistical analysis of the age and occupation of each member. The entries for members include a narrative sketch of each man's education, occupation, professional and political careers, and military experience. In addition, there is an evaluation of the member's stand on broad areas of legislative concern. This material was drawn from official records of secession conventions and state legislatures as well as contemporary newspaper accounts. Four appendixes supplement the entries on the individual members: "Sessions of the Confederate Congress," "Membership of the Confederate Congress," "Standing Committees of the Confederate Congress," and "Maps of Occupied Confederate Territory 1861–1864" (which indicates Confederate territory lost at the end of each year).

Reviewed in: CWH   24 (March 78) 88–90

JAH   64 (March 78) 1119–1120

JSO   44 (Feb. 78) 121–123

LAH   19 (Fall 78) 473–474

NCH   55 (Autumn 78) 448–449

100   Warner, Ezra J., and W. Buck Yearns. *Biographical Register of the Confederate Congress.* Baton Rouge, La.: Louisiana State University Press, 1975. xxii, pp. : ill., photographs, maps. Includes appendixes.

ISBN: 0-8071-0092-7   LC: 74-77329

Warner and Yearns have included a narrative sketch of each member who served in the Confederate Congress. Entries describe each man's education, occupation, professional and political careers, and military experience. There is also an evaluation of the voting record of the members on selected issues.

Reviewed in: JAH   63 (Sept. 76) 421

                JSO   42 (Aug. 76) 431

101 Waugh, John C. *The Class of 1846: From West Point to Appomattox—Stonewall Jackson, George McClellan and Their Brothers.* New York: Warner Books, 1994. xvi, 635 pp. : ill. Includes index and references.

ISBN: 0-446-5159-49   LC: 92-50532

The main characters in this volume, thirty-four of them, were all members of the West Point class of 1846. George B. McClellan, Thomas "Stonewall" Jackson, A. P. Hill, and George E. Pickett are among them, and Waugh has provided brief biographical sketches of their lives up to the rebellion. The members of the class fought in three wars, and twenty of them became generals. Waugh chronicles their training, their personalities, and the events in which they made names for themselves, drawing on letters, diaries, and personal accounts for this collective biography.

Reviewed in: LIJ   119 (Feb. 1, 94) 98

                NYT   (June 12, 94) 23

102 Werlich, David P. *Admiral of the Amazon: John Randolph Tucker, His Confederate Colleagues, and Peru.* Charlottesville, Va.: University Press of Virginia, 1990. xv, 353 pp. : ill., photographs, maps. Includes index, bibliography, and references.

ISBN: 0-8139-1270-9   LC: 89-77279

Using public archives and private manuscript collections, Werlich places former Confederate naval officers in a broader context than usual and tells, for the first time, the story of Confederate expatriots in South America. John Randolph Tucker began his career in the United States Navy in 1827. In 1861 Commander Tucker resigned his commission to offer his services to the Confederacy. Tucker served with the James River Squadron and saw action at the battle of Hampton Roads. Later, he commanded the Confederate squadron at Charleston;

and at the battle of Sayler's Creek, the final major field engagement of the war, Tucker was the last of Robert E. Lee's major commanders to surrender. Unable to resume his naval career at the end of the war, Tucker accepted a commission as a rear admiral in the Peruvian navy to assist Peru and Chile in their war with Spain. Faced with strong opposition from both within and outside the Peruvian navy, Tucker resigned after only eight months. Realizing that there was little prospect of finding employment in the United States, Tucker tried farming in the Amazon region. Eventually he became president of the Hydrographic Commission of the Amazon, a Peruvian agency that charted the headwaters of the Amazon for steam navigation.

> *Reviewed in:*   CHO   28 (May 91) 1557
> JAH   78 (Dec. 91) 1093
> JSO   58 (Aug. 92) 541

103 Wert, Jeffrey D. *General James Longstreet: The Confederacy's Most Controversial Soldier.* New York: Simon & Schuster, 1993. 527 pp. : ill., photographs, maps. Includes index, bibliography, and references.

ISBN: 0-671-70921-6   LC: 93-28953

James Longstreet was Robert E. Lee's senior lieutenant in the Army of Northern Virginia. Longstreet was a superb battlefield commander with great tactical skill. Wert provides an extensive examination of the general's military career. He focuses on Longstreet's conduct in a number of engagements, including the Peninsula campaign, the Second Battle of Manassas, Antietam, Fredericksburg, Gettysburg, Chickamauga, and the Battle of the Wilderness. Longstreet often disapproved of the tactics of his superiors—in particular, Lee. Wert maintains that Longstreet's military skills have been overlooked by historians because he fell from favor in the postwar years by aligning himself with the radical Republicans. He received several patronage appointments after the war, including those as surveyor of customs for the port of New Orleans, deputy collector of internal revenue, and minister to Turkey. The text is supplemented with useful maps.

> *Reviewed in:*   HRN   22 (Spring 94) 106
> LIJ   118 (Nov. 1, 93) 102
> NYT   (Nov. 28, 93) 34

104 Wiley, Bell Irvin. *Confederate Women*. Westport, Conn.: Greenwood Press, 1975. xiv, 204 pp. : ill., photographs. Includes index, bibliography, and references.

ISBN: 0-8371-7534-8   LC: 74-5995

The essays in this volume were first presented as a series of lectures. The first three are biographical portraits of women who were all together first in Washington, D.C., as the wives of U.S. senators in the United States Congress and later in Richmond as the wives of highly placed Confederate officials. Wiley selected these women because they were married to members of the ruling elite and because in his estimation they represent "distinct types of Southern womanhood." The first essay examines the life of Mary Boykin Chesnut, author of *Diary from Dixie*. Married to a United States senator who later became a military aide to Jefferson Davis, Chesnut is described by Wiley as a "childless intellectual." Wiley considers his second subject, Virginia Tunstall Clay, to be the "inveterate Southern belle." Clay's husband served as a senator in both the United States Senate and in the Senate of the Confederate States of America. Varina Howell Davis, the wife of Confederate President Jefferson Davis, is the subject of Wiley's third essay. The final essay is a discussion of Southern women and the role they played in providing a livelihood for themselves and their families and in supporting the military effort.

Reviewed in: CWH   21 (Sept. 75) 284–285

JAH   62 (March 76) 998–999

JSO   41 (Nov. 75) 559–560

NCH   52 (Summer 75) 315–316

105 Wills, Brian. *A Battle from the Start: The Life of Nathan Bedford Forrest*. New York: HarperCollins Publishers, 1992. xix, 457 pp. : ill., maps. Includes index and references.

ISBN: 0-060-1683-23   LC: 91-58380

This is the most thorough biography available on the life and career of Nathan Bedford Forrest. He rose rapidly through the ranks to lieutenant general, living his life and his military career on the edge of danger, and attempting to control his anger and his fate. Wills has included a map of the Western theater of the Civil War that shows Forrest's principal engagements with federal forces from 1861 to 1865.

Reviewed in: JAH   80 (Sept. 93) 688

JSO   59 (Aug. 93) 567–568
LIJ   117 (June 1, 92) 140

106 Wilson, Clyde Norman. *Carolina Cavalier: The Life and Mind of James Johnston Pettigrew.* Athens, Ga.: University of Georgia Press, 1990. xiv, 303 pp. Includes index and references.

ISBN: 0-820-3120-10   LC: 89-020136

Although mostly thought of as a Confederate general, prominent in the battle of Gettysburg, James Johnston Pettigrew was not an atypical Southern aristocrat: an astronomer, a traveler, a lawyer, and a politician. His life makes for interesting reading in this dissertation turned biography. Well illustrated, it is similarly enlarged by a chronology of Pettigrew's life. An intellectual born into the cult of chivalry, his experience in wartime "characterized the entire existence of the abortive southern nation."

Reviewed in: AHR   96 (June 91) 957
          CWH   37 (June 91) 155–157
          GHQ   75 (Summer 91) 437–439
          JAH   78 (Dec. 91) 1072–1073
          JSO   58 (May 92) 344–345
          SCH   92 (April 91) 132–134Help

Cavalry Operations

107 Jones, James Pickett. *Yankee Blitzkrieg: Wilson's Raid through Alabama and Georgia.* Athens, Ga.: University of Georgia Press, 1976. xvi, 256 pp. Includes index and bibliography.

ISBN: 0-820-3037-04   LC: 74-015206

By March 1865 the Confederacy was on the verge of collapse. One reviewer has called it ironic for the North to launch its greatest cavalry actions with some thirteen thousand cavalrymen just at that time. James Harrison Wilson's raiders left their camps along the Tennessee River in March 1865 with talk of prolonged rebel resistance in the Deep South. Wilson was confident that his large, well-trained cavalry corps could deny the Confederates a stronghold in the heart of Alabama and Georgia in an area that had previously been untouched. Others have called his action not a blitzkrieg but *Uberflussigkrieg,* a redundant war. As Wilson destroyed iron works, factories, and ordnance stores, his campaign was overshadowed by other contemporary events, such as Robert E. Lee's surrender, Abraham Lincoln's assassination, and the Fall of Richmond. Jones contends that Wilson's raid is still significant not only for its role in the defeat of the Confederacy but for its place in the history of mounted warfare.

Reviewed in:	AHR	82 (Oct. 77) 1074
	CWH	23 (March 77) 87–89
	FHQ	56 (July 77) 91–93
	GHQ	61 (Spring 77) 93–95
	JAH	64 (June 77) 160–161
	JSO	43 (Aug. 77) 463–464

108 Longacre, Edward G. *Mounted Raids of the Civil War.* South Brunswick, N.J.: A. S. Barnes and Co., 1975. 348 pp. : ill., photographs. Includes index and bibliography.

ISBN: 0-498-01171-2   LC: 73-151

Because of the speed and mobility afforded him by the horse, the cavalryman rendered more-frequent and more-arduous service than the infantryman. His most important assignment was striking at the enemy unexpectedly to gather intelligence and to inflict the maximum amount of damage in the minimum amount of time. Longacre's excellent introduction discusses the general rules used by Civil War leaders to evaluate the success or failure of cavalry raids. He delineates the ideal conditions as well as the number of officers and men needed to meet these conditions. Longacre then discusses twelve cavalry raids, six Union and six Confederate.

Reviewed in:	AHR	81 (Dec. 76) 1252
	CWT	15 (July 76) 49
	JAH	63 (Sept. 76) 424–425
	JSO	42 (Aug. 76) 436–437

Cities and States

109 Ash, Stephen V. *Middle Tennessee Society Transformed, 1860–1870: War and Peace in the Upper South.* Baton Rouge, La.: Louisiana State University Press, 1988. xiii, 299 pp. Includes bibliography.

ISBN: 0-807-1140-06   LC: 87-3337

The thirteen tobacco-growing counties of middle Tennessee are the primary focus of this study. These counties had characteristics distinct from the highland farms and the cotton belt. The large slave population and economic prosperity of the region contrasted with the economy of the highlands, but the area's absence of cotton set it apart from the Deep South also, artificially forming what Ash describes as the "Third South." Ash has researched the social history of the region, occupied by the Union Army for a period of three years, from secession to Reconstruction. Generalizing from census data and refining the information through the use of local resources and records, Ash found that when the region was faced with secession the white community stood united. Middle Tennessee was one of the most fought-over regions of the South and one of the North's first conquests. With the Union victories in 1862 at Forts Henry and Donelson, Ash sees the destruction of this Tennessee economy and society. When it became obvious that the slave owners no longer had control, Ash says that the slaves walked off the land. After 1865 the land was again an area of conflict and change. Blacks went to the segregated cities in large numbers, while rural white and city migrants formed the Ku Klux Klan to retain the old ways. Information is appended on the sampling and quantitative techniques Ash used and the occupations of the family heads in the 1860 and 1870 census samples.

Reviewed in: AHR   94 (Dec. 89) 1480–1481

CWH   35 (March 89) 81–83

JSO   56 (Feb. 90) 121–123

NCH   65 (Oct. 88) 494–495

RKH   86 (Autumn 88) 388–389

110 Cooling, Benjamin Franklin. *Symbol, Sword, and Shield: Defending Washington during the Civil War.* Hamden, Conn.: Archon Books, 1975. 300 pp. : ill., photographs, maps, tables. Includes index, references, and appendix.

ISBN: 0-208-01479-9   LC: 74-28025

Cooling claims that the Civil War transformed Washington, D.C., from a provincial capital to the "nerve center of a major nation." He maintains that the Army of the Potomac had a twofold mission. First, it was charged with defeating the Confederate forces that were defending Richmond. Its responsibility was to defend Washington as part of a "team" effort that also included field fortifications, heavy ordnance, garrisons, and a mobile maneuver force. Cooling delineates the history of the physical defenses of Washington from the election of Lincoln to the end of the conflict. He describes the thirty-seven-mile-long fortification chain connected by lines of earthworks on which were mounted the most powerful guns of the time. Cooling

Charleston, South Carolina

also discusses George B. McClellan and comments on the debate regarding whether or not the general neglected the defenses of the capital. The appendix lists the forts in the Washington area that are administered by the United States National Park Service.

Reviewed in: AHR   81 (June 76) 668

CWH   21 (Dec. 75) 364–365

CWT   15 (Dec. 76) 47–48

JSO   42 (Feb. 76) 126–127

111 Dougan, Michael B. *Confederate Arkansas: The People and Politics of a Frontier State in Wartime*. Tuscaloosa, Ala.: University of Alabama Press, 1976. viii, 165 pp. Includes index and bibliography.

ISBN: 0-817-3523-09   LC: 76-016117

Beginning with antebellum Arkansas and taking the reader through secession and the war's end, Dougan has sought to portray a state's life through newspapers, letters, diaries, official reports, and other contemporary sources. Although most of the book centers on prewar Arkansas, the state suffered greatly in the war years. It was repeatedly invaded and occupied by Northern armies, its farms suffered crop failures, and it saw much internal strife caused by the great numbers of people who remained loyal to the Union or turned against the Confederacy. By 1865 Arkansas was in a condition of almost total collapse. As a doctoral dissertation, this work was awarded the 1972 Baruch Award for the best work pertaining to the Confederacy.

Reviewed in: AHR   83 (Feb. 78) 276–277

CWH   23 (Sept. 77) 269–270

HRN   5 (Aug. 77) 198

JSO   43 (Nov. 77) 620–621

NCH   54 (Summer 77) 326–327

112 Harrison, Lowell H. *The Civil War in Kentucky*. Lexington, Ky.: University Press of Kentucky, 1975. ix, 115 pp. : ill., maps. Includes bibliography and references.

ISBN: 0-8131-0209-X   LC: 75-3545

The state of Kentucky was vitally important to the Union cause, both militarily and psychologically. Although thirty thousand Kentuckians served in the Confederate Army, Kentucky remained loyal to the Union. When the state adopted a policy of neutrality for several months, a group of citizens formed a rival government that was admitted to the Confederate States of America. Harrison provides a brief overview of the struggle over secession in the state. The core of his study focuses on military operations within Kentucky, although it also explores the political, legal, constitutional, and cultural aspects of the conflict. The text is supplemented by maps.

Reviewed in: CWH   23 (Sept. 77) 264–265

JAH   63 (June 76) 136

RKH   74 (April 76) 126–128

113 Lucas, Marion Brunson. *Sherman and the Burning of Columbia.* College Station, Tex.: Texas A & M University Press, 1976. 188 pp. Includes index and bibliography.

ISBN: 0-890-9601-86   LC: 76-017979

The capture and occupation of Columbia, South Carolina, by William Tecumseh Sherman and the Union forces has caused controversy since the events occurred. Lucas's analysis has it that blunders on both sides contributed to the disaster that further drove a wedge between the North and the South, even after the war. Researching through official records, newspapers, public documents, and secondary sources, he finds the truth to be far different from the mythology of the events. Sherman had been blamed for personally setting the fires, and packs of drunken soldiers were thought to have roamed the streets beating and assaulting the citizens. This impartial analysis by Lucas reveals that both military and civil authorities made mistakes. Flames from bales of cotton that were ordered burned in the streets were further fueled by high winds. Union commanders did not destroy the large amounts of liquor stored in the city or stop its distribution to the men. Although looting and rioting did occur and a third of the city was in ashes, Lucas found that many of the troops did help fight the inextinguishable fires. To Lucas the principal demons in this drama were cotton, whiskey, and wind. Appendixes include "Inventory of Ordnance Stores Captured in Columbia, South Carolina, February 17, 1865," and "Soldiers Directory of Public Officers [e.g. Quartermasters, Surgeons, and so forth] in Columbia."

Reviewed in: AHR   82 (June 77) 747

JAH   64 (Dec. 77) 801

LIJ   102 (Feb. 1, 77) 381

114 McKay, Ernest A. *The Civil War and New York City.* Syracuse, N.Y.: Syracuse University Press, 1990. xv, 377 pp. : ill. Includes references.

ISBN: 0-8156-0246-4   LC: 90-32799

New York City, in all its diversity, found its populace divided over the city's relationship with the South even though the city's economy was heavily dependent on trade and commerce with the Southern states. It was just as divided over the questions of secession and abolition. Even as they supplied the Union with troops, money, and supplies, New Yorkers still had sympathy for the Southern cause. The draft riots in New York City brought out the worst in its inhabitants; what had begun as opposition to conscription ended in a deadly race riot. Author McKay reviews chronologically the panorama of social, political, and economic events, and the reactions to them. Clashes of ideology and prejudice had existed in this commercial city from the first settlements by the Dutch to the influx of immigrants in the nineteenth century. The semblance of order and cohesiveness allowed the daily routine of trade to proceed. With the rise in immigration and the increased imbalance in wealth, the new ideas of abolition and secession forced hidden tensions to the top. The previous indifference to slavery could no longer exist. McKay explores the life of the city on all levels—from the politicians, whose corruption was rampant, to the lower classes, whose poverty became undeniable—and the rush to arms by many of the city's men.

Reviewed in:	AHR	96 (Oct. 91) 1295–1296
	CWH	38 (June 92) 185–187
	JAH	78 (Sept. 91) 676–677
	JSH	58 (May 92) 358–359
	RAH	19 (Sept. 91) 363–369

115 Marten, James. *Texas Divided: Loyalty and Dissent in the Lone Star State, 1856–1874.* Lexington, Ky.: University Press of Kentucky, 1990. x, 246 pp. Includes references.

ISBN: 0-813-1170-03   LC: 89-48256

Much of the challenge to the Confederate Texas was not the result of the external forces of the Civil War but, rather, of its size and location; dissension came from within its borders. Marten's discussion centers around the Unionists in Texas, those who became dissenters during the war years, and the wartime behavior of the predominant ethnic groups in Texas at the time: the blacks, the Germans, and the Hispanics. Marten's analysis of this "loyalty" and "dissension" is verified by biographical references to prominent Texans as representative of the shared experiences of others.

Reviewed in: AHR   96 (June 91) 964

CHO   28 (Oct. 90) 374

JAH   78 (June 91) 334

116 Maslowski, Peter. *Treason Must Be Made Odious: Military Occupation and Wartime Reconstruction in Nashville, Tennessee, 1862–1865.* Millwood, N.Y.: KTO Press, 1978. xvii, 173 pp. Includes index and bibliography.

ISBN: 0-527-62185-4   LC: 78-016799

The Union Army's occupation of Nashville, Tennessee, has broad implications for the understanding of the war years and postwar Reconstruction. Maslowski considers the Union activities in the capital a "microcosm" of the Reconstruction effort and discusses the difficulties that were encountered, such as nonbattlefield activities and a hostile civilian population. According to Maslowski, most studies concentrate on the postwar years, whereas he feels that concentrating on a local case history affords insight into wartime civil and military relations and into the Reconstruction efforts. There were several reasons he chose Nashville for his research: the city was captured early in the war, its diversified economy relied as much on the North as the South, and it had only a modest dependence upon slavery. The failure of Reconstruction in Nashville could provide insights into its failure in the South as a whole.

Reviewed in: AHR   84 (Dec. 79) 1481

CHO   16 (Sept. 79) 910

JAH   66 (Dec. 79) 661

LIJ   104 (Feb. 15, 79) 490

117 Paludan, Phillip Shaw. *Victims: A True Story of the Civil War.* Knoxville, Tenn.: University of Tennessee Press, 1981. xvi, 144 pp. Includes index, references, and appendix.

ISBN: 0-8704-931-67   LC: 81-2578

This collection of thematic historiographical essays presents the true story of thirteen suspected Union partisans from the isolated rural community of Shelton Laurel, North Carolina, who were massacred by Confederate rangers in January 1863. The victims, ranging in age from thirteen to fifty-nine, had allegedly participated in a Unionist reign of terror in nearby Marshall, the county seat. In retelling the story of the massacre and its effect on the small Appalachian community, Paludan interweaves the stories of the individuals, the community, and the nation into a coherent whole that connects social, economic, and political forces with military events. In the midst of battles in which hundreds and thousands died, Paludan focuses on death on a smaller, more-personal scale. He concentrates on the clash between the relatively static kinship culture of the Appalachians and the more-volatile, modern values that were at the center of the conflict between the North and the South.

> *Reviewed in:* AHR 87 (Oct. 82) 1167–1168
> FHQ 61 (Oct. 82) 199–201
> GHQ 66 (Fall 82) 396–397
> JAH 69 (Sept. 82) 455
> JSO 48 (Aug. 82) 436–437
> VMH 90 (Oct. 82) 515–516

118 Wubben, Hubert H. *Civil War Iowa and the Copperhead Movement.* Ames, Iowa: Iowa State University Press, 1980. xi, 280 pp. : ill. Includes index and bibliography.

ISBN: 0-8138-112-01   LC: 79-23407

Wubben explores the economic, cultural, and social life of the Iowan populace, using as his guide the newspapers of the Civil War years. Included are tables to explain voting and party representations, which showed that although Iowa Democrats could not shake the conservative label of Copperhead, and could not unseat the entrenched Republicans, they did maintain a minority-party status for years to come. Other historians have explored the political arena in Civil War Iowa, and although Wubben's does not appear to be the definitive study, it is one that deserves attention. He traces the origins of the Copperheads and war Democrats, and the competition they had with the Iowa Republicans.

> *Reviewed in:* AHR 86 (April 81) 549
> CWH 27 (June 81) 185–186
> CWT 20 (June 81) 48

HIS   44 (Feb. 82) 277–278
JAH   67 (March 81) 930–931
MIA   45 (April 81) 99

Civil Rights

119   Neely, Mark E., Jr. *The Fate of Liberty: Abraham Lincoln and Civil Liberties.* New York: Oxford University Press, 1991. xvii, 278 pp. Includes index and references.

ISBN: 0-19-506496-8   LC: 90-31907

This book provides a comprehensive view of the issue of civil liberties under Lincoln within the context of politics, and it examines the practical impact on civil liberties of the policies Abraham Lincoln developed to save the Union. Neely believes that Lincoln was more

3rd US Colored Troops banner

concerned with prosecuting the war than he was with persecuting his opponents. He considers Lincoln's suspension of habeas corpus a "well intentioned attempt" to deal with a broad range of unanticipated events, such as hostility to the draft and the possible threat to Washington, D.C., arising from uncertainty over Maryland's possible secession. The book includes a discussion of the history of habeas corpus in American history. In an attempt to determine whether arrests were mainly of the Democratic opposition, Neely examines contemporary arrest records to determine who was arrested when the writ of habeas corpus was suspended and why. He also looks at various abuses that occurred under martial law, including torture of suspected deserters, antisemitism among Union generals and officers, and the practice of seizing civilian hostages. Neely consulted letters of prisoners, memoirs, and records of federal prisons and military courts. He concedes that there were obvious abuses of power and widespread injustice, but there was no deliberate plan to silence dissent or suppress opposition.

Reviewed in: AHR   97 (April 92) 619–620

CWH   37 (Dec. 91) 343–345

GHQ   75 (Fall 91) 642–644

JAH   78 (Dec. 91) 1091–1092

NCH   69 (April 92) 245–246

RAH   20 (March 92) 55–58

Commerce and Finance

120 Abbott, Richard H. *Cotton and Capital: Boston Businessmen and Antislavery Reform, 1854–1868.* Amherst, Mass.: University of Massachusetts Press, 1991. x, 249 pp. Includes index, bibliography, and references.

ISBN: 0-87023-749-7   LC: 91-14137

This study covers the years from 1854 to 1868, from the passage of the Kansas Nebraska Act to the election of Ulysses S. Grant. Drawing on manuscript sources as well as other primary and secondary materials, Abbott examines how a select group of forty Boston businessmen took up the antislavery cause and eventually joined the Republican Party. The lives and careers of six men—Amos A. Lawrence, Edward Atkinson, John Murray Forbes, George Luther Stearns, Eli Thayer, and Edward Evertt Hale—provide the focus of Abbott's study. Lawrence, Atkinson, and Forbes supplied the organizing energy, creative vision, and money that enabled these men to establish a number of voluntary organizations designed to promote the cause of black freedom. The first organization established was the New England Emigrant Aid Company. During the war these businessmen operated a New England branch of the United States Sanitary Commission, an Emancipation League, and a committee to recruit black soldiers for the Union Army. Abbott points out that for the most part the men involved in these enterprises were guided by practical, not moral, considerations. They translated their concern for economic profit into a concern for freedom, arguing that the abolition of black slavery would have significant benefits for white Americans because they believed that slavery threatened the economic development of the whole nation.

Reviewed in: AHR   98 (Feb. 93) 246

HRN   20 (Summer 92) 147

JEH   53 (Sept. 93) 680

JSH   59 (Aug. 93) 551

121 Ball, Douglas B. *Financial Failure and Confederate Defeat.* Urbana, Ill.: University of Illinois Press, 1991. xi, 329 pp. : ill., tables. Includes index, references, and appendixes.

ISBN: 0-252-01755-2   LC: 90-10831

Ball believes that it was not unrealistic for the Confederate States of America to expect it to be successful in achieving independence. He contends that the failure of the Confederate economic policy and the South's ultimate defeat resulted from inept political leadership rather than a lack of resources or the absence of an industrial base. He begins with a discussion of the accepted financial wisdom of the day and examines the South's cotton foreign exchange, debt management, currency, and fiscal policies. There is also an informative reappraisal of the Erlanger Loan and a listing of Confederate loans between 1861 and 1865. Using private correspondence and public debates among

Southern political leaders, Ball analyzes the reasoning employed by the Confederate government and concludes that in fiscal matters, both Jefferson Davis and C. G. Memminger were incompetent. The final chapter of the book and the appendixes present a counterfactual economic and military strategy for the Confederacy that Ball maintains would have resulted in a more successful war effort.

Reviewed in: AHR   97 (April 92) 619

LIJ   116 (Jan. 91) 118

122 Daddysman, James W. *The Matamoros Trade: Confederate Commerce, Diplomacy, and Intrigue.* Newark, Del.: University of Delaware Press, 1984. 215 pp. : ill. Includes bibliography.

ISBN: 0-874-1321-50   LC: 81-72031

Matamoros, Mexico, situated between Mexico and Texas, had a unique geographic and political position during the blockade of the Confederate ports in that it lay just outside the American jurisdiction. It provided the way by which the Confederacy and entrepreneurs could export Southern cotton to Europe in exchange for needed goods. This trade route resulted in numerous fortunes and did not gain the full force of development by the Confederacy; nor did the North see its way to bringing it to a halt. Daddysman brings the fragmented information together to supplement earlier work done on this borderland territory.

Reviewed in: AHR   90 (April 85) 492

CHO   22 (Oct. 84) 334

JAH   71 (Dec. 84) 642

123 DeCredico, Mary A. *Patriotism for Profit: Georgia's Urban Entrepreneurs and the Confederate War Effort.* Chapel Hill, N.C.: University of North Carolina Press, 1990. xx, 211 pp. : ill. Includes index and references.

ISBN: 08-0781-891-7   LC: 89-39132

Addressing the debates between the continuity of the old South and the new, DeCredico focuses her attention on the industrial mobilization of the South during and after the Civil War. The entrepreneurial processes of Augusta, Atlanta, and Columbus experienced considerable growth, according to DeCredico, because of the importance of the railroad and Confederate armaments throughout the war, while Savannah had its economic difficulties caused by the blockade. She stresses the importance of the entrepreneurial tradition, even though the four cities had different economic histories and recovered from the war at different times.

Reviewed in: AHR   96 (June 91) 965
                  JAH   78 (Sept. 91) 678
                  JEH   52 (March 92) 247
                  JSO   58 (Fall 94) 148

Education

124   Butchart, Ronald E. *Northern Schools, Southern Blacks and Reconstruction: Freedmen's Education, 1862–1875.* Westport, Conn.: Greenwood Press, 1980. xiv, 309 pp. : ill., graph, tables. Includes index, bibliography, and references.

ISBN: 0-313-22073-5   LC: 79-8949

Butchart presents a revisionist interpretation of the work of the secular and religious aid societies, and of the Freedmen's Bureau, in their effort to educate former slaves. In his analysis of the ideas of the Northerners who organized education for freed slaves, he maintains that Reconstruction began early in the war, as the Union Army came into contact with slaves, and continued long after the political compromise of 1877. According to Butchart, Reconstruction was "a struggle to establish the contours of postslavery southern society—its mode of production, class structure and class relations, culture, ambience and institutions." He faults all groups involved in the effort to educate blacks for emphasizing traditional subjects and methods and for using materials that taught docility and accommodation to the white power structure. The program for black literacy failed because it was not coupled with land distribution and legal or financial assistance.

Reviewed in: AHR 86 (Oct. 81) 931

JAH 68 (Dec. 81) 676

JMH 66 (Summer 81) 156

LIJ 105 (Aug. 80) 1627

125 Morris, Robert C. *Reading, 'Riting, and Reconstruction: The Education of Freedmen in the South, 1861–1870.* Chicago, Ill.: University of Chicago Press, 1981. xv, 341 pp. : ill., photographs. Includes index, bibliography, and references.

ISBN: 0-226-53928-8   LC: 80-25370

This book presents a comprehensive account of the controversial Northern-based program to educate former slaves that began during the early months of the Civil War and continued until 1870. Under the auspices of the Freedman's Bureau, more than fifty secular and religious organizations established schools and colleges, and provided teachers to work in them. The bureau coordinated educational programs in seventeen states and in the District of Columbia. Morris consulted a wide range of manuscript sources, and he has provided detailed information about the backgrounds, the politics, and the social and racial attitudes of the teachers and administrators who staffed the schools. He has also included detailed descriptions of the instructional materials used in the classroom. Although he acknowledges that many of those involved in this effort were motivated by idealism and a genuine desire to improve the lives of the former slaves through education, a significant number of these Northern educators were white supremacists whose first priority was to maintain social stability. They were not necessarily interested in supplying the former slaves with the educational training that would enable them to work for the economic, legal, and political reforms that would ensure racial equality. For many, education meant social control, not social equality.

Reviewed in: AHR 87 (Dec. 82) 1467

JAH 69 (Dec. 82) 708

JAS 17 (Aug. 83) 306

JSH 48 (Aug. 82) 438

RAH 10 (Sept. 82) 364

Foreign Public Opinion

126   Foner, Philip S. *British Labor and the American Civil War.* New York: Holmes & Meier Publishers, 1981. 135 pp. Includes index, bibliography, and references.

ISBN: 0-8419-0671-8   LC: 80-26162

This is the first book-length study of the role of British workers during the American Civil War. Foner supports the traditional view that even though the textile workers of Lancashire were put out of work by the cotton famine, they supported the Northern cause. He claims that the Emancipation Proclamation helped rally support among British laborers and that the war itself was a major factor in the growth of working-class internationalism in Britain during the 1860s. Foner moves his argument a step beyond that of other historians, however, asserting that the working class successfully restrained the British government from becoming officially involved in the conflict on the side of the Confederacy.

> *Reviewed in:*   AHR   88 (April 83) 529
>
>   JSO   48 (Aug. 80) 438

127   Jenkins, Brian A. *Britain and the War for the Union.* 2 vols. Montreal: McGill-Queens University Press, 1974. Includes index and bibliography.

ISBN: 0-7735-0184-3 (vol. 1) LC: 74-77503

           0-7735-0354-4 (vol. 2)

This two-volume set is Jenkins's examination of Britain's response to the American Civil War. The first volume deals with Anglo-American relations between November 1860 and the spring of 1862, focusing mainly on diplomatic relations. Four main themes are conveyed: Confederate diplomacy toward Great Britain, the policy of Britain to the North and South and Canada, the role of Canada in Anglo-American relations, and United States government diplomacy toward Great Britain. The second volume continues with the last nine months of 1862 through to the end of the war. Broader in scope than the first volume, it focuses on a variety of problems. Jenkins's thesis is that British neutrality was not based on principle or public opinion but rather on fear of intervention. He analyzes the ideas of Union and Confederate sympathizers and explores Anglo-American diplomacy, the naval and legal problems that were evident, and the government's attempt to relieve Lancashire's problems before foreign intervention was necessary. Jenkins combines both recent scholarship and an extensive use of original documents.

> Reviewed in: CWH   27 (Sept. 81) 282–285
> JAH   68 (Sept. 81) 393
> JAS   16 (April 82) 131–132
> JSO   47 (Nov. 81) 614–615

Foreign Relations

128 Cook, Adrian. *The Alabama Claims: American Politics and Anglo-American Relations, 1865–1872.* Ithaca, N.Y.: Cornell University Press, 1975. 261 pp. Includes index, bibliography, and references.

ISBN: 0-8014-0893-8   LC: 74-10408

Cook presents a thoroughly documented account of the negotiations surrounding the Alabama claims, the American demands for compensation from Great Britain for unneutral acts during the Civil War. He delineates the roles of the chief participants on both sides and emphasizes the relationship between the domestic political considerations of the Ulysses S. Grant administration and the settlement with Great Britain. Cook carefully recounts the actions of Secretary of State Hamilton Fish, whom he believes was so completely devoted to Grant that he readily subordinated diplomatic requirements to partisan political necessities. The claims were not settled until seven years after the fighting ended. Cook asserts that the settlement was more a result of luck and the British government's eagerness to settle the matter than of any diplomatic skill on Fish's part.

> *Reviewed in:* AHR 81 (Dec. 76) 1254
>
> HRN 3 (Sept. 75) 254
>
> JSO 41 (Nov. 75) 562–563

129 Cortada, James W. *Spain and the American Civil War: Relations at Mid-Century, 1855–1868.* Philadelphia: American Philosophical Society, 1980. Transactions of the American Philosophical Society, vol. 70, part 4. 121 pp. Includes index and bibliography.

ISSN: 0065-9746   ISBN: 0-871-69704-1   LC: 79-054276

Using Spanish archival sources, Spanish newspapers, and foreign office archives in Great Britain and France, Cortada has contributed to the understanding of American diplomatic history during the midnineteenth century; particularly significant because the balance of power in Europe and the New World was changing. The study focuses on the problems of slavery, economics, and imperialism through the 1850s and 1860s and on the study of Civil War diplomacy. In this light Cortada examines Spain's diplomatic relations with America in terms of her attitude toward Latin America. According to Cortada, even though Spaniards ranked their relationship with Europe as first, in terms of political importance, in reality Spain's greater diplomatic influence was in the New World. An examination of Spain's Latin American policy depends on understanding the relationship with America.

> *Reviewed in:* AHR 86 (June 81) 651–652

130 Crook, D.P. *The North, The South, and the Powers.* New York: John Wiley and Sons, 1974. x, 405 pp. : ill., maps, charts. Includes index and bibliography.

ISBN: 0-471-18855-7   LC: 73-16355

Crook has produced a narrative history of Civil War diplomacy that focuses on the interrelationships among the United States, Great Britain, and France. Relations between the United States and the lesser powers such as Spain, Austria, and Russia are also discussed. Crook contends that the war threatened the balance of power of the Western hemisphere and that one important result of the conflict was the war's marking an end to an intimate phase in Anglo-American relations. The text is supplemented with useful maps.

Reviewed in: AHR   80 (Oct. 75) 1049

CHO   11 (Oct. 74) 1204

LAH   18 (Winter 77) 110–111

131 Ferris, Norman B. *Desperate Diplomacy: William H. Seward's Foreign Policy.* Knoxville, Tenn.: University of Tennessee Press, 1976. ix, 265 pp. Includes index and bibliography.

ISBN: 0-8704-9170-9   LC: 75-5509

Focusing more on the relations with Great Britain than on William Henry Seward's policy of 1861, Ferris views Seward in a favorable light, contending that Seward tried to forestall Britain's recognition of the Confederacy and its intervention in the war. Ferris's story of the 1861 diplomacy is based on an examination of public and private sources as well as contemporary pamphlets and newspapers.

Reviewed in: AHR   82 (Feb. 77) 183

CWH   23 (March 77) 82–84

CWT   16 (Jan. 78) 49

HRN   5 (Nov.–Dec. 76) 26

JAH   64 (June 77) 159–160

JSO   43 (Aug. 77) 459–460

132 Ferris, Norman B. *The Trent Affair: A Diplomatic Crisis.* Knoxville, Tenn.: University of Tennessee Press, 1977. xi, 280 pp. Includes index, bibliography, and references.

ISBN: 0-87049-169-5   LC: 76-28304

This is a thoroughly researched and well-written account of the most serious diplomatic crisis of the Civil War. It recounts the events of the seizure of two Confederate emissaries, James Mason and John Slidell, who were passengers on the British mail steamer *Trent,* by Captain Charles D. Wilkes, of the United States warship *San Jacinto.* Ferris examines the activities, motives, and relationships of the leading players on both sides of the Atlantic. He believes that the *Trent* seizure in itself was not enough to touch off the violent reaction but that a "strong barrier of misunderstanding" was already in place before Wilkes acted. Unlike others, Ferris does not believe that the press played an inflammatory role in the incident. He asserts that American political leaders fanned the flames of discord with their rhetoric and that Secretary of State Seward was primarily responsible for preserving the peace.

Reviewed in:	AHR	82 (Dec. 77) 1331–1332
	CWH	24 (Sept. 78) 271–272
	HRN	6 (Jan. 78) 54
	JAH	65 (June 78) 176–177
	JSO	44 (May 78) 313–314
	THQ	36 (Fall 77) 428–429

133 Jones, Howard. *Union in Peril: The Crisis over British Intervention in the Civil War.* Chapel Hill, N.C.: University of North Carolina Press, 1992. xiii, 300 pp. : ill. Includes index and references.

ISBN: 0-8078-2048-2   LC: 92-053619

Supplementing his work with portraits and contemporary political cartoons from London's *Punch,* Jones focuses on the views and policies of British Foreign Secretary Lord John Russell, a leading advocate of British intervention in the American Civil War, and on the views of other British Cabinet officials from the period between 1860 and November 1862. British concerns and misperceptions all seemed to be pulling Britain toward intervention on behalf of the Confederacy. Jones's study explains how others prevailed over Russell and kept Britain from making the serious mistake of engaging in a third Anglo-American war.

Reviewed in:	CHO	3 (March 93) 1228
	JAH	80 (Sept. 93) 687
	LIJ	117 (Nov. 1, 92) 102

134 Warren, Gordon. *Fountain of Discontent: The Trent Affair and Freedom of the Seas.* Boston, Mass.: Northeastern University Press, 1981. xiv, 301 pp. : ill., photographs. Includes index, bibliography, and references.

ISBN: 0-9303-5012-X   LC: 80-24499

Neutral and belligerent rights had long been a cause of conflict between the United States and Great Britain when Union naval captain Charles Wilkes removed two Confederate diplomats, James Mason and John Slidell, from the British mail ship *Trent* in November 1861.

Acting on his own accord, Wilkes violated one of the most important principles of American diplomacy and international law, the freedom of the seas. His action precipitated the crisis that almost brought England into the American Civil War on the side of the Confederacy. Using a wide range of manuscript sources, including the personal papers of the major participants as well as contemporary newspapers and periodicals, Warren explains the diplomatic background of the *Trent* affair, the day-to-day events of the six-week crisis and its resolution. His discussion of international law as it applied to the *Trent* case is especially notable.

Reviewed in: AHR   87 (Oct. 82) 1169

HRN   10 (July 82) 205

JAH   69 (Sept. 82) 456–457

JSO   48 (May 82) 289

General

135   *Atlas for the American Civil War.* Wayne, N.J.: Avery Publishing Group, 1986. 58 pp. : ill., maps.

ISBN: 0-8952-9302-1   LC: 88-675005

Cadets at the United States Military Academy have studied the campaigns of the American Civil War for more than a century. This atlas, of more than seventy-five maps, was designed to support the text they use in their studies. It provides less detailed graphic treatment than the classic atlas they used before but places greater emphasis on the totality of the war. The authors have relied somewhat on the previous work used at West Point, *The West Point Atlas of American Wars* by Vincent J. Esposito. The graphics and maps are clear and in color.

Reviewed in: JSO   54 (Feb. 88) 119

136 Barney, William L. *Flawed Victory: A New Perspective on the Civil War.* New York: Praeger, 1975. xi, 215 pp. : ill., map. Includes index and bibliography.

ISBN: 0-275-52040-4/0-275-85040-4(paper)   LC: 74-14989

Barney labels the Civil War a watershed of American history. He contends that the conflict was proof of the collapse of the original union. The work of the Founding Fathers proved inadequate, and the union had to be formed again. Each chapter in this book views the war and its outcome from a different angle. One chapter provides a succinct account of military operations, another examines the federal authorities' changing approach to the war, and a third looks at the relationship between blacks and the war.

Reviewed in: CHO   12 (May 75) 446

HRN   3 (April 75) 139–140

LIJ   100 (Jan. 15, 75) 122

137 Bosse, David C. *Civil War Newspaper Maps: A Historical Atlas.* Baltimore, Md.: Johns Hopkins University Press, 1993. x, 162 pp. : ill., photographs, maps. Includes index, bibliography, and appendix.

ISBN: 0-8018-4553-X   LC: 92-33942

Eyewitness accounts of the Civil War and newspaper correspondents' stories were often accompanied by maps. In some cases newspapers provided the only cartographic records of military operations. This atlas illustrates celebrated and obscure battles and campaigns fought from Pennsylvania to Louisiana and Missouri to Georgia. A brief overview of the military event and a commentary on the map itself accompany each entry. For most battles the map selected was the first to appear in the daily newspapers at the time. For some battles an additional map is included to illustrate particularly significant differences in cartography. Each entry includes a short bibliography of additional reports on the battle. The introduction includes a discussion of the development of journalistic cartography.

Reviewed in: CHO   31 (March 94) 1203

138 Catton, Bruce. *Reflections on the Civil War.* Edited by John Leekley. Garden City, N.Y.: Doubleday, 1981. xxiv, 246 pp. : ill. Includes index.

ISBN: 0-385-06347-4   LC: 79-6164

Catton moves beyond the rudimentary facades of the war to examine what he considers to be the essential meaning and consequences of the conflict. He identifies a number of contributing factors, including slavery, the prevailing emotional climate, and the strengths and weaknesses of the opposing leaders. Catton also examines the experience of army life for the common soldier. The text is accompanied by a collection of sketches made by John B. Geyser, a young Union soldier.

Reviewed in: CWH   28 (June 82) 176–177

LAH   23 (Winter 82) 82–83

RKH   80 (Autumn 82) 462–463

VMH   90 (July 82) 386–387

139 Culpepper, Marilyn Mayer. *Trials and Triumphs: Women of the American Civil War.* East Lansing, Mich.: Michigan State University Press, 1991. x, 427 pp. : ill., photographs. Includes bibliography.

ISBN: 0-87013-296-2   LC: 91-52579

Little has been written about the women during the Civil War who endured hardships on the homefront and of those who ventured to the sites of the combat. Using the diaries and correspondence of more than five hundred women, Culpepper provides insights into their lives. She examines how the war shaped their attitudes and altered their responsibilities, permitting them to break out of the "cult of domesticity." Culpepper bases her research on the eyewitness accounts of white women, including as little interpretative analysis as possible and letting the women speak for themselves through their writing. Her research presents the realities of middle-class white women's lives by revealing their anxiety and depravation, the nature of their nursing experiences, and their reflections on slavery and politics.

Reviewed in: JAH 80 (Dec. 93) 1097

140 Current, Richard. *Lincoln's Loyalists: Union Soldiers from the Confederacy.* Boston, Mass.: Northeastern University Press, 1992. ix, 253 pp. : ill., maps. Includes bibliographical references and index.

ISBN: 1-5555-3124-5   LC: 91-47876

Current, basing his story essentially on information from the *War of the Rebellion* and other primary sources, has brought forward the neglected story of the thousands of white Southerners who fought for the Union in the Civil War. According to Current, Union military units were raised in all of the Confederate states except South Carolina, their makeup differing little economically or socially from their Confederate counterparts. Most of these Southern Unionists, however, were unlikely to own slaves even though they usually were proslavery antiabolitionists. Approximately 75 percent of the men who made up these units came from the mountain regions of the Appalachians and Ozarks. At least one hundred thousand white Southerners served in the Union military, according to Current's calculations. They had a difficult time of it. While government authorities cared for the families of Union soldiers in the North, the families and properties of Southern loyalists did not have such protection and were left to face the hostilities and revenge of their Confederate neighbors. Included is an appendix that assesses the number of men who fought.

> *Reviewed in:*   AHR   98 (June 93) 949
>   LIJ   117 (May 1, 92) 96

141 *Encyclopedia of the Confederacy.* 4 vols. Editor in chief, Richard N. Current. New York: Simon & Schuster, 1993. ill., photographs, maps, tables. Includes bibliographies and references.

ISBN: 0-13-275991-8(set)   LC: 93-4133

This four-volume encyclopedia is a significant reference work that covers a wide range of topics related to the Confederacy: social, military, cultural, and economic. There are biographies of leading political and military figures; descriptions of forts, cities, and battles; and in-depth essays on the causes of the war. The entries include bibliographies, and they are cross-referenced. There are sixty-seven maps and a number of reproductions of etchings.

> *Reviewed in:*   CRL   55 (Sept. 94) 420
>   LIJ   119 (April 15, 94) 39
>   JMH   58 (July 94) 527

142 Faust, Drew Gilpin. *The Creation of Confederate Nationalism: Ideology and Identity in the Civil War South.* Baton Rouge, La.: Louisiana State University Press, 1988. 110 pp. Includes index and references.

ISBN: 0-807-1150-96   LC: 88-009036

These essays, revised and somewhat-expanded versions of the Walter Lynwood Fleming Lectures delivered in 1987, explore the meaning of Confederate nationalism for wartime Southerners. The chapters include "The Problem of Confederate Nationalism," "Religion, Politics and Confederate Nationalism," "The Sin of Extortion and the Dynamics of Confederate Identity," and "Confederate Nationalism and Slavery Reform." They survey a variety of primary sources and the roles of teachers, ministers, planters, journalists, and others, to analyze Southern culture. It is said that in Faust's opinion Confederate culture was a natural result of antebellum beliefs. Faust's story is that of the wartime shifts in Southern society, the elite upper classes becoming increasingly dependent upon the support of the general public.

Reviewed in:	AHR	95 (Oct. 90) 1293
	CWH	36 (Sept. 90) 275–277
	FHQ	68 (Oct. 89) 231–232
	GHQ	74 (Spring 90) 171–172
	JAH	76 (March 90) 1272–1273
	JSO	56 (Aug. 90) 538–540

143 Faust, Drew Gilpin. *Southern Stories: Slaveholders in Peace and War.* Columbia, Mo.: University of Missouri Press, 1992. viii, 252 pp. Includes index.

ISBN: 0-8262-0865-7   LC: 92-20632

Faust has assembled ten essays on a wide range of topics that help to illustrate an evolution of interests: the political culture of the antebellum South; the conflict between the private and public cultures of white Southern women; an analysis of the novel *Macaria,* with its warnings about the limits of freedom women had from male dominance during the war; and the story of Lizzie Neblett, who after her husband went to war struggled with the violence needed to maintain slave discipline and the nonviolent norms of Southern women. Faust's telling of the stories shows that there was a way for Southerners to interpret their history to themselves. Educated white Southerners wrote to explain themselves to the world and to themselves. They told their stories in diaries, sermons, novels, and songs, as they searched for personal identity and the role of gender in the Confederate South.

Reviewed in:	CHO	30 (April 93) 1377
	JSO	60 (May 94) 399

144 Geary, James W. *We Need Men: The Union Draft and the Civil War.* DeKalb, Ill.: Northern Illinois University Press, 1991. xvii, 264 pp. : ill., photographs, tables. Includes index, bibliography, references, and appendix.

ISBN: 0-87580-157-9   LC: 90-21636

Within two years of the firing on Fort Sumter, both the North and the South had enacted conscription laws. This book provides a general, analytical history of the draft in the North, examining how it evolved and how it affected Northerners and their attitudes toward military service. It provides a synthesis of the military, social, and political aspects of the draft. Geary's principal focus is on matters directly related to conscription rather than on other mobilization issues, such as logistics or general recruitment policies and practices. He comments on congressional debates related to military service, the administration of the conscription laws that were enacted, and the effects that bounties and substitutes had on the equity of the draft. Geary's research indicates that men from modest backgrounds were not forced to serve in disproportionate numbers. While the wealthy paid for their own substitutes, the poor joined insurance clubs or obtained support from the community to pay for substitutes. Geary concludes that conscription practices during the Civil War were more equitable than most methods used to raise an army during the twentieth century.

Reviewed in:

AHR	97 (Dec. 92) 1598	
CHO	29 (Nov. 91) 508	
JSO	59 (Feb. 93) 148	
LIJ	116 (May 15, 91) 93	

Confederate recruits

145 *Historical Times Illustrated Encyclopedia of the Civil War.* Senior Editor Patricia L. Faust. New York: Harper & Row, 1986. xxiv, 849 pp. : ill., photographs, maps.

ISBN: 0-0618-1261-7   LC: 86-45095

This one-volume reference work has been a long-going project of Historical Times, Inc. It provides the historical profession and the general public with serious and balanced information on all aspects of the Civil War. Its five editors and sixty-two authors have assembled more than two thousand written entries on the generals, battles, politicians, women, correspondents, and photographers. It is enhanced by one thousand photographs and other illustrations. Information on technical topics such as telegraphy and railroads, as well as art and music, round out this important tool. The amount of basic information found in this single volume makes that aspect alone well worth consulting it. The team of writers represents both traditional and nontraditional backgrounds, further balancing the contents of the encyclopedia.

Reviewed in: LAT   (Nov. 3, 91) 18
              RSR   17 (April 89) 66

146 Kunhardt, Philip B. *A New Birth of Freedom: Lincoln at Gettysburg.* Boston: Little, Brown and Company, 1983. vii, 263 pp. : ill., photographs, map. Includes index and appendix.

ISBN: 0-316-50600-1   LC: 83-16167

The focus of Kunhardt's book is Lincoln's Gettysburg Address—why and how he delivered it and how he wrote it. The author begins with a discussion of Abraham Lincoln's early life and political career, tracing events in Lincoln's background that led him to deliver the address. Kunhardt also identifies traces of the origin of the address in remarks that Lincoln made to his secretary, John Hay, soon after the outbreak of the war. Kunhardt uses books, newspapers, letters, diaries, and scrapbooks to present a thorough account of Lincoln's trip to Gettysburg and the days preceding it. The appendix contains the seven known versions of the Gettysburg Address.

Reviewed in: LIJ 108 (Nov. 15, 83) 2157

147 Lowry, Thomas P. *The Story the Soldiers Wouldn't Tell: Sex in the Civil War.* Mechanicsburg, Pa.: Stackpole Books, 1994. xiv, 209 pp. : ill. Includes index and bibliography.

ISBN: 0-811-7151-59   LC: 94-1401

It has been easy to dismiss the notion of promiscuity or sexual misconduct by soldiers of the blue and gray. Little information is readily available, and Victorian sensibilities and the romantic aura of gentlemen going off to fight the Civil War have made documentation scarce. But as in war of any kind, with men far from home for long periods of time, passion can be bred as it was for the soldiers of the 1860s. Lowry has been able to discover material in books, manuscripts, and newspapers to produce this study of sexual behavior during the Civil War. With more than 7,500 prostitutes in the vicinities of New York and Washington, Lowry was able to study prostitution and the ensuing outbreak of venereal diseases in those areas. Pornography was readily available, rape occurred, contraception was available, and general promiscuity was not exceptional.

Reviewed in: NYT   (June 12, 94) 24

148 McPherson, James M. *Abraham Lincoln and the Second American Revolution.* New York: Oxford University Press, 1991. xiii, 173 pp. Includes index, bibliography, and references.

ISBN: 0-19-505542-X   LC: 90-6885

McPherson calls the Civil War a new revolution that gave the United States a "new birth of freedom." The seven essays in this volume examine the events of the war from several perspectives. They provide an analysis of the development of Lincoln's strategy as the limited war turned into an all-out struggle to secure total victory. McPherson identifies the revolutionary nature of the Civil War in the abolition of slavery, the destruction of the social structure of the old South, and the shift in the balance of power between the North and the South. He also explores the ways in which the war transformed the American concepts of liberty and freedom.

Reviewed in: AHR   95 (Feb. 90) 260–262
CWH   34 (Dec. 88) 344–347
HRN   17 (Winter 89) 44–45
JAH   75 (March 89) 1333–1334
JSO   55 (Aug. 89) 460–461
RAH   17 (June 89) 214–218

149 McPherson, James M. *Battle Cry of Freedom: The Era of the Civil War.* New York: Oxford University Press, 1988. xix, 904 pp. : ill., photographs, maps. Includes index and bibliography.

ISBN: 0-195-0386-30   LC: 87-11045

To develop his central theme of "the multiple meanings of slavery and freedom, and how they dissolved and re-formed into new patterns in the crucible of war," McPherson begins with an examination of the United States at midcentury. He then provides the reader with a clear and understandable narrative framework that weaves together the complex social, economic, and political relationships that characterized American society in the second half of the nineteenth century. McPherson supplements his descriptions of the war's major campaigns with discussions of conscription, medicine, slavery, and the Free Soil party among other topics, to provide a comprehensive analysis of the era. The text is supplemented with photographs and more than twenty clear, useful maps, which illustrate important battles.

Reviewed in: JSO   58 (Nov. 92) 724

NYT   (June 20, 91) 13

RAH   20 (March 92) 55

150 McPherson, James M. *Ordeal by Fire : The Civil War and Reconstruction.* New York: Alfred A. Knopf, 1981. xviii, 694, xxxii pp. : ill., photographs, maps. Includes index, bibliography, references, and glossary.

ISBN: 0-3943-1206-6   LC: 81-11832

McPherson claims that the Civil War was the central event in the American historical consciousness. It preserved the nation from destruction and determined what it would be. This book is organized around the concept of modernization. The author maintains that the war and its aftermath were important stages of the process of modernization for the United States. The impulse for the process of change came from New England, and the Republican party became the expression of the modernization impulse. The text is supplemented by illustrations, charts, and maps.

Reviewed in: CHO   19 (June 82) 1480

JAH   69 (Dec. 82) 705

JSO   48 (Aug. 82) 431

LIJ   107 (Feb. 15, 82) 456

151 McPherson, James M. *What They Fought For, 1861–1865.* Baton Rouge: Louisiana State University Press, 1994. xv, 88 pp. Includes index and references.

ISBN: 08-07119-040   LC: 93-36934

McPherson, in preparation for a larger work, examined hundreds of diaries and letters of Union and Confederate soldiers in an attempt to explore the motives for their enlisting and fighting in the Civil War. He states that he reached conclusions different from those of other historians—for example, a large number of men on both sides of the conflict were "intensely aware" of the issues at stake and were "passionately concerned" about them. The reasons for this he attributes to the high degree of literacy, the fact that most of the men were volunteers, that the soldiers came from a highly political and democratic society, and that they voted often even during the war years. Liberty and republicanism were themes McPherson found in these letters. Both Confederate and Union soldiers were fighting to preserve the legacy of 1776, the South fighting for independence from what they regarded as a the tyrannical government and the Union to preserve the nation its founders had created.

Reviewed in: LAT   (April 24, 94) 6

LIJ   119 (Feb. 1, 94) 98

NYT   (June 12, 94) 22

152   Parish, Peter. *The American Civil War.* New York: Holmes & Meier Publishers, 1975. 750 pp. : ill., photographs, maps, and charts. Includes index, bibliography, references, and chronology.

ISBN: 0-8419-0176-7/0-8419-0197-X(paper)   LC: 74-84660

Parish presents an excellent synthesis of Civil War scholarship. He asserts that the issue of slavery was the focus of the controversy and that the war was the "central event of American history." Parish uses the war as a "lens" to focus on longer-term changes that were taking place in the United States in the middle of the nineteenth century. He relates the military action of the war to political developments and the wider concerns of society. The text is supplemented with population charts based on the 1860 census and with a number of useful maps.

Reviewed in: AHR   81 (Oct. 76) 976–977

CWT   15 (Jan. 77) 48–49

GAH   60 (Fall 76) 295–296

JAH   62 (March 76) 996–998

JSO   42 (Feb. 76) 125–126

153   Potter, David Morris. *The Impending Crisis, 1848–1861.* Edited by Don E. Fehrenbacher. New York: Harper & Row, 1976. xv, 638 pp. : ill. Includes index and bibliography.

ISBN: 0-06-013403-8   LC: 75-6354

Winner of the Pulitzer Prize in history for 1977, this work was begun by Potter, who wrote until his death, and was completed by Fehrenbacher. It is part of the New American Nation series and is one of the best studies of the crucial decade before the Civil War. The work affords an important balance of issues and controversies with Potter's own judgments. The authors concentrate on the political issues that arose after the Mexican War, when the United States acquired California and the southwest territories: the Wilmot Proviso, the Compromise of 1850, Dred Scott and Harpers' Ferry, and the other complex problems of slavery, expansion, and sectionalism—all of which would eventually lead the country into civil war.

Reviewed in: HRN   4 (May 76) 138

JAH   63 (Dec. 76) 719

JSO   43 (Feb. 77) 103

154 Powell, Lawrence N. *New Masters: Northern Planters during the Civil War and Reconstruction.* New Haven, Conn.: Yale University Press, 1980. xiv, 253 pp. : ill., tables. Includes index, bibliography, and references.

ISBN: 0-300-02217-4   LC: 79-64226

Powell presents the story of the Northerners who settled in the South before and immediately following Appomattox intending to become planters. From his study of 524 Northerners who settled in six states in the lower South, he developed a profile of most of those who went south as young and well-educated, with business or professional, rather than agricultural, backgrounds. Powell found that 70 percent of the Northerners who attempted to earn a living as planters were from New York, Massachusetts, Illinois, and Ohio. Many were discouraged by poor crops in 1866 and 1867. Powell provides insights into the social forces at work during this time and illuminates the cultural contrasts between Northerners and Southerners, blacks and whites.

Reviewed in: LIJ   105 (March 1, 80) 612

NYT   (May 4, 80) 9

155 Roland, Charles P. *An American Iliad: The Story of the Civil War.* University Press of Kentucky, 1991. xii, 289 pp. : ill., photographs, maps. Includes index and bibliography.

ISBN: 0-8131-1737-2   LC: 90-38392

Roland claims that the Union victory forever changed the course of American history in the same way that the Greek victory over Troy changed the course of Western history. His emphasis is on the military action, but he explains the major political, economic, diplomatic, social, and cultural developments of the time in relation to the war effort. Roland also includes brief biographical and character sketches of leading civilian and military figures. There is an especially useful discussion of the constitutional problems faced by Abraham Lincoln and, in particular, the issue of freedom of speech. Roland concludes that Lincoln emerged as a superior war leader because of his tenacity of purpose in pursuing his goal of preserving the Union and, at the same time, maintaining a degree of flexibility—as witnessed by his acceptance of the emancipation of the slaves as a war aim.

Reviewed in: LIJ   115 (Oct. 15, 90) 95

JSO   58 (Aug. 92) 546

156   Smith, Page. *Trial by Fire: A People's History of the Civil War and Reconstruction.* New York: McGraw-Hill, 1982. xvi, 1038 pp. : ill.

ISBN: 0-0705-8571-7   LC: 81-18573

Smith calls the Civil War the "most titanic" internal struggle a nation had ever experienced. Basic questions of race relations, equality, and democracy were held in abeyance until the outcome of the war was settled. In Smith's view the South could not sustain itself against the strength of Generals Ulysses S. Grant and William Tecumseh Sherman and the Union Army soldiers both black and white. Its resolve was broken by the emancipation of the slaves and the politics of Lincoln. This work is a mix of popular history and scholarship to illuminate the ordeal of the common man and woman who endured the suffering and the sacrifice. Smith shares with others the view that the combination of a weak commitment to black rights in the North and Southern racism undid the military and African American reconstruction.

Reviewed in: HRN   11 (May 83) 149

LIJ   107 (Sept. 1, 82) 1658

157   Stampp, Kenneth M. *The Imperiled Union: Essays on the Background of the Civil War.* New York: Oxford University Press, 1980. xv, 320 pp. Includes index.

ISBN: 01-95026-721   LC: 79-20276

Stampp, one of the great scholars of the Civil War, has compiled a collection of his essays dating from 1945 to the present. He represents the generations of historians who believed in the value of historical research on the Civil War—and particularly research into contemporary sources. Stampp is said to be a historian "holding the scales of justice," and he believed that the preservation of the Union was important. The essays included in this volume review conflicting theories of the causes of the Civil War, the constitutional debate over the nature of the Union, the political crisis of the 1850s, and the controversial question of why the Confederacy lost the war.

> Reviewed in: CHO   18 (Nov. 80) 453
>
> JSO   47 (May 81) 296
>
> RAH   8 (Dec. 80) 511

158 Thomas, Emory M. *The Confederate Nation, 1861–1865.* New York: Harper & Row, 1979. xvi, 384 pp. : ill., photographs, maps. Includes index, bibliography, and appendix.

ISBN: 0-06-014252-9   LC: 76-26255

This imaginatively interpretative work integrates military and political events within a broader framework. Thomas discusses major battles, Confederate politics and diplomacy, and the social and economic life of the South. His thesis is that the Confederacy began as a political manifestation of the ideology of the Southern planter class, which was based on an agrarian slave-labor economy that prized individualism and states' rights. In order to preserve this lifestyle, the Confederate States of America was established. Therefore, according to Thomas, in the beginning the Confederate revolution was essentially a conservative movement intended to preserve the regional status quo. After the first year of the war, however, things changed. Military setbacks coupled with fiscal worries contributed to a generally lower morale. To ensure the Confederacy's survival, a new ideology was adopted, one that allowed for greater centralization of political power, more control over domestic industry and foreign commerce, and the development of more class consciousness by the lower and middle classes. The text is supplemented with maps. The appendix presents the text of the Constitution of the Confederate States of America.

> Reviewed in: AHR   84 (Dec. 79) 1481
>
> FHQ   59 (July 80) 93–95
>
> JAH   66 (Dec. 79) 654
>
> JSO   45 (Nov. 79) 611
>
> RAH   8 (March 80) 57

159 Trudeau, Noah Andre. *Out of the Storm: The End of the Civil War, April–June 1865.* Boston: Little, Brown and Company, 1994. xvi, 470 pp. : ill., maps. Includes index and references.

ISBN: 03-1685-328-3   LC: 93-34683

The afternoon in April 1865 when General Robert E. Lee surrendered at Appomattox did not put an immediate end to the war. Battles on sea and land continued to rage on for several months. Trudeau completes his trilogy on the last year of the war with vivid details of the final military campaigns, the sinking of the *Sultana* as it transported former prisoners of war to their homes up north, the munitions explosion that leveled a large section of Mobile, the hunt for Abraham Lincoln's assassin, and the pursuit and capture of Jefferson Davis. These events would be followed by the return of thousands of veterans to civilian life and the effects of emancipation and industrialization on American society. Trudeau's narrative documents life in a new South and the attempt to redefine itself after surrender.

Reviewed in: NYT (June 12, 94) 22

160 Vandiver, Frank E. *Blood Brothers: A Short History of the Civil War.* College Station, Tex.: Texas A & M University Press, 1992. xii, 209 pp. : ill., maps. Includes index and references.

ISBN: 08-9096-523-4   LC: 92-10985

Vandiver, a distinguished historian of the Civil War, has expanded what was to be an encyclopedia article on the military history of the war into a brief, yet major, work on the Civil War as a whole. The work contains an analysis of military operations and the new war machinery, as well as assessments of key leaders. The book is based on both recent and classic scholarship. An important bibliographic essay and numerous photographs are included.

Reviewed in: JAH   80 (March 94) 1475

JMH   57 (Oct. 93) 7204

JSO   60 (May 94) 401

LIJ   117 (Oct. 10, 92) 82

161 Wills, Gary. *Lincoln at Gettysburg: The Words that Remade America.* New York: Simon & Schuster, 1992. 317 pp. Includes index and references.

ISBN: 0-671-76956-1   LC: 92-003546

Reviewers have suggested that one of the most important aspects of the Gettysburg Address is the importance it sheds on Abraham Lincoln's Emancipation Proclamation. This work by Wills is a thorough analysis of the three-minute speech, a line-by-line, word-by-word study of the speech that Wills compares to other funeral orations. There is substantial discussion of the spoken text itself and the variations published in the newspapers, of the preparation of the site in Gettysburg before it could become the cemetery, and of Edward Everett, whose oratory preceded Lincoln's short remarks. Wills offers a vivid description of the devastation of the battlefield, the burning of the animals, the hastily and barely buried bodies of the eight thousand men who died here—making the entire field a burial ground. In preparation for this ceremony, the fields were cleansed, the bodies reburied, order and dignity restored to the grounds, and the federal government assessed to the states to support the cemetery and reburials. Photographs, maps of the grounds, and plans for the cemetery all add to an understanding of Lincoln's interest in the rural cemetery movement and his determination to dedicate a final, peaceful resting place for all those who gave their lives.

> *Reviewed in:*   LIJ   117 (Nov. 1, 92) 99
>
> NYT   (June 7, 92) 1

162 Wyatt-Brown, Bertram. *Yankee Saints and Southern Sinners.* Baton Rouge, La.: Louisiana State University Press, 1985. xi, 227 pp. Includes index and references.

ISBN: 0-8071-1244-5   LC: 85-8112

Using a multidisciplinary approach that incorporates insights from sociology, anthropology, and psychology, Wyatt-Brown explores the ethical differences—especially regarding honor, liberty, and slavery—that divided the North and the South. He assesses the forces in the years preceding the war that produced an abolitionist, reform-minded society in the North and a rural, slaveholding South. The first half of the book examines the relationship between the abolitionists and the evangelical culture. Wyatt-Brown investigates the role that conscience played in the abolitionist movement and places these reformers within the context of the larger religious movements in the North. The second half of the book explores the ethical spirit of the South. The author discusses the regional differences over the meaning and applicability of honor and shame. Then he develops a cultural definition of honor to clarify the nature of Southern political language.

> *Reviewed in:*   CHO   23 (June 86) 1599
>
> JAH   73 (Sept. 86) 434

Historiography

163 Beringer, Richard E., Herman Hattaway, Archer Jones, and William N. Still, Jr. *Why the South Lost the Civil War.* Athens, Ga.: University of Georgia Press, 1986. xi, 582 pp. : ill., maps. Includes index and bibliography.

ISBN: 0-8203-0815-3   LC: 85-8638

This revisionist work sets forth the theme that when the South lost the will to win, it lost the war. More-traditional views state that the South was worn out and had been defeated by superior strategy, superior industrial power, and larger forces. To these authors the overwhelming reason for the defeat was that the nationalism that created the Confederate States of America could not lead the states to independence. The authors state that their analysis demonstrates the relationship between military success and morale. The Confederate nationalism could not sustain itself with the losses on the battlefield.

> *Reviewed in:*   AHR   92 (June 87) 748
>
> APS   495 (Jan. 88) 173–174
>
> JAH   74 (Sept. 87) 523
>
> JEH   48 (Dec. 88) 972–973

164 Current, Richard N. *Arguing with Historians: Essays on the Historical and the Unhistorical.* Middletown, Conn.: Wesleyan University Press, 1987. 208 pp. Includes index.

ISBN: 08-19551-872   LC: 87-13682

This book is a collection of eleven incisive and provocative essays in which Current responds, either positively or negatively, to what he considers some of the important historiographical trends of the past half century relating to the Civil War. Written over the course of almost forty years, these essays possess a certain unity. They are all concerned with the themes of nationalism and sectionalism, and how they are manifested in the relationship between blacks and whites in the United States. In these essays Current cautions historians that they must scrupulously adhere to the facts as he attempts to correct what he believes are errors of interpretation in the writings of others. Current examines the interpretation of the lives and careers of several prominent individuals including Abraham Lincoln, Thaddeus Stevens, and Jefferson Davis. In "President Grant and the Continuing Civil War," he argues that Ulysses S. Grant made a commendable effort to enforce programs developed to ensure voting rights for African Americans and that, because of this, he deserves a much more positive political reputation. Current also writes about ethnicity, reconstruction, and minority rights. In "Carpetbaggers Reconsidered" he raises doubts about the familiar stereotype of Northern political adventurers who sought to control the South. And in "Fictional History: Vidal, Haley, Styron," he maintains that some novelists have exerted a greater influence than most historians on popular conceptions of the American past.

    Reviewed in: AHR   94 (June 89) 848–849

                     JAH   77 (June 90) 270–272

165 Sewell, Richard H. *The House Divided: Sectionalism and Civil War, 1848–1865.* Baltimore, Md.: Johns Hopkins University Press, 1988. 223 pp. Includes bibliography.

ISBN: 08-01835-313   LC: 87-14305

   Sewell synthesizes the work of many scholars to reinforce and refocus the thinking about the origins of the Civil War on slavery as the main reason for sectionalism and the ensuing conflict. The South remained, in Sewell's view, trapped in its localism while the Northern economy flourished.

    Reviewed in: AHR   94 (Oct. 89) 1177

                     CWH 35 (June 89) 180–181

                     HRN 17 (Fall 88) 9

                     JAH   75 (March 89) 1332–1333

                     JSO   55 (Aug. 89) 496–497

                     LAH 30 (Winter 89) 97–98

166 *Why the Confederacy Lost.* Edited by Gabor S. Boritt. New York: Oxford University Press, 1992. 209 pp. Includes references.

ISBN: 0-1950-7405-X LC: 91-44291

This collection includes the following essays: "American Victory, American Defeat," by James M. McPherson; "Military Means, Political Ends: Strategy," by Archer Jones; "'Upon Their Success Hang Momentous Interests': Generals," by Gary W. Gallagher; "The Perseverance of the Soldiers," by Reid Mitchell; "Black Glory: The African-American Role in Union Victory," by Joseph Glatthaar. These essays written by Civil War scholars challenge the conclusion that Northern advantages and Southern weaknesses were not the deciding factors in the outcome of the Civil War. Rather, the writings reach back to the primary factor of the battlefield as the place where the war was ultimately won and lost, despite other factors that may have been in play.

Reviewed in: HRN   21 (Spring 93) 106
            LIJ   117 (Feb. 15, 92) 183

Literature and the War

167 *Classics of Civil War Fiction.* Edited by David Madden and Peggy Bach. Jackson, Miss.: University Press of Mississippi, 1991. viii, 223 pp. Includes bibliography.

ISBN: 0-87805-522-3/0-87805-541-X(paper)   LC: 91-16947

There is little extant literary criticism devoted to the fiction that was written about the Civil War. This collection of original essays examines the different criteria that may be applied when analyzing Northern or Southern literature. There are essays on Ambrose Bierce's *Tales of Soldiers and Civilians,* Stephen Crane's *The Red Badge of Courage,* Evelyn Scott's *The Wave,* and William Faulkner's *Absalom! Absalom!* The bibliography is a selected listing of novels, stories, poems, and plays related to the war.

Reviewed in: ALI   64 (Sept. 92) 606
            NCL   49 (Sept. 92) 266
            VQR   68 (Spring 92) 48

168 Furtwangler, Albert. *Assassin on Stage: Brutus, Hamlet and the Death of Lincoln.* Urbana, Ill.: University of Illinois Press, 1991. x, 168 pp. : ill., diagrams, and photographs. Includes index and references.

ISBN: 0-25201-746-3   LC: 90-38627

Furtwangler relates Abraham Lincoln's assassination to classical politics and tragedy and to the transformation of America's political and cultural life. Focusing on *Julius Caesar* and *Hamlet,* works that he labels "meditations on the art of political murder," Furtwangler examines how political murder and tragedy have affected modern history. Weaving together literature and history, he traces the careers of John Wilkes Booth and Edwin Booth, and analyzes their portrayals of Hamlet (Edwin) and Brutus (John Wilkes). According to Furtwangler, Lincoln's death marks the dividing point between the idealism of the revolutionary era and the anguish of the post–Civil War years. He believes that Shakespearean tragedy "serves as a measure for the mythic power of Lincoln's assassination."

Reviewed in: JAH   19 (June 92) 282

169 Garner, Stanton. *The Civil War World of Herman Melville.* Lawrence, Kans.: University Press of Kansas, 1993. xii, 544 pp. : ill., photographs. Includes index and references.

ISBN: 0-7006-0602-5   LC: 93-640

Garner traces Melville's life and writings from the time of John Brown's raid in 1859 through the publication of *Battle Pieces and Aspects of the War* (1866), which he considers one of Melville's most underrated works. Garner's purpose is to place Melville the poet and his book *Battle Pieces* within the contexts of time and place, and to suggest the intent of individual poems. He considers Melville within the broader contexts of his reading, his political beliefs, his travels, his extended family, and the social circles he moved in. Melville did not join the army or the navy, nor did he work for the civil government. Garner maintains that Melville abhorred the destruction brought about by the war but that this lack of active involvement did not signify Melville's detachment, emotionally or intellectually, from the conflict.

Reviewed in: CHO   31 (Feb. 94) 934
            HRN   22 (Spring 94) 105
            NYT   (Oct. 3, 93) 44

170 *The Real War Will Never Get in the Books: Selections from Writers during the Civil War.* Edited by Louis P. Masur. New York: Oxford University Press, 1993. x, 301 pp. : ill., photographs. Includes index and references.

ISBN: 0-19-506868-8   LC: 92-24446

This is a selection of excerpts from letters, journal entries, articles, and speeches written during the Civil War. The editor has attempted to provide a balanced overview by including selections from a racial, regional, and sexual cross-section. There are contributions from Henry Adams, Louisa May Alcott, Frederick Douglass, Nathaniel Hawthorne, Herman Melville, and Walt Whitman, among others. The selections reveal connections among the political, the personal, and the creative. They illustrate how art grows out of experience and how experience is understood through literary art. Each chapter begins with a brief biographical sketch.

Reviewed in: LIJ   118 (June 1, 93) 152
                  NYR   41 (April 7, 94) 36

Manuscripts

171 Library of Congress. Manuscript Division. *Civil War Manuscripts: A Guide to the Collections in the Manuscript Division of the Library of Congress.* Compiled by John R. Sellers. Washington, D.C.: Library of Congress, 1986. xvii, 391 pp.

ISBN: 08-4440-381-4   LC: 81-607105

The Library of Congress manuscript collections consist largely of the personal papers of prominent Americans, as opposed to official government records, which are held by the National Archives and Records Administration. This bibliography of manuscripts also contains an extensive index and numerous portraits, many of which have been autographed by their subjects, which materials have been reproduced from an album in the James Wadsworth family papers. This subject guide to more than one thousand separately identifiable collections evolved from a checklist produced in 1965–1967 by Lloyd A. Dunlap. Sellers provides a lengthy introduction to the types of information that can be found in the collections: the manufacture and use of aerial reconnaissance balloons and the function of the U.S. Aeronautic Corps; the organization of philanthropic societies; prisoners of war; the role of women in the war; and the effects of the federal, state, and local bounty systems to enlist soldiers. Many letters testify to early enthusiasm for the war and the official solicitation for higher ranks in black regiments. There is much on religion during the period and extensive representation of the effects of the war on Southern blacks. Students of military engineering, military intelligence, or Civil War medicine will find much to examine in the collections. A section explains the use of the guide and the index. All of the collections provide information such as occupation of the writer, dates, number of items, and a brief description of the contents. Example:

> 54
>
> Barton, Clara Harlowe (1821–1912)   Nurse, USA
>   Papers, 1834–1918. ca. 70,000 items.
>   Correspondence, diary, lectures, newspaper clippings, and miscellaneous items relating, in part, to Miss Barton's work with sick and wounded soldiers. Also includes postwar correspondence with the families of missing prisoners of war and a list of Union soldiers buried at Andersonville, Ga.
>   Finding aid available.

Reviewed in: JAH 76 (March 88) 1423–1424

Medical Care

172 Maher, Sister Mary Denis. *To Bind Up the Wounds: Catholic Sister Nurses in the U.S. Civil War.* Westport, Conn.: Greenwood Press, 1989. x, 178 pp. : ill., photographs. Includes index and bibliography.

ISBN: 0-313-26458-9   LC: 89-2217

This is a study of a topic previously ignored in standard histories of the Civil War—the work of the nursing nuns who cared for the sick and wounded in both the North and the South. In all, six hundred nurses from twenty-one communities and twelve orders were involved in the provision of medical care. The focus of this volume is the work done by the Sisters of Charity who had previously staffed the Baltimore Infirmary and the St. Louis Mullanphy Hospital. Using diocesan and convent records, Maher constructs a "composite" picture of Roman Catholic nursing sisters. Accustomed to living and working in organized groups, they were committed to poverty and were willing to live and work in the harsh conditions that existed in army field hospitals. They regarded nursing as a religious calling and viewed themselves as carrying on an established tradition rather than as functioning as feminist pioneers. Maher claims that nursing religious were in demand by surgeons because they rarely challenged orders and did not question military authority. At the beginning of the war, nursing was not generally recognized as a suitable job outside the home for women, so the religious communities were often the only source of trained nurses when the hostilities began. Maher maintains that their work during the war brought the nuns' nursing abilities to the attention of the

Union hospital

American public and that they served as role models for other women, helping to pave the way for professional training for women nurses.

> *Reviewed in:*   AHR   96 (Oct. 91) 1295
> CWH   37 (June 91) 175–176
> JAH   77 (Dec. 90) 1032–1033
> JMI   54 (July 90) 352

173 Oates, Stephen B. *A Woman of Valor: Clara Barton and the Civil War.* New York: Free Press, 1994. x, 527 pp. : ill., map. Includes index and references.

ISBN: 0-0292-3405-0   LC: 93-38830

Clara Barton, a Massachusetts woman who would come to found the American Red Cross, saw firsthand the horrors of war and how adept the armies of the blue and gray became in killing one another. Improvements in military technology went far beyond advances in medicine. Barton nursed thousands of Union soldiers, gave them the little she could to relieve their thirst or protect them from the cold. In Andersonville Prison she led the effort to identify the Union dead after the war. Oates writes of this one dedicated woman who voluntarily put herself within these horrors in an attempt to soften the real human suffering amidst the death and destruction.

> *Reviewed in:*   CHO   32 (Sept. 94) 196
> LIJ   119 (April 1, 94) 108
> NYT   (June 12, 94) 14

174 Olmsted, Frederick Law. *Defending the Union: The Civil War and the U.S. Sanitary Commission, 1861–1863.* Jane Turner Censer editor. Baltimore, Md.: Johns Hopkins University Press, 1986. 757 pp. : ill., photographs, maps. Includes bibliography.

ISBN: 0-8018-3067-2   LC: 85-24044

The fourth volume of Olmsted's papers represents those years Olmsted helped organize and serve as general secretary of the United States Sanitary Commission. The mission of the commission was to supplement the work of the Union Army's Medical Bureau in caring for the large volunteer army. The stated purpose of the project was to publish in annotated form the most significant of Olmsted's writings. The documents demonstrate that despite Olmsted's feeling of failure within the commission, he did have considerable impact. The wide scope of his activities for the commission, investigative reports from behind the lines during the Civil War, and the author's opinions of government policies concerning slavery are all within the documents chosen by the editor. The documents are complemented by a sixty-page introduction that summarizes the work and events relating to the creation of the Sanitary Commission and presents Olmsted's strong belief in the abolition of slavery. Also valuable are a biographical directory, complete with portraits and additional sources of biographical information; extensive and informative notes following each letter and document; and an Olmsted chronology.

> Reviewed in: GHQ   72 (Summer 88) 372–374
> JSO   54 (Feb. 88) 116–118

Military Arts and Science

175 Connelly, Thomas Lawrence. *Autumn of Glory: The Army of Tennessee, 1862–1865.* Baton Rouge, La.: Louisiana State University Press, 1971. ix, 558 pp. : ill., photographs, maps. Includes index and bibliography.

ISBN: 0-8071-0445-0   LC: 70-122353

Using manuscript and archival collections, contemporary newspapers, and personal accounts, Connelly relates the history of the Army of Tennessee from late 1862 until the Confederacy's surrender in 1865. According to Connelly, the chief problem of the Army of Tennessee was command discord, the feuding and lack of communication among officers. In addition to being "crippled by poor leadership," the army's performance was hindered by military politics and internal dissension. Connelly provides an expert analysis of the army's command relationships, which he feels suffered as a result of poor direction from Richmond and which diverted talent and manpower from strategic areas. Connelly also blames Jefferson Davis for many of the Army of Tennessee's problems, asserting that Davis frequently intervened in military operations without adequate knowledge of the problems at hand.

Reviewed in: AHR   79 (Oct. 74) 1266–1267

176 Daniel, Larry J. *Soldiering in the Army of Tennessee: A Portrait of Life in a Confederate Army.* Chapel Hill, N.C.: University of North Carolina Press, 1991. xvi, 231 pp. : ill., photographs, maps, and tables. Includes index, bibliography, and references.

ISBN: 0-8078-2004-0   LC: 91-50250

Using letters from nearly 350 soldiers and scores of memoirs and unit histories, Daniel focuses on the men in the ranks of the Army of Tennessee. He examines how the men felt about their officers and their Union counterparts, what they thought of the course of the war, how they were clothed and fed, and how they spent their time. As a result of his research, Daniel concludes that the Confederate soldiers in the Eastern and Western theaters were more alike than different. The main difference was the way the different armies sustained morale. He believes that, unlike the Army of Northern Virginia, the Army of Tennessee could not maintain its cohesiveness through confidence in its leadership or as a result of battlefield victories. Rather, the soldiers in the Western theater were bound by a sense of commitment instilled through religious fervor and a "perverse pride" that developed as a result of the common experience of serving under losing generals.

Reviewed in: JAH   65 (Dec. 78) 788–789
                   JSO   44 (Aug. 78) 470–471
                   MIR   58 (June 78) 95–96

177 Glatthaar, Joseph T. *Partners in Command: The Relationship between Leaders in the Civil War.* New York: Free Press, 1994. xi, 286 pp. : ill., maps. Includes index and references.

ISBN: 0-029-1181-74   LC: 93-25954

Bringing together material on nine prominent Civil War figures, Glatthaar demonstrates that the societal and industrial changes before the war prompted changes in the technique of military command. War had become complicated. The size and complexity of this first modern war impelled Abraham Lincoln and Jefferson Davis to use these new relationships to interact with top field generals and, in turn, with their subordinates. This collection of essays describes the relationships between Robert E. Lee and Thomas "Stonewall" Jackson, Lincoln and George B. McClellan, Davis and Joseph E. Johnston, Ulysses S. Grant and David D. Porter, and Lincoln and Grant. Some of the partnerships worked and some did not, and in war the consequences can be crucial. These six partnerships were selected because of Glatthaar's perceptions of the critical effect the partnerships would have on the success or failure of the armed forces under their commands. This study deals with the highest levels of command and, therefore, what he terms the operational levels of war, not battlefield tactics.

Reviewed in: NYT (June 12, 94) 15

178 Hagerman, Edward. *The American Civil War and the Origins of Modern Warfare: Ideas, Organization, and Field Command.* Bloomington: Indiana University Press, 1988. 366 pp. : ill. Includes bibliography.

ISBN: 0-253-30546-2   LC: 87-046015

The Civil War proved to be a new era in land warfare; the impact of technology challenged the traditional type of arms as the devastating effect of increased firepower challenged the tactics of warfare. The offensive and defensive ranks dug the trenches. Hagerman analyzes the evolution of field warfare and supply, manpower, firepower, and transportation. He compares the two theaters of operation—with an emphasis on the emergence of trench warfare in the East, Virginia, and the West, mainly Tennessee and Georgia. As Hagerman also shows, technological advances such as the telegraph, observation balloons, the signal corps, and the railroad to move and supply troops affected the field operations too.

Reviewed in: AHR 95 (June 90) 914
CWH 35 (June 89) 172–176
HRN 17 (Spring 89) 103
JAH 76 (Dec. 89) 939–940
JSO 56 (May 90) 357–358
RAH 17 (Dec. 89) 552–558

179 Jones, Archer. *Civil War Command and Strategy: The Process of Victory and Defeat.* New York: Free Press, 1992. xi, 338 pp. : ill., map, diagrams. Includes index, bibliography, and appendixes.

ISBN: 0-02-916635-7   LC: 91-44224

Jones provides a general synthesis of current scholarship, including his own, and places Civil War military history in the broader context of the evolution of modern warfare. In analyzing the level of competence demonstrated during the war, he examines the ways in which military and political considerations affected the formulation of strategy. Jones contends that both belligerents had effective systems of command and that on average the civilian and military leaders performed well. In his assessments of some of the more important battles of the war, Jones hypothesizes about the effect of alternative outcomes. The text is supplemented by two interesting appendixes: "The European Art of War" presents a history of the European tactical systems and logistical methods that influenced tactics and logistics during the Civil War, and the second appendix traces the development of the United States Army.

> *Reviewed in:*   JAH   80 (Sept. 93) 687
>
> JSO   59 (Aug. 93) 557
>
> LIJ   117 (March 15, 93) 100

180   Linderman, Gerald F. *Embattled Courage : The Experience of Combat in the American Civil War.* New York: Free Press, 1987. x, 357 pp. : ill., photographs. Includes index and bibliography.

ISBN: 0-02919-760-0   LC: 86-33515

This book examines the relationship between courage, the "soldier's cardinal virtue and talisman," and combat. Linderman maintains that each war is really two: the war witnessed by civilians and the war fought by soldiers. His narrative moves beyond the battlefields to examine the perceptions of the troops who were actually involved in the fighting. Linderman focuses on those who volunteered during the first two years of the conflict and went on to fight in most of the major battles in the East and with General William Tecumseh Sherman. For the most part these men were white, educated, and from families prominent in the social, economic, and political life of the time. Drawing on their eyewitness accounts and reminiscences, Linderman provides an inside look at these soldiers' disillusionment and the ways in which they struggled to reconcile what they encountered with what they expected to find. The bibliography is especially useful because it includes references to a number of primary source materials.

> *Reviewed in:*   AHR   94 (Feb. 89) 219–220
>
> FHQ   68 (July 89) 104–105
>
> JAH   75 (Dec. 88) 954–955
>
> JSH   22 (Spring 89) 559–561

JSO   54 (Nov. 88) 668–670
RAH   16 (June 88) 222–226

181   McMurry, Richard M. *Two Great Rebel Armies: An Essay in Confederate Military History*. Chapel Hill, N.C.: University of North Carolina Press, 1989. xvi, 204 pp. : ill., map, tables. Includes index, bibliography, references, and appendix.

ISBN: 0-8078-1819-4   LC: 88-14374

During the course of the Civil War, the Confederate government organized approximately two dozen armies. Most were small commands that remained in existence for short periods. The two largest and longest-lived were the Army of Tennessee and the Army of Northern Virginia. The latter was the main military strength of the Confederacy east of the Appalachians. It was involved in many of the most significant battles of the war and enjoyed considerable success. In contrast, the Army of Tennessee lost almost every battle it ever fought, and it has been largely ignored by historians. McMurry compares the two armies and addresses the question of why the Army of Northern Virginia was more successful. He discusses the role of the Tennessee and Virginia state military organizations, the characteristics of the federal opponents in each theater, and other political, logistical, and geographic factors. McMurry contends that Robert E. Lee was correct in calling for a holding action in the West and the mounting of a major effort for victory in the East.

Reviewed in: AHR   95 (Oct. 90) 1294–1295
CWH   36 (March 90) 69–70
JAH   76 (March 90) 1273–1274
JSO   56 (Aug. 90) 541–543
LAH   31 (Winter 90) 96–97
RAH   17 (Dec. 89) 552–558

182   McWhiney, Grady, and Perry D. Jamieson. *Attack and Die: Civil War Military Tactics and the Southern Heritage*. Tuscaloosa, Ala.: University of Alabama Press, 1982. xv, 209 pp. : ill., maps, tables. Includes index, bibliography, and references.

ISBN: 0-8173-0073-2   LC: 81-902

McWhiney discusses Confederate military history within the context of Southern social history. He attempts to distinguish between Southern and Northern military tactics and concludes that the Confederate defeat was in part the result of the Southerners' proclivity for outmoded offensive tactics. Confederate commanders did not appreciate the significance of the increased range and killing power of the rifled musket, and they did not adapt their tactics to account for the enormous advantage that technological change had given to the defense. The text is supplemented with tables that include a comparison of losses sustained by eight Confederate commanders and a comparison of casualties suffered by Confederate and Union commanders.

Reviewed in:	AHR	88 (April 83) 475–476
	CWH	28 (Sept. 82) 274–276
	GHQ	67 (Spring 83) 125–127
	HRN	11 (Nov.–Dec. 82) 36–37
	JSO	49 (Feb. 83) 128–129
	MIR	62 (Dec. 82) 79–80

183 Radley, Kenneth. *Rebel Watchdog: The Confederate States Army Provost Guard.* Baton Rouge, La.: Louisiana State University Press, 1989. xvii, 340 pp. : ill., photographs, and maps. Includes index, bibliography, and appendixes.

ISBN: 0-8071-1468-5   LC: 88-30338

This pathbreaking study of the Confederate Provost Marshall system examines a little-known aspect of Confederate military history. The activities of the provost marshals, or military police force, were sanctioned by the Articles of War adopted on March 6, 1861, which also provided for military courts to try army personnel. The provost marshals, under the command of General John H. Winder, were charged with maintaining army discipline, tracking down deserters, and guarding prisoners of war. As the war continued, the provost system's duties were broadened to include preserving civilian discipline. Radley comments that lack of discipline was an ongoing problem in the Confederate Army. Southerners had a history of self-determination and eventually came to detest the provost marshals, who were accused of favoritism, incompetence, abuse of power, and theft. This study also examines the background of provost officers, the poor organizational structure that eventually led to the system's failure, and the passport policy adopted by the Confederate government.

Reviewed in:	AHR	95 (Dec. 90) 1634
	CWH	36 (June 90) 185–187
	JAH	77 (Sept. 90) 678–679
	JSO	57 (May 91) 332–333

LAH   31 (Spring 90) 215–217
NCH   67 (April 90) 270–271

184 Robertson, James I. *Soldiers Blue and Gray*. Columbia, S.C.: University of South Carolina Press, 1988. ix, 278 pp. : ill. Includes index and bibliography.

ISBN: 0-8724-9572-8   LC: 88-17408

Robertson, a student of Bell I. Wiley, has supplemented Wiley's classic studies on the common Civil War soldiers, *The Life of Johnny Reb* and *The Life of Billy Yank*, by searching for new evidence to support the classic interpretation. He does not dispute the findings, nor does he incorporate revisionist studies, but he does write with great respect for the soldiers, using many of their own writings to retell the nature of the battles, camp and prison life, and other topics. Many of the soldiers were extremely observant and had much to criticize: the disorganization of the officers, the boredom, the food. Robertson lets their letters speak for themselves.

Reviewed in: CWH   35 (Sept. 89) 267–269
JAH   76 (Dec. 89) 940
JSO   56 (Feb. 90) 123–125
NCH   66 (April 89) 252–253
SCH   90 (Oct. 89) 328–329
VMH   98 (April 90) 309

Military Offenses

185 Alotta, Robert I. *Civil War Justice: Union Army Executions under Lincoln*. Shippensburg, Pa.: White Mane Publishing Co., 1989. xi, 234 pp. : ill., photographs. Includes index, bibliography, and appendixes.

ISBN: 0-9425-9710-9   LC: 88-36680

Alotta provides a general overview of the system of military justice that was in place at the time of the Civil War and how it was modified to accommodate wartime expediency. He also explains the rituals of military executions and their effect on those who witnessed them. Information is provided regarding 276 Union soldiers who were officially executed between 1861 and 1866. According to Alotta, many of these men were black or foreign born, a circumstance that he claims resulted in their being underpaid and that indicated prejudice on the part of military officials, who generally favored the testimony of commanding officers over that of enlisted men. The author also contends that in large measure, Abraham Lincoln should be held responsible for the executions of many of these men because of what Alotta sees as his "lack of management skills, his vacillation in regard to military justice decisions, and his complete disregard for the Constitution."

Reviewed in: JSO 56 (Nov. 90) 762–763

Native Americans

186 Danziger, Edmund Jefferson. *Indians and Bureaucrats: Administering the Reservation Policy during the Civil War.* Urbana, Ill.: University of Illinois Press, 1974. x, 240 pp. Includes bibliography.

ISBN: 0-2520-0314-4   LC: 73-085486

Using both government and contemporary sources, this comprehensive study of the administration of Indian affairs during the Civil War years offers insights into the period and the crisis connected with the "Indian problem," westward expansion, and nineteenth-century ethnocentricism. Westward expansion into the new territories and Indian pacification were policy conflicts. Indian-white relations were not improved by the Civil War. The problems with the reservation policies, the field officers' administration of the policies, and the rights of Native Americans were caught in the nation's preoccupation with slavery and the war. Plagued by whiskey and hucksters, broken treaties, racism, patronage appointments to the Indian Service, and the misplaced priorities of the Indian Service, the Native Americans found their welfare placed far below the desire for white expansionism. Lincoln had little time for Civil Service reform, and without leadership from the top, reform of Indian Services could not take place. The failure of the reservation system and the concept of assimilation further entrenched the corruption and the plight of native peoples.

> *Reviewed in:*　HRN　3 (May–June 75) 165
>
> 　　　　　　　JAH　62 (March 76) 1002–1003

187　Hauptman, Laurence M. *The Iroquois in the Civil War: From Battlefield to Reservation.* Syracuse, N.Y.: Syracuse University Press, 1993. xiii, 214 pp. : ill., photographs, maps. Includes index, bibliography, and references.

ISBN: 0-8156-0272-3　LC: 92-3741

Hauptman presents the first in-depth study of the participation of Iroquois in the war and the effects this service had on them. Using archival records, letters, and diaries, he discusses their war service as commissioned and noncommissioned officers, and as cavalry and foot soldiers in units such as the 132nd New York State Volunteer Infantry and the 14th Wisconsin Volunteer Infantry. Hauptman assesses the rate of the Iroquois military volunteerism, their loyalty to the Union, and their efforts to maintain their lands, sovereignty, and cultural identity during the conflict. One of the most notable members of the Iroquois nation whom Hauptman discusses is Ely S. Parker, who served as Ulysses S. Grant's military secretary and was present at the surrender at Appomattox.

> *Reviewed in:*　AHR　99 (June 94) 972
>
> 　　　　　　　CHO　30 (June 93) 1692
>
> 　　　　　　　JAH　81 (Sept. 94) 709
>
> 　　　　　　　LIJ　117 (Oct. 15, 92) 117

188　Nichols, David A. *Lincoln and the Indians: Civil War Policy and Politics.* Columbia, Mo.: University of Missouri Press, 1978. vii, 223 pp. Includes index and bibliography.

ISBN: 0-8262-0231-4   LC: 77-12196

Although not a product of the war itself, the Indian policy and the corrupt Indian office were inherited by Abraham Lincoln. Nichols has documented how the office was used for personal and political purposes to the disadvantage of Native Americans; fraud and theft were rampant. Lincoln had the demands of the war and the settling of white pioneers as his priorities. It was not, as Nichols writes, until the Minnesota Sioux war of 1862 that Lincoln had to face the severe corruption of the Indian Office system. Indian affairs were not detached from the mainstream of Civil War history; they were not always marginal to Lincoln. The corruption was part of the intrinsic bureaucratic maze of financial, political, social, and military problems.

Reviewed in:	AHR	84 (Oct. 79) 1162
	CHO	15 (Sept. 78) 943
	JAH	66 (June 79) 943
	JSH	45 (May 79) 282

Naval Operations

189 Hearn, Chester G. *Gray Raiders of the Sea: How Eight Confederate Warships Destroyed the Union's High Seas Commerce.* Camden, Maine: International Marine Publishing, 1992. xv, 351 pp. : ill., photographs, maps. Includes index, references, and appendixes.

ISBN: 0-87742-279-6   LC: 91-18618

Hearn relates the story of the eight Confederate cruisers that were charged by Confederate Naval Secretary Stephen R. Mallory with dismantling the American carrying trade and forcing wealthy shippers to press the government for a peaceful settlement. The author provides a detailed account of the exploits of the *Sumter,* the *Nash-*

Confederate river defense ram *Stonewall Jackson*

ville, the *Georgia,* the *Tallahassee,* the *Chickamauga,* the *Alabama,* the *Florida,* and the *Shenandoah,* which among them captured, looted, or burned one hundred thousand tons of United States goods. Hearn's analysis is based on memoirs, United States Department of the Navy official records of the Union and Confederate Navies, contemporary newspaper accounts, and secondary sources. He also discusses the support that the Confederacy received for its efforts from Great Britain, which was anxious to regain dominance of the merchant trade. The appendix lists the capture of each Confederate cruiser.

Reviewed in: CHO   29 (April 92) 1290
                 HRN   21 (Spring 93) 106

190 Turner, Maxine T. *Navy Gray: The Story of the Confederate Navy on the Chattahoochee and Apalachicola Rivers.* Tuscaloosa, Ala.: University of Alabama Press, 1988. 357 pp. ill. Includes bibliography.

ISBN: 0-817-3031-62   LC: 86-016047

Using financial records, business correspondence, and employment records, Turner offers analysis of the naval activity on these two rivers as the Confederate Navy's reach into new technology and new industries was hampered by construction delays, manpower and supply shortages, and government bureaucracy.

Reviewed in: CWH   35 (June 89) 186–187
                 CWT   27 (Nov. 89) 16
                 FHQ   67 (Jan. 89) 359–361
                 GHQ   73 (Spring 89) 139–140
                 JAH   76 (June 89) 266–267
                 JSO   55 (Nov. 89) 731–732

Boat attack on Ft. Sumter

191 Wise, Stephen R. *Lifeline of the Confederacy: Blockade Running during the Civil War.* Columbia, S.C.: University of South Carolina Press, 1989. xi, 403 pp. : ill., photographs, maps. Includes index, bibliography, references, and appendixes.

ISBN: 0-87249-554-X   LC: 88-20524

This is a definitive study of Confederate blockade-running operations and their effect on the war effort. Wise uses earlier accounts, previously unused manuscript and newspaper accounts, records from the Admiralty courts, and consul dispatches to present a detailed explanation of how cargoes were obtained and brought in, where they were landed, and how they aided the war effort. He emphasizes the importance of efforts to organize foreign supplies both within and outside the Confederacy. Wise relates the story of Confederate purchasing in England and Europe, and puts the Erlanger Loan into perspective. There are also discussions of important companies and individuals involved in blockade-running operations. The text is supplemented with twenty-one impressive appendixes which relate the antebellum value of imports and exports for Southern ports, the descriptions of blockade runners that cleared various ports and their destinations, and more.

Reviewed in: CWH   36 (March 90) 82–83
                  FHQ   68 (April 90) 490–492

JSO   56 (Aug. 90) 543–544
SCH   91 (Jan. 90) 53–54
VMH 98 (April 90) 324–326

Personal Narratives

192 Alexander, Edward Porter. *Fighting for the Confederacy: The Personal Recollections of General Edward Porter Alexander.* Edited by Gary W. Gallagher. Chapel Hill, N.C.: University of North Carolina Press, 1989. xxvii, 664 pp. : ill. Includes explanatory notes and index.

ISBN: 0-8078-1848-8   LC: 88-37667

Alexander was a skilled engineer artillerist and staff officer who participated in almost all of the major battles in the Eastern theater of operations. His abilities brought him into close contact with the Confederate high command. Written at the urging of his children, who wanted to know more about his war experiences, *Fighting for the Confederacy* is an intimate, candid account of Alexander's personal encounters with Generals Pierre Beauregard, Joseph E. Johnston, and Robert E. Lee, among others. The text is accompanied by reproductions of the seventy-six illustrations that appeared in Alexander's original manuscript—including diagrams, sketches, and maps in the author's own hand. The narrative, which reflects Alexander's insightful opinions and judgments, is enhanced by the editor's detailed endnotes, which supply the necessary background and explanations to allow for a fuller understanding of the author's recollections. This book, which was actually written first, compliments Alexander's other account of the war, *Military Memoirs of a Confederate : A Critical Narrative,* published earlier, which presented a more objective history of Lee's army.

Reviewed in: CWH   36 (June 90) 167–169

FHQ   69 (Oct. 90) 237–238

JAH   77 (Sept. 90) 679–680

JSO   57 (Feb. 91) 118–119

LAH   31 (Summer 90) 312–315

NCH   67 (April 90) 272

193 Averell, William Woods. *Ten Years in the Saddle: The Civil War Memoirs of William Woods Averell, 1851–1862.* Edited by Edward K. Eckert and Nicholas J. Amato. San Rafael, Calif.: Presidio Press, 1979. xiii, 443 pp. : ill., photographs, maps. Includes index, bibliography, and references.

ISBN: 0-89141-024-4   LC: 77-73551

Averell was a Union cavalry general from Bath, New York. While attending West Point, he began keeping a diary in which he recorded his experiences as a cadet as well as his service with the Mounted Rifles in New Mexico during the Navajo wars. In 1891 Averell began working on a memoir based on his diary. In it he provides information about his war service, including descriptions of his staff duties, the history and function of the cavalry, and his role in the organization of the Third Pennsylvania Cavalry. He also discusses the battlefield action he saw at Bull Run and on the Bermuda Hundred Peninsula. In 1864 Averell was removed from command of the cavalry in the Shenandoah Valley by General Sheridan. In the epilogue the editors use Averell's correspondence to discuss his relationship with Philip H. Sheridan. They conclude that Averell was a capable company and regimental commander who had the misfortune to rise above his level of competence. There is also a discussion of Averell's postwar career as a businessman and diplomat.

Reviewed in: CHO   16 (Sept. 79) 905

CWH   29 (Sept. 83) 270–271

MIA   45 (April 81) 101

194 Bellard, Alfred. *Gone for a Soldier: The Civil War Memoirs of Private Alfred Bellard.* Edited by Davis Herbert Donald. Boston: Little, Brown and Company, 1975. xxii, 298 pp. : ill., photographs, maps, drawings. Includes biographical index and appendix.

ISBN: 0-316-08833-0   LC: 75-19220

This memoir by Alfred Bellard, a private volunteer soldier of the Fifth New Jersey Infantry, is unique because it combines prose with seventy-five colorful pictures of the primitive type drawn by the author. Bellard, who seemed to enjoy army life despite its many hardships, provides a lively account of the life of ordinary soldiers—what they wore, cooked and ate, and how they spent their leisure time. Bellard was a carpenter's apprentice from Hudson City, New Jersey, when he enlisted in the army in August 1861. Because he was very attached to his family and wanted them to know what he was doing, he kept a pocket diary on a daily basis. Once a week he sent long letters, often illustrated with sketches, to his family, who carefully preserved all the materials he sent. This memoir, compiled in the 1880s, is based on Bellard's recollections and on the materials his family kept. It presents eyewitness accounts of some of the more important battles of the war. Bellard served with General George B. McClellan on the Bermuda Hundred Peninsula, participated in the rout at Second Bull Run, and was with General Ambrose E. Burnside at Fredericksburg. After he was wounded at Chancellorsville, Bellard served in the provost marshall's guard that was assigned to keep order in Washington, D.C. During this tour of duty, he witnessed Jubal Early's raid on the city in 1864. Bellard's narrative extends until the summer of 1864, when he left the service. For comparative purposes, the editor provides three accounts by Bellard of the Battle of Fredericksburg—in the memoir, the entry from his pocket diary, and his letter to his father from Falmouth, Virginia, on December 16, 1862. There is also a listing of the officers who served in Company C, Fifth New Jersey Infantry, between August 1861 and May 1863.

Reviewed in: CHO   13 (March 76) 129

                            CWT   30 (Dec. 91) 63

                            JSH   42 (Feb. 77) 134–135

                            LIJ   101 (Jan. 15, 76) 331

195 Brewster, Charles Harvey. *When This Cruel War Is Over: The Civil War Letters of Charles Harvey Brewster.* Edited with an introduction by David W. Blight. Amherst, Mass.: University of Massachusetts Press, 1992. x, 366 pp. Includes references.

ISBN: 0-08723-773-X   LC: 91-038861

Charles Harvey Brewster was twenty-seven years old when he entered the army. Left for posterity are 133 of the original 192 letters that provide an account of the experiences of a young soldier who survived seven major campaigns. These important letters were written with an eye for detail, commenting on unit politics, the evolution of military tactics, unburied corpses, and unattended wounded. This antislavery Republican admitted his fears and openly expressed support for emancipation, yet he was a typical mid-nineteenth century racist. Because he was a man of conviction, Brewster's letters make compelling reading. Sections of the letters are briefly annotated to serve as a guide to names and places. In all, the letters stand on their own as a chronicle about the meaning of the Civil War. Included are four of the letters Brewster's daughter Mary Kate apparently edited and made into a journal.

Reviewed in:	CHO	30 (Jan. 93) 867
	JAH	80 (Sept. 93) 689
	LIJ	117 (June 1, 92) 136

196 *"Broke by the War": Letters of a Slave Trader.* Edited by Edmund L. Drago. Columbia, S.C.: University of South Carolina Press, 1991. x, 152 pp. Includes references.

ISBN: 0-87249-763-1   LC: 91-17887

This is a collection of letters written between 1852 and 1857 by a South Carolina slave trader, A. J. McElveen, to his employer, Ziba B. Oakes, an affluent Charleston broker. The letters provide valuable insights into the slave-trading world and its effect on both slaves and traders. A variety of topics is covered, including the destruction of slave families, the pursuit of fugitive slaves, and the active involvement in the slave trade by professionals such as doctors, lawyers, and brokers. Drago considers the slave traders to have been "hard-headed businessmen pursuing profits according to well-established practices." Most of the wealthier traders were pillars of the community; those who were less successful viewed the trade as an honest way to support their families. McElveen's letters tend to bolster Drago's contentions. It is clear from the correspondence that McElveen admired Oakes's prosperous lifestyle and that he sought to emulate his employer's profit-making business practices.

Reviewed in:	JAH	79 (Dec. 92) 1173
	JEH	52 (Dec. 92) 961
	JSO	59 (May 93) 372
	RAH	20 (Dec. 92) 501

197 *The Brothers' War: Civil War Letters to Their Loved Ones from the Blue and Gray.* Edited by Annette Tapert. New York: Time Books, 1988. xiv, 242 pp. Includes index.

ISBN: 0-8129-1634-4   LC: 88-040160

Balancing Yankee and Confederate, officers and enlisted men, the editor has put together a volume of letters to show the Civil War as personal experience. Reading these letters—which provide witness to every crucial campaign and battle, as well as tell of life in camp (the disease, the bravery, and the stoicism)—makes us realize that the stories cannot be forgotten. Tapert chose some of the letters for historical significance but most for their prose, their emotional content, and anecdotes. They have been put into chronological order with some linking text. At the beginning of the war, a man's sense of inner quality was more important than rank. What Tapert as editor saw was that the early letter writers did not see that the war would be won not by moral superiority but, rather, by railroads and munitions. It was the first modern war, and slowly the letter writers began to understand that it would not end quickly. Tapert notes how impressive it is that no matter what side the letter writer fought on, the letters have the same tone and quality. Each side believed in the absolute rightness of the cause. Readers learn that it was not the blood and death that made the bloodiest American war so memorable to the men who fought it and wrote about it; rather, it was the "pumped up glory of the bugles and the guns" that initiated the letters, made the veterans wrap them in ribbons, put them away, and eventually "obscure and reinvent" their memories.

> *Reviewed in:* CWH 35 (Sept. 89) 273–274
>
> CWT 28 (Sept.–Oct. 89) 28–29
>
> JMI 52 (Feb. 90) 66–67

198 Bull, Rice C. *Soldiering: The Civil War Diary of Rice C. Bull, 123rd New York Volunteer Infantry.* Edited by K. Jack Bauer. San Rafael, Calif.: Presidio Press, 1977. x, 259 pp. : ill. Includes index and bibliography.

ISBN: 0-8914-1014-7   LC: 76-58758

Born in 1842, Rice C. Bull joined the 123rd New York in 1862. After the unit served with the 12th Corps in 1863, the 123rd spent the remainder of the war participating with the forces of Major General William Tecumseh Sherman. Bull saw action in the Atlanta campaign. This account of Bull's experiences, written by him in 1913, was based on the diary he kept during the war and the letters he wrote from 1862 to 1865.

> *Reviewed in:*   JAH   65 (Dec. 78) 788
>
> JSO   44 (Aug. 78) 470

199 *Civil War Diary of Sarah Morgan.* Edited by Charles East. Athens, Ga.: University of Georgia Press, 1991. xii, 626 pp. : ill., photographs, maps. Includes index.

ISBN: 0-8203-1357-2   LC: 91-2161

Sarah Morgan's diary, which chronicles a young woman's emotional development, is significant because it contributes to an understanding of the character of elite Southern women's political and social allegiances. In her diary, which she began at age nineteen in the early days of 1862, Morgan combines an intense loyalty to the Confederacy, and the class and racial hierarchies it represented, with an ambiguous attitude regarding her position as a woman in a patriarchal society. During the war Morgan lived in and around New Orleans, and the five books that make up her diary portray the daily life in this corner of the Confederacy.

> *Reviewed in:*   JAH   79 (Dec. 92) 1181
>
> JSO   59 (May 93) 386

200 Conolly, Thomas. *An Irishman in Dixie: Thomas Conolly's Diary of the Fall of the Confederacy.* Edited by Nelson D. Lankford. Columbia, S.C.: University of South Carolina Press, 1988. xi, 154 pp. Includes index and references.

ISBN: 0-8724-9555-8   LC: 88-001143

Thomas Conolly, an Irish Protestant and a member of Parliament, was heir to a dynasty and owner of Castletown House in Ireland. An ardent supporter of the Confederacy, Conolly sailed to America in the last weeks of the war, hoping to exchange cargo for cotton to reap a profit. He maintained a continued optimism about the victory of the Confederacy and its eventual independence. His expedition from February 23, 1865, to May 26, 1865, was hampered by ship problems; but he did manage to make it to the South, where he was received with great enthusiasm by Robert E. Lee, Jefferson Davis, and other prominent citizens. His diary is filled with vivid and frank descriptions of the conditions and the people of the South. Well edited, with important identifying notes, the diary is also enhanced with illustrations. Appendix A explains the editorial process; footnotes appear at the first mention of every individual for ease of identification. Additional appendixes include a chronology of Conolly's life and a chronology of his American travels.

Reviewed in: CWH   35 (Dec. 89) 343–345

CWT   27 (Dec. 88) 44

FHQ   68 (Oct. 89) 234–235

JSO   56 (Feb. 90) 130–131

NCH   66 (Jan. 89) 104–105

VMH   98 (April 90) 326–328

201 *Confederate Foreign Agent: The European Diary of Major Edward C. Anderson.* Edited with prologue and epilogue by W. Stanley Hoole. Tuscaloosa, Ala.: University of Alabama Press, 1976. viii, 161 pp. Includes index and references.

ISBN: not available   LC: 76-374426

Edward C. Anderson, a former lieutenant in the United States Navy who served several times as mayor of Savannah, Georgia, was commissioned a major in the Confederate Army in April 1861. The following month he was dispatched to Europe with instructions to procure arms and other supplies for the Confederacy before the Union blockade was fully implemented. Anderson was also charged with investigating the activities of a Confederate agent named Caleb Huse. Anderson spent six months in London, where he exonerated Huse and conducted himself well. He also acquired and outfitted the *Fingal,* which eventually transported $250,000 worth of war materiel to the Confederate States of America. The *Fingal's* cargo represented the single largest shipment of supplies to reach the Confederacy during the war. Anderson's diary records his activities from the time of his departure for London until shortly after his return. The diary brings to light many unknown facts about Confederate activities in Europe. Following his European service Anderson was offered the post of assistant secretary of war in the Confederate government. After he declined the offer, he was promoted to colonel and placed in command of the coastal defenses of Georgia. Hoole's epilogue summarizes Anderson's career as a two-term mayor of Reconstruction Savannah and as a businessman until his death in 1883.

Reviewed in: JSO   43 (Aug. 77) 460–461

CWT   16 (Nov. 77) 50

202 *Fallen Leaves: The Civil War Letters of Major Henry Livermore Abbott.* Edited by Robert Garth Scott. Kent, Ohio: Kent State University Press, 1991. xiv, 266 pp. : ill., photographs. Includes index, bibliography, and references.

ISBN: 0-87338-440-7   LC: 91-8019

Major Henry Livermore Abbott was a highly respected officer who distinguished himself in every battle he fought. Abbott was an ardent Democrat who was opposed to Abraham Lincoln's policies on emancipation, conscription, and the suspension of civil liberties. Although he was reluctant to join, Abbott enlisted in the Twentieth Massachusetts Volunteer Infantry. At first he thought he was too timid to fight, but he soon came to long for action in a major battle. Abbott's letters relate his experiences from his first encounter with combat at Ball's Bluff until his last at the start of the Wilderness Campaign, where he died of a stomach wound. Scott's introduction includes a biographical sketch that places the letters in context. He called Abbott "without question, the most widely known, most highly respected officer of his rank ever to serve in the Army of the Potomac."

> *Reviewed in:*   CHO   29 (May 92) 1454
> LIJ   116 (Oct. 15, 91) 90
> NYT   (Nov. 17, 91) 1
> VQR   68 (Spring 92) 54

203 Geer, Allen Morgan. *The Civil War Diary of Allen Morgan Geer: Twentieth Regiment, Illinois Volunteers.* Edited by Mary Ann Andersen. Tappan, N.Y.: R. C. Appleman, 1977. xxii, 306 pp. : ill., photograph, map. Includes bibliography, references, and appendix.

ISBN: not available   LC: 77-3830

Geer—who was born in Cooperstown, New York, and reared in Illinois and Wisconsin—spent most of his adult life in Missouri. The entries in his diary cover a long period of time, June 1861 through mid-July 1865, and provide insightful evaluations of a variety of political and military issues. Geer began the war as a private and advanced to the rank of lieutenant. Along the way he saw service in a variety of roles, fighting soldier, hospital orderly, member of the provost guard, and special mounted escort. He reveals himself as a sober, sensitive, intellectual individual as he relates details of a number of battles— including those at Forts Henry and Donelson, Shiloh, Vicksburg, Atlanta—and the Carolinas campaign.

Reviewed in: CWT   17 (Dec. 78) 46
            JSO   44 (May 78) 313

204 Gooding, Corporal James Henry. *On the Altar of Freedom: A Black Soldier's Civil War Letters from the Front.* Edited by Virginia Matzke Adams. Amherst, Mass.: University of Massachusetts Press, 1991. xxxvii, 139 pp. : ill., photographs, maps. Includes index and appendixes.

ISBN: 0-87023-745-4   LC: 91-0039

This is a collection of forty-eight letters from James Henry Gooding—an original member of the Fifty-fourth Massachusetts Infantry Regiment, one of the Union's black regiments, to his hometown newspaper, the *New Bedford Mercury.* These letters are especially noteworthy because they represent the only sustained contemporaneous account of life in a black regiment. Gooding enlisted in the United States Army in February 1863. His first letter, dated in March of that year, details life in training camp. In July 1863 Gooding participated in the Union assault on Fort Wagner near Charleston Harbor in South Carolina. His regiment's unflinching behavior during this encounter helped to ensure the permanency of the Union policy of enlisting blacks. In his letters Corporal Gooding describes camp life, the excessive amount of drilling and training that recruits endured, and his desire for combat. He expresses some of the concerns of many African Americans at the time (1863–1864) and describes the hardships faced by the families of black soldiers. Gooding also urges other blacks to sacrifice for the Union. His letters reveal him to be an observant, well-informed, fluent writer who is passionately committed to the Union, to liberty, and to black rights. He was wounded at the battle of Olustee, Florida, taken prisoner, and sent to Andersonville Prison, where he died in July 1864.

Reviewed in: CHO   29 (April 92) 1290
            LIJ   116 (Oct. 1, 91) 120
            NYT   (Nov. 17, 91) 1

205 *A Grand Army of Black Men: Letters from African-American Soldiers in the Union Army, 1861–1865.* Edited by Edwin S. Redkey. Cambridge: Cambridge University Press, 1992. xix, 302 pp.

ISBN: 0-5214-3400-9/0-5214-3998-1(paper)   LC: 92-14632

Of the two hundred thousand African Americans who served in the Union army and navy during the Civil War, the majority were former slaves. Although they did not leave behind an extensive collection of diaries and journals, their wartime experiences are taken from a selection of letters published in black and abolitionist newspapers during the war years. Redkey provides a short history of the two nationally read newspapers published by African Americans during the Civil War: the Philadelphia *Christian Recorder,* which was an official organ of the African Methodist Episcopal Church, and the New York City *Weekly Anglo-African,* which was the main voice of the black soldiers of the North. The other paper from which letters were drawn was the weekly Boston *Pine and Palm,* the official organ of the Haitian Emigration Bureau and the African Civilization Society. The letters are arranged in chapters by broad topics. Redkey clearly shows that the letter writers had a real sense of being African Americans and considered themselves pioneers in the struggle for racial equality. The focus of the letters is on army life, black soldiers in white units, fighting a war in different parts of the South, troops on occupation duty, and civil rights issues such as citizenship and voting privileges, equal pay, and complaints against racism.

Reviewed in: CHO   30 (April 93) 1377

JAH   80 (March 94) 1476

JMH   57 (July 93) 572

JSO   60 (May 94) 4104

206 *The Granite Farm Letters: The Civil War Correspondence of Edgeworth and Sallie Bird.* Edited with an introduction by John Rozier. Athens, Ga.: University of Georgia Press, 1988. xxvi, 300 pp. Includes index and bibliography.

ISBN: 0-820-31042-5   LC: 88-13978

Members of the elite families of planters in middle Georgia, the Birds lived the life of the stereotypical antebellum South, where money was available for education and travel and where the ownership of slaves made the pursuit of politics and hunting possible. Their correspondence was extensive; unfortunately many of Sallie's letters were not saved. Rozier has included letters from 1861 to the death of Edgeworth in 1867, and his unobtrusive editing lets the letters speak for themselves. Individuals mentioned in the letters are identified for the reader. These are the letters of educated, caring individuals, theirs was a family that lived in authentic antebellum culture and society. Bird, a defender and product of the old regime, would even give his wife advice on her careful treatment of the slaves while he was stationed at the front lines. It was the system of slavery that made their lives comfortable, and the intrusion of the war and the beginning of slave revolts were facts that could not be avoided.

> *Reviewed in:*   CWH   35 (Sept. 89) 269–270
> FHQ   68 (April 90) 494–497
> GHQ   74 (Summer 90) 324–326
> JSO   56 (Aug. 90) 540–541
> NCH   66 (Oct. 89) 483–484

207 Grant, Julia Dent. *The Personal Memoirs of Julia Dent Grant.* Edited by John Y. Simon. New York: G. P. Putnam's Sons, 1975. 346 pp. : ill., photographs. Includes index and references.

ISBN: 0-399-11386-X   LC: 74-79648

These memoirs are a direct transcription of Julia Grant's reminiscences as they were dictated to her oldest son and later to a secretary. Grant began the memoir in 1887, two years after her husband's death, and completed it in 1890. She spent most of the war at her husband's side. Almost one-half of her memoir is devoted to these battlefield years and provides an accurate, day-to-day account of the fighting she witnessed. Grant also includes a detailed accounting of her childhood on her father's Missouri plantation, White Haven, as well as of her courtship and early marriage. In addition to a discussion of her years in the White House as the president's wife, Grant tells the story of the couple's triumphant world tour in 1877–1879. The text is supplemented with genealogies of the Grant and Dent families and an essay entitled "The First Lady as an Author," which includes a bibliography of books written by the wives of presidents from Abigail Adams to Edith Wilson.

> *Reviewed in:*   AHR   81 (June 76) 669–670
> CWH   21 (Sept. 75) 285–287
> JAH   62 (Dec. 75) 702–703

208 Hawks, Esther Hill. *A Woman Doctor's Civil War: Esther Hill Hawks' Diary.* Edited by Gerald Schwartz. Columbia, S.C.: University of South Carolina Press, 1989. ix, 289 pp. : ill., photograph, maps. Includes bibliography.

ISBN: 0-87249-435-7/0-87249-622-8(paper)   LC: 84-11998

A dedicated abolitionist, humanitarian, and supporter of women's rights, Hawks was one of America's first female physicians. She was married in 1854 and graduated from medical school three years later. The war gave her the opportunity to transform her ideals into action. In 1862 she left New Hampshire with her husband, also a doctor, to work in South Carolina on behalf of the National Freedman's Aid Association of New York. Hawks's diary, in which she recorded her experiences and observations, covers the period between October 1862 and November 1866. During the time that Hawks and her husband lived on the Sea Islands of South Carolina, she worked primarily as a teacher. Hawks travelled widely in South Carolina and Northern Florida, and recorded her observations of the transition she observed among African Americans moving from a condition of slavery to freedom. She also includes her firsthand observations regarding the special problems of African-American education. Hawks's diary is especially important because of the insights it provides regarding gender roles during this period.

Reviewed in: CHO   23 (Feb. 86) 918

JSO   52 (Feb. 86) 115

209 *Hearth and Knapsack: The Ladley Letters, 1857–1880.* Edited by Carl M. Becker and Ritchie Thomas. Athens, Ohio: Ohio University Press, 1988. xxiii, 414 pp. Includes index and bibliography.

ISBN: 0-8214-0885-2   LC: 87-30687

The correspondence of Oscar Ladley, who was a twenty-three-year-old volunteer in the Union Army, to his widowed mother and sisters in Ohio begins in 1861. He begins by sharing with them the details of army life, and they their concerns about casualty lists and the difficulties they face with high prices and scarcities. Half way through the book, there are no longer any letters from home, only those written by Ladley. From these the reader gains insight into the evolving career of a professional soldier. They also serve to document what success meant to young men who sought in a military life what they could not attain in civilian life. With a moderate degree of education, and without the backing of family income, he was able to obtain a commission through some political friends of his family. A glossary to identify the names that appear in the Ladley letters is appended, as is a chronology of Ladley's life, roster, and engagements with which he was associated.

Reviewed in: CWH   35 (Sept. 89) 273–274

FHQ   69 (Jan. 91) 367–368

210 Heyward, Pauline DeCaradeuc. *A Confederate Lady Comes of Age: The Journal of Pauline DeCaradeuc Heyward, 1863–1888.* Edited by Mary D. Robertson. Columbia, S.C.: University of South Carolina Press, 1992. xxi, 160 pp. : ill. Includes index and bibliography.

ISBN: 0-87249-782-8   LC: 91-25091

Pauline DeCaradeuc Heyward, born into a wealthy, French-Catholic family in 1843, began her diary on her plantation in 1863 to record the day-to-day events of the war from the perspective of a young Southern woman convinced of the "rightness of the southern cause." Intelligent and cultured, she led a privileged life. Her journal sheds light on the role of women in Southern society. She hoped the Confederacy would be victorious, even as she watched her plantation being destroyed by the Union troops and the Confederacy going down in defeat. Her diary records not only the danger and desperation that women on the homefront had to face but also their struggle to preserve their way of life. A prologue provides details on the history of the family from 1792, and Robertson has unobtrusively annotated the entries, setting them into their historical context and providing information on the principal characters mentioned in the journal. This work is part of an ongoing series of women's diaries and letters of the nineteenth-century South that enable women to speak for themselves on issues important to them.

Reviewed in: JAH   80 (Sept. 93) 692

JSO   59 (Aug. 93) 563

211 Lauderdale, John Vance. *Wounded River: The Civil War Letters of John Vance Lauderdale, M.D.* Edited by Peter Josyph. East Lansing, Mich.: Michigan State University Press, 1993. xii, 241 pp. : ill., photographs, map. Includes index, bibliography, references and appendixes.

ISBN: 0-8701-3328-4   LC: 92-56959

John Vance Lauderdale practiced medicine in New York City before the war began. He became a civilian contract surgeon with the Union Army and served as a surgeon aboard the United States Army hospital ship *D. A. January* between April and August 1862. The *January* carried the wounded from as far south as Memphis to hospitals in the north along the upper Ohio and Mississippi Rivers. Peter Josyph, an expert on Civil War medicine, summarizes the state of the medical arts at the time in his introduction. The book is divided into three parts. Part 1 includes Lauderdale's letters home to his sister while he was serving on the *January*. Part 2 includes letters that were written while he was completing his medical training at Bellevue Hospital in New York City. Part 3 presents his letters from the frontier where Lauderdale served as a regular army surgeon. Lauderdale's letters describe the New York City draft riots and relay his impressions of river life, Confederate morale, abolitionists, slavery, and Abraham Lincoln's assassination.

> *Reviewed in:*   CHO   31 (Nov. 93) 526
>
> HRN   22 (Summer 94) 151
>
> NYT   (Dec. 5, 93) 58

212   Lee, Elizabeth Blair. *Wartime Washington: The Civil War Letters of Elizabeth Blair Lee*. Edited by Virginia Jeans Laas. Chicago: University of Illinois Press, 1991. xii, 552 pp. : ill., photographs, maps. Includes index and bibliography.

ISBN: 0-252-01802-8   LC: 90-25762

Elizabeth Blair Lee was a daughter of the Southern aristocracy. Well born and well bred, she worked for her family's interests in Washington political and social circles. Her husband, Samuel Phillips Lee, was a Union naval officer. While he was at sea, Elizabeth lived with her parents in Blair House across the street from the White House, which put her at the center of politics and society in Washington. Elizabeth was an intelligent, perceptive correspondent. The 368 letters reprinted here provide a civilian point of view of military events. The text is supplemented with useful maps.

> *Reviewed in:*   CHO   29 (June 92) 1604
>
> LIJ   116 (Aug. 91) 110
>
> JAH   80 (Sept. 93) 691
>
> JSO   59 (May 93) 388

213   McClellan, George B. *The Civil War Papers of George B. McClellan: Selected Correspondence, 1860–1865*. Edited by Stephen W. Sears. New York: Ticknor & Fields, 1989. xv, 651 pp. : ill., photograph. Includes indexes.

ISBN: 0-89919-337-4   LC: 88-29447

Sears presents 813 documents in this volume, including 260 that have never before been published. In addition to McClellan's candid letters about himself, his motivation, and his intentions, there are also campaign plans, strategic papers, and material related to McClellan's tactical decisions. These documents focus on the general's military operations and political machinations from the Battle of Antietam through the election of 1864. McClellan is presented in a wide variety of wartime roles: army commander, theater commander, battlefield tactician, military executive, political partisan, and presidential candidate. Sears claims that McClellan was "possessed by demons." He believed that federal officials were conspiring against him and that the Confederacy always faced him with a considerably larger force than was actually the case. Each time he lost the courage to fight, the general believed he was preserving his army to fight again.

> *Reviewed in:*   CWH   35 (Dec. 89) 329–323
>
> JSO   57 (Feb. 91) 113–115

214   *Make Me a Map of the Valley: The Civil War Journal of Stonewall Jackson's Topographer.* Edited by Archie P. McDonald. Dallas, Tex.: Southern Methodist University Press, 1973. xxxvii, 352 pp. : ill., maps. Includes index, bibliography, and references.

ISBN: 0-87074-137-3   LC: 73-82036

Jedediah Hotchkiss contributed almost one-half of the Confederate maps that appeared in the *Atlas of the War of the Rebellion,* and he is considered by many historians to be the foremost mapmaker of the Civil War. This journal relates to his war service between March 10, 1862, and April 18, 1865. The volume's editor, McDonald, provides a comprehensive biographical sketch in the introduction. Hotchkiss, who was a self-taught engineer and cartographer, produced maps for Thomas "Stonewall" Jackson and succeeding commanders of the Second Corps of the Army of Northern Virginia. His first assignment was to make a map of the Shenandoah Valley for Jackson. A distinctive feature of Hotchkiss's maps was his use of different-colored pencils for greater clarity in the definition of surface features. This journal is also important because it provides information on Jackson and Robert E. Lee, as well as problems of command and accounts of various battles fought in Virginia.

> *Reviewed in:*   CWH   20 (June 74) 184–185
>
> HRN   2 (May–June 74) 160
>
> JAH   62 (June 75) 139–140
>
> JSO   40 (Aug. 74) 489–490

215   *Mary Chesnut's Civil War.* Edited by C. Vann Woodward. New Haven, Conn.: Yale University Press, 1981. lviii, 886 pp. : ill. Includes index and explanatory notes.

ISBN: 0-300-02459-2   LC: 80-36661

Mary Chesnut, wife of a prominent Confederate politician, recorded events that occurred between February 1861 and July 1865 in
what she referred to as her "journal" or her "notes." Eventually,
Chesnut's journal would fill more than twenty-five hundred pages of
forty-eight copy books, which she kept under lock and key during the
war. In this journal Chesnut conveys a sense of the chaos that characterized her daily life. During the 1870s and 1880s Chesnut began
revising her journal, occasionally filling in some gaps from memory, to
prepare it for publication. Following her death, Chesnut's reminiscences were further edited, and abridged versions of what purported to
be her work were published under the title *A Diary from Dixie* in
1905 and 1949. In this volume, C. Vann Woodward presents the
memoir that Chesnut prepared in the 1880s as the authorized text,
occasionally supplementing it with journal entries from the 1860s.
Some scholars did not agree with the decision to consider the revised
memoir an authorized text; nevertheless, Chesnut's very readable
prose brings to life the historic crisis she experienced.

Reviewed in:	AHR	87 (Feb. 82) 261–262
	CWH	27 (Sept. 81) 280–282
	HRN	9 (Sept. 81) 224–225
	JAH	68 (March 82) 939–941
	JSO	47 (Nov. 81) 585–592
	RAH	10 (March 82) 54–59

216 Merrick, Morgan Wolfe. *From Desert to Bayou: The Civil War
Journal and Sketches of Morgan Wolfe Merrick.* El Paso, Tex.:
Texas Western Press, 1991. vi, 134 pp. : ill. Includes index and
bibliography.

ISBN: 0-87404-218-6   LC: 91-065178

Merrick joined Lieutenant Colonel John Robert Baylor's Second
Mounted Rifles in 1861, a Confederate unit sent west to occupy Fort
Davis on the Trans-Pecos. This illustrated journal of Morgan Wolfe
Merrick's experiences and observations of the Confederate invasion of
the New Mexico Territory is filled with memorable incidents and detailed sketches of Mescalero Apache chiefs whom Merrick encountered. It also includes descriptions of battles fought in Louisiana, as
well as of encampments at Stein's Peak and Cooke's Canyon and of
forts Davis and Fillmore. Merrick also records details of a feud be-

tween two Confederate commanders, Colonel Baylor and Brigadier General H. H. Sibley.

> *Reviewed in:*   JSO 59 (Nov. 93) 766

217 Mitchell, Reid. *Civil War Soldiers*. New York: Viking, 1988. xi, 274 pp. Includes index and bibliography.

ISBN: 0-6708-1742-2   LC: 87-040565

Using letters and diaries to recreate the wartime experiences of Civil War soldiers, Mitchell finds reasons why Northern and Southern men went to war, what they thought of their enemies, and how they responded to combat. Without differentiation between Union and Confederate soldiers, white men on both sides initially showed firm resolve for their cause. Eventually, however, both sides often found themselves descending into savagery and blatant racism. What Mitchell offers is not new, but it is a complete view of the soldiers' world.

> *Reviewed in:*   AHR   95 (June 90) 910–911
> CWH   35 (June 89) 187–188
> GHQ   74 (Summer 90) 322–324
> HRN   17 (Spring 89) 102
> JSO   56 (Feb. 90) 123–125
> MIR   69 (Sept. 89) 110–111

218 Osborn, Thomas Ward. *The Fiery Trail: A Union Officer's Account of Sherman's Last Campaigns*. Edited with an introduction by Richard Harwell and Philip N. Racine. Knoxville, Tenn.: University of Tennessee Press, 1986. 238 pp. : ill., maps. Includes bibliography.

ISBN: 0-8704-9500-3   LC: 85-027620

Major Thomas W. Osborn was chief of artillery in the Union Army of Tennessee and accompanied General William Tecumseh Sherman on his Southern campaigns; these are his letters and dairies that reconstruct military activities and battlefield anecdotes. He was not a romantic warrior but rather a technician who was able to see the benefits and losses of the actions of war. Lengthy notes clarify and amplify each letter, and engravings and maps enhance the pages. An introduction presents a biographical sketch of Osborn, his place in the military, and background on Sherman's March to the Sea and through the Carolinas.

Reviewed in: CWH   34 (March 88) 87–88
                 JSO   54 (Feb. 88) 123–124
                 THQ   47 (Spring 88) 55

219 Russell, Sir William Howard. *William Howard Russell's Civil War: Private Diary and Letters, 1861–1862.* Edited by Martin Crawford. Athens, Ga.: University of Georgia Press, 1992. li, 252 pp. : ill. Includes index and references.

ISBN: 0-8203-1369-6   LC: 91-14194

Sir William Howard Russell, celebrated Crimean correspondent for the *Times* of London, came to New York in March 1861 to report on the American Civil War. He spent time in New York and Washington with Abraham Lincoln, Secretary of State William Henry Seward, and other top Union leaders. After traveling south and meeting with Jefferson Davis, among others, he returned to Washington but was forced to leave the United States after the battles at Manassas. Because he despised slavery and was pro-Union he was not appreciated in the South. After denouncing aspects of American life that he did not like, he also was not liked in the North. His honest, and often harsh, opinions made unbiased reporting difficult and led the Army to restrict his access to the field of operations. Russell returned home in April 1862, and we are left to read of the attitudes of this important observer.

Reviewed in: JAH   80 (Dec. 93) 1100
                 JSO   60 (Feb. 94) 147
                 LIJ   117 (June 15, 92) 84

220 Seabury, Caroline. *The Diary of Caroline Seabury, 1854–1863.* Edited by Suzanne L. Bunkers. Madison, Wisc.: University of Wisconsin Press, 1991. xi, 148 pp. : ill.

ISBN: 0-299-12870-9/0-299-12874-1(paper)   LC: 90-50640

Caroline Seabury was an unmarried, middle-class, white Northern woman who spent nine years teaching French to daughters of wealthy Southerners. She arrived in Columbus, Mississippi, in 1854 and left shortly after the fall of Vicksburg in 1863. Seabury began her diary on her voyage south and continued it until her escape back beyond Union lines. Approximately one-third of the diary is concerned with her wartime experiences. Seabury's account of her journey north is especially interesting because it demonstrates the hazards of wartime travel and particularly the problems encountered by women

travelers. It also discusses the declining morale of poor white Southerners who increasingly resented waging a rich man's war.

Reviewed in: CHO   29 (Jan. 92) 804

                 JAH   79 (Dec. 92) 1171

221   Seymour, William J. *The Civil War Memoirs of Captain William J. Seymour: Reminiscences of a Louisiana Tiger.* Edited by Terry L. Jones. Baton Rouge, La.: Louisiana State University Press, 1991. 162 pp. : ill., maps. Includes index, bibliography, and references.

ISBN: 0-8071-1646-7   LC: 90-49919

William J. Seymour's memoirs provide the only existing documentation of several key events during the war. For example, his is the
only known Confederate first-person account of the battle of Fort
Jackson. His reminiscences make up also the only extant account by a
field or staff officer who served in the First Louisiana Brigade in the
Army of Northern Virginia. The book begins with an account of
Seymour's service as a volunteer aide to Confederate General Johnson
K. Duncan during the 1862 New Orleans campaign. Most of the book
consists of Seymour's recollections of his service as a volunteer aide to
Harry T. Hays, commander of the First Louisiana Brigade. There are
firsthand accounts of the fighting at Chancellorsville and of the Wilderness and Shenandoah Valley campaigns. Seymour is a perceptive
and articulate commentator who provides critical analysis of the tactics and strategies employed by the Confederate army.

Reviewed in: CHO   29 (Jan. 92) 806

                 LIJ   116 (July 91) 112

                 JSO   59 (Feb. 93) 147

222   Shaw, Robert Gould. *Blue-Eyed Child of Fortune: The Civil War Letters of Colonel Robert Gould Shaw.* Edited by Russell Duncan. Athens, Ga.: University of Georgia Press, 1992. xxiii, 421 pp. Includes index and references.

ISBN: 0-820-31459-5   LC: 91-46644

Supplemented by photographs, Robert Gould Shaw's letters are
introduced by a biographical essay in which Duncan acknowledges
that everything about Shaw made him seem larger than life. The letters
and the introduction combine to form a rich biographical and documentary history of an extraordinary soldier. Dropping out of Harvard
and rushing to join the Union army, Shaw reluctantly accepted the

unpopular command of the black troops of the Fifty-fourth Massachusetts Infantry Regiment. Although Shaw came from an abolitionist family, his parents felt that the war was not theirs. Shaw for a time was indifferent about slavery and struggled with his own preconceptions about black inferiority, yet he made a complete turnaround. The men of the Fifty-fourth educated him even as their actions led others to reexamine their own beliefs. Shortly before his death he demanded that his soldiers receive the same pay as the white soldiers. Shaw led the charge against the impregnable Fort Wagner in Charleston, his men turning the fort into a "national stage" to demonstrate the valor of his "colored troops." As Shaw put it, the heroic fighting of thousands of black troops made the Proclamation of Emancipation a reality. Killed at the fortress and thrown into a mass grave with his men, he was eulogized in verse by Ralph Waldo Emerson and James Russell Lowell. Shaw was also the subject of a sculpture by Saint-Gaudens and was immortalized in the film *Glory*.

Reviewed in:	AHR	95 (June 90) 910–911
	CWH	35 (June 89) 187–188
	GHQ	74 (Summer 90) 322–324
	HRN	17 (Spring 89) 102
	JSO	56 (Feb. 90) 123–125
	MIR	69 (Sept. 89) 110–111

223 *Such Are the Trials: The Civil War Diaries of Jacob Gantz.* Edited by Kathleen Davis. Ames, Iowa: Iowa State University Press, 1991. xiv, 122 pp. : ill., photographs, maps. Includes index and appendixes.

ISBN: 0-8138-0947-9   LC: 90-48636

Jacob Gantz traveled with the Fourth Iowa Cavalry into Missouri, Arkansas, Mississippi, and Alabama. He spent much of his time as a cook, and his diaries present camp life in detail particularly the constant search for provisions for both men and horses. The diaries provide the reader with an understanding of the day-to-day operations of the workings of a cavalry unit. Perhaps their most valuable contributions to the documentation of the war, however, are their detailed accounts of military action in northern Mississippi during the summer of 1864 and in Missouri in the fall of the same year. Two highlights of Gantz's memoirs are his description of the Union expedition against Nathan Bedford Forrest that culminated in the battle of Harrisburg and his recollections of the Fourth Iowa's participation in the Union campaign against Sterling Price in Missouri.

Reviewed in: JSO   59 (Feb. 93) 146

224 *Thomas Morris Chester, Black Civil War Correspondent: His Dispatches from the Virginia Front.* Edited with a biographical essay and notes by R. J. M. Blackett. Baton Rouge, La.: Louisiana State University Press, 1989. xvi, 375 pp. : ill., photograph, maps.

ISBN: 0-80711-516-9   LC: 89-30169

Blackett has divided this book into two sections. The first is a biographical sketch of Thomas Morris Chester, the son of a former slave, who was born in Harrisburg, Pennsylvania, in 1834. When he was eighteen years old, Chester settled in Liberia, where he founded a newspaper and served as the head of a school for immigrants. By January 1863 Chester had returned to the United States. He was appointed captain of a volunteer black regiment from Harrisburg. In 1864 the *Philadelphia Press* commissioned Chester to report on the war and, more specifically, to cover the activities of black troops at the Virginia front. Chester was the first black correspondent of the *Philadelphia Press* and the only black correspondent for a major daily paper during the war. His dispatches filed between August 1864 and June 1865 provide the most sustained and thorough account of the activities of black soldiers. Writing under the nom de plume of Rollin, Chester vividly described the camp life of the black troops on the Virginia front, their performance in military engagements, and the reaction toward them of Confederate troops and civilians. In addition, Chester described the fall of Richmond as well as the beginning of reconstruction efforts in and around the city. Following the war Chester became a European agent for the Garnet League, a freedmen's aid society. He traveled in Europe and Russia, earned a law degree in England, and became the first African American admitted to the English bar. In 1871 Chester returned to the United States and settled in New Orleans, where he practiced law and was active in local politics. He died in 1892. In the second section of the book, Chester's Civil War dispatches are reproduced along with Blackett's annotations. The dispatches are arranged chronologically leading up to the fall of Richmond.

Reviewed in: CWH   37 (March 91) 89–91
                 GHQ   74 (Fall 90) 531–532
                 JAH   77 (Dec. 90) 1035–1036
                 JSO   57 (Aug. 91) 528–529
                 NCH   67 (July 90) 378–379

225 Ward, William Walker. *"For the Sake of My Country": The Diary of Colonel W. W. Ward, Ninth Tennessee Cavalry, Morgan's Brigade, C.S.A.* Edited by R. B. Rosenburg. Murfreesboro, Tenn.: Southern Heritage Press, 1992. vii, 164 pp. : ill. Includes index and references.

ISBN: 0-963-1963-32/0-163-1963-24(paper)   LC: 92-64044

An addition to the Confederate Nation series, this diary of a Tennessee Unionist who enlisted in the Confederacy after his state seceded is important for several reasons. W. W. Ward served in several army units: the Seventh Tennessee Infantry, the Ninth and Fifteenth Tennessee Cavalry, and the First Kentucky Battalion. His diary begins with his arrival in March 1864, however, at Fort Delaware, a Union POW prison. Ward's account of prison life is more balanced than other accounts. His observations, made as an officer, show a different side of prison life. Later he was transferred to a prison ship off the coast of Charleston and his diary relates the experiences of a prisoner exchange by an actual participant.

Reviewed in: JSO   60 (May 94) 410

226 Welsh, Peter. *Irish Green and Union Blue: The Civil War Letters of Peter Welsh, Color Sergeant, Twenty-eighth Regiment, Massachusetts Volunteers.* Edited by Lawrence Frederick Kohl with Margaret Cosse Richard. New York: Fordham University Press, 1986. xxii, 170 pp. : ill., maps. Includes index and bibliographies.

ISBN: 0-82321-163-0   LC: 86-80619

The letters of Sergeant Peter Welsh, an Irish American who fought in the Civil War, have been preserved by his family for generations. Persons and events referred to in letters are biographically and historically identified in the book whenever possible. Grammar and spelling have been retained as originally written. The letters document the feelings of a man deeply committed to the Union cause. They were written to his frail wife who did not share his views but, rather, longed for the end of their separation. Welsh fought with a distinctively Irish American regiment and became the flag bearer for Irish nationalism. The success of the Union, to Welsh and his fellow Irishmen, was necessary if America was to remain free, providing a future haven for those who sought a better life.

Reviewed in: CWH   34 (March 88) 90–91
HRN   16 (Fall 87) 9
MIA   52 (April 88) 103

227 Whitman, George Washington. *Civil War Letters of George Washington Whitman.* Edited by Jerome M. Loring. Durham, N.C.: Duke University Press, 1975. xiii, 173 pp. : ill., photographs. Includes index and appendix.

ISBN: 0-8223-0331-0   LC: 74-83788

George Washington Whitman, the younger brother of Walt Whitman, served with the Union Army from 1861 until the end of the conflict. This book is a collection of letters written by Whitman to his mother and brother. He experienced a good deal of action on the battlefield and was a prisoner of war for more than six months. His letters contain information on army life as well as descriptions of conditions in Confederate prisons. The book is arranged in three parts. The introduction includes a detailed discussion of the Whitman family that describes the relationship among George, his mother, and Walt. The first part presents a series of sixty-one letters, and the appendixes include George's diary, in which he recorded his wartime experiences.

> *Reviewed in:*   CHO   12 (Jan. 76) 1450
> HRN   4 (Nov.–Dec. 75) 40
> JSO   42 (May 76) 286–287
> LIJ   100 (Nov. 15, 75) 2140

228 Williams, Hiram Smith. *This War So Horrible: The Civil War Diary of Hiram Smith Williams.* Edited by Lewis N. Wynne and Robert A. Taylor. Tuscaloosa, Ala.: University of Alabama Press, 1993. xvii, 175 pp. : ill., maps. Includes index and bibliography.

ISBN: 0-8173-0642-0   LC: 92-25867

Hiram Smith Williams was a New Jersey carriage maker who moved to Alabama in 1859. The editors propose three reasons to explain why Williams joined the Confederate Army soon after moving south. First, they claim that Williams was a social creature who enjoyed the company of others. Caught up in the excitement of the moment, he may have enlisted because his friends were doing the same. Second, Williams was satisfied with his work as a carpenter and mechanic in the shipyards of Mobile, Alabama, and military service provided him with a reason and the means to remain in the city. Finally, the editors speculate that Williams may have enlisted to avoid being drafted. He and a number of his friends joined the Fortieth Alabama Volunteer Infantry Regiment when it was formed in May 1862. Williams took advantage of his skills as a carpenter to secure duty away from the front lines by becoming a member of the Pioneer Corps of General Alexander P. Stewart. The Pioneer Corps was a specialized unit that built bridges, hospitals, and fortifications. Williams's diary, which captures the hardships and humor of a soldier's life, is significant because little has been written about Stewart's Pioneer Corps.

Reviewed in: CHO   31 (Sept. 93) 208

229 *Your True Marcus: The Civil War Letters of a Jewish Colonel.* Edited by Frank L. Byrne and Jean Powers Soman. Kent, Ohio: Kent State University Press, 1985. xi, 353 pp. : ill., photographs, maps. Includes index and bibliography.

ISBN: 0-87338-306-0   LC: 84-12266

This is a collection of 119 letters written by Marcus Spiegel to his wife, Caroline. Spiegel was born in Germany and emigrated to the United States following the 1848 uprisings. He moved to Ohio and became an itinerant peddler. After his marriage Spiegel worked in a successful produce and commission business. When the war broke out, he helped to organize a unit of volunteers and was commissioned an officer. Eventually he became a colonel. Spiegel was one of the few Jewish officers, from either the North or the South, to serve during the war. He saw active duty from early 1862 until his death on May 4, 1864, from wounds sustained in a battle near Alexandria, Louisiana.

Reviewed in: HRN   13 (May–June 85) 125

Pictorial Works

230 *The Embattled Confederacy.* Volume 3 of The Image of War, 1861–1865. Edited by William C. Davis. Garden City: Doubleday, 1982. 464 pp. : ill., photographs, map. Includes index.

ISBN: 0-3851-5468-2   LC: 81-43240

Although the Union troops had been driven from Virginia by September 1862 and the armies of Robert E. Lee and Thomas "Stonewall" Jackson had been victorious over Union forces at the Second Battle of Manassas, the tide was turning against the South. The camera was there to record the huge losses at Antietam and at Fredericksburg, where the price of victory was high. The Civil War proved to be the perfect vehicle for the public's new fascination with photography. In this third volume of the series The Image of War, 1861–1865, more than 650 photographs, many of them previously unpublished, are accompanied by essays: "The Bloodiest Day: Antietam," by James I. Robertson, Jr.; "The Fury of Fredericksburg," by Peter J. Parrish; "Strangling the South" (the new navy), by James M. Merrill; "New Bern In North Carolina" and "Slaves No More," by Dudley T. Cornish; "Washington at War" and "Chancellorsville, Lee's Greatest Triumph," by Frank E. Vandiver; "The South At War," by Charles P. Roland; and "The Guns at Gettysburg," by William A. Frassanito. There are numerous photographs of women on the homefront, freedmen, battle landscapes, naval vessels and their crews, and Washington, D.C.

Reviewed in:	CWH	29 (March 83) 74
	GHQ	67 (Summer 83) 248–249
	JSO	49 (August 83) 461–462
	RKH	81 (Summer 83) 232–235

231 *The End of an Era.* Volume 6 of The Image of War, 1861–1865. Edited by William C. Davis. Garden City, N.Y.: Doubleday, 1984. 469 pp. : ill., photographs.

ISBN: 0-385-1828-21   LC: 82-45884

Volume 6 of The Image of War, 1861–1865, the final volume in this epic compilation, comprises photographs and essays of the armies of Ulysses S. Grant and Robert E. Lee battling in the year-long siege of Petersburg and of Sherman's March to the Sea. Peace is made, Lincoln is mourned, and parades of veterans fill the streets. All of the photographs are captioned and accompanied by informative essays. In this volume they include "The Modern Army," by Russell F. Weigley; "Damn the Torpedoes!" by Charles R. Haberlein, Jr.; "Houghton at the Front: A Portfolio" and "The Great March," by John G. Barrett; "Petersburg Besieged," by Richard J. Sommers; "Richmond, City and Capital at War," by Emory M. Thomas; "An End at Last," by Louis Manarin; and "The Last Unpleasantness," by William C. Davis. This final volume also includes an index to the entire series.

Reviewed in: JSO   52 (May 86) 312

LIJ   109 (Nov. 1, 84) 2064

232   *Fighting for Time.* Volume 4 of The Image of War, 1861–1865. Edited by William C. Davis. Garden City, N.Y.: Doubleday, 1983. 464 pp. : ill., photographs, map.

ISBN: 0-385-18280-5   LC: 82-453663

Each chapter in this volume begins with an introductory essay that provides a context for the photographs included. A broad range of subjects is covered. One chapter chronicles the siege of Charleston and another the operations of the Confederate raiders who attacked Union shipping. There are essays about prisons and hospitals. One series of photographs portrays life in the navy and another life in the cavalry.

Reviewed in: JSO   52 (May 86) 312

233   Frassanito, William A. *Gettysburg: A Journey in Time.* New York: Charles Scribner's Sons, 1975. 248 pp. : ill., photographs, maps. Includes index and references.

ISBN: 0-684-13924-3   LC: 74-10597

This is a study of the photographs taken of the battlefield and of the dead after the fighting at the battle of Gettysburg. It is the first systematic study of the Gettysburg photographs as a group. Frassanito, who worked as a guide at Gettysburg National Park, is interested in telling the story of the photographers who went to the battlefield, soon after the fighting ended and for several years after, to record its appearance. He has identified works by Mathew Brady, Alexander Gardner, Timothy O'Sullivan, and some lesser-known photographers such as Charles and Isaac Tyson. The book presents a comparative study of the work of these men and provides revisions in the authorship, date, and subject of a number of photographs. Frassanito examined more than 230 images during the course of his research. This book presents his selections of the important samples along with his own photographs of key places on the battlefields and his own maps, which indicate relative camera positions. The photographs are supplemented with a brief description of the fighting.

Reviewed in: CWH   21 (Dec. 75) 366–367

JSO   41 (Nov. 75) 560–561

LAH   17 (Fall 76) 473–474

VMH   83 (Oct. 75) 499–500

234 Frassanito, William A. *Grant and Lee: The Virginia Campaign, 1864–1865.* New York: Charles Scribner's Sons, 1983. 442 pp. : ill., photographs, maps. Includes index and references.

ISBN: 0-684-17873-7   LC: 82-42673

This photo-essay chronicles Ulysses S. Grant's Virginia campaign during the final year of the war, and it supplies insight into how photographers recorded military engagements by providing a detailed analysis of their surviving work. Frassanito located original glass-plate negatives in the Library of Congress and has assembled 255 photographs. He identified the photographers, verified the photographs' original captions, and whenever possible photographed the present-day site from the same camera position. The accompanying maps indicate camera positions in relation to battle lines. The photographs depict entrenchments, river crossings, headquarters of commanders, sites of battles, and the dead and wounded. In addition to providing a thorough examination and analysis of each of the photographs, the author discusses the individual photographers.

Reviewed in: HRN   12 (July–Aug. 1984) 165
                  PUW   230 (Aug. 29, 86) 393

235 *The Guns of '62.* Volume 2 of The Image of War, 1861–1865. Edited by William C. Davis. Garden City, N.Y.: Doubleday, 1982. 460 pp. : ill., photographs, map. Includes index.

ISBN: 0-385-1546-74   LC: 81-43151

The second volume of The Image of War, 1861–1865 series contains more than 650 captioned photographs of various aspects of the war. The camera was still not able to capture action scenes because of the state of the technology. Photographers, however, were able to find soldiers attempting to make their tents as homelike as possible, and they could record the African American as servant, laborer, and enlisted man. The camera was able to capture the pictures of the ironclads and the river fleets, graphically disputing the notion that the Civil War was a romantic adventure. As with other volumes in the series, the photographs are accompanied by several essays: "The New Ironclads," by William N. Still; "The Peninsula Campaign," by Emory M. Thomas; "In Camp with the Union Soldiers," by Bell Wiley; and "The Conquest of the Mississippi," by Charles L. Dufour.

Reviewed in: CWH   28 (June 82) 189–190

MIR   63 (March 83) 90–91

RKH   81 (Spring 83) 216–217

236 Holzer, Harold, Gabor S. Boritt, and Mark E. Neely, Jr. *The Lincoln Image: Abraham Lincoln and the Popular Print.* New York: Charles Scribner's Sons, 1984. xxi, 234 pp. : ill. Includes index and references.

ISBN: 0-684-18972-3   LC: 83-21291

This book was based on an exhibit held at Gettysburg College, offering not a new interpretation of Abraham Lincoln as martyr, man, or President, but rather a collection of numerous illustrations that demonstrates how Lincoln was presented to the public by artists, engravers, lithographers, and photographers. The anecdote is related that, although the students who came to hear Lincoln's remarks at the Gettysburg cemetery had never seen him in person, they recognized him immediately. Print portraits had made the face of an unknown politician the best known face in the country. Newspapers of the Civil War did not have the capability of reproducing photographs, but the public's huge need to know what these heroic men looked like brought about the commercial publication and distribution of political lithographs and engravings. These images hung in homes as frequently as celebrity pictures might hang today. With the various prints and photographs are other materials that help to explain the relationship among the images, the printmakers' craft, and the political climate.

Reviewed in: AHR   89 (Dec. 84) 1395

              HRN   14 (Sept.–Oct. 85) 7

237 *Leslie's Illustrated Civil War.* Jackson, Miss.: University Press of Mississippi, 1992. xii, 256 pp. : ill.

ISBN: 0-878-0556-73   LC: 92-8815

Originally published as *The Soldier in Our Civil War,* abridged edition 1894, this facsimile work consists of woodcut engravings taken from issues of Frank Leslie's illustrated newspaper published between 1861 and 1865. As in other wars and conflicts, the families of those in uniform are always anxious for images and word from the front. Although photography was available, it could not yet capture action pictures. Leslie tried to fill the void by sending into action artists and illustrators who could capture the action on paper, mail their works to Leslie's newspapers or to *Harper's,* and have engravers trace them for publication. An introduction by John E. Stanchak provides information on the experiences of the illustrators' backgrounds and on the ideological rivalry between *Harper's* and Leslie.

Reviewed in: LIJ   117 (July 1992) 132

NYT   (Sept. 20, 1992) 404

238   *Shadows of the Storm*. Volume 1 of The Image of War, 1861–1865. Edited by William C. Davis. Garden City, N.Y.: Doubleday, 1981. 464 pp. : ill., photographs, map.

ISBN: 0-385-15466-6   LC: 80-1659

The more than 650 photographs in this volume were all made from either original prints or negatives. More than one-half of them have never been seen before. They chronicle the last days of peace, the firing on Fort Sumter, and the First Battle of Bull Run. One chapter examines the lives and work of the photographers who chronicled the conflict. Another discusses the work of the Confederate photographer J. D. Edwards. Each chapter begins with an essay that provides a context for the photographs.

Reviewed in: CHO   19 (Dec. 81) 551

JSO   48 (May 82) 288

239   *The South Besieged*. Volume 5 of The Image of War, 1861–1865. Edited by William C. Davis. Garden City, N.Y.: Doubleday, 1983. 461 pp. : ill., photographs, map. Includes index.

ISBN: 0-385-18281-3   LC: 82-45399

This volume provides a pictorial account of the Shenandoah Campaign of William Henry Sheridan, the impact of the Union navy, the war in the West, the Wilderness Campaign, and the war for Tennessee. Each of the chapters begins with an essay that provides the context for the accompanying photographs. A unique feature is a portfolio of remarkable photographs taken during the destruction of Atlanta.

Reviewed in: JSO   52 (May 86) 312

240   Ward, Geoffrey C. *The Civil War: An Illustrated History*. Narrative by Geoffrey C. Ward. Based on a documentary filmscript by Geoffrey C. Ward, Ric Burns, and Ken Burns. New York: Alfred A. Knopf, 1990. xix, 425 pp. : ill., photographs, maps. Includes index and references.

ISBN: 0-3945-6285-2   LC: 89-43475

Closely following the text of the Ken Burns's film series *The Civil War*, the authors have used the words of many people across the wide spectrum of mid-nineteenth-century America. The words of Jefferson Davis and Frederick Douglass are interspersed with those of obscure individuals; the centrality of slavery marks the cause of the war, and emancipation is central as the war progresses. Several important essays are included: "Why the War Came" by Don E. Fehrenbacher; "War and Politics," by James M. McPherson; "What the War Made Us," by C. Vann Woodward; and "Who Freed the Slaves?" by Barbara J. Fields. The bulk of the narratives center on military events. A selection of photographs illustrates the text. Ward has provided a good introduction to the people and the events of the war.

Reviewed in: JSO   58 (May 92) 353–355
LIJ   115 (Sept. 1, 90) 236
NYT   (Sept. 9, 90) 26

Politics and Government

241 Alexander, Thomas Benjamin, and Richard E. Beringer. *The Anatomy of the Confederate Congress: A Study of the Influences of Member Characteristics on Legislative Voting Behavior, 1861–1865*. Nashville, Tenn.: Vanderbilt University Press, 1972. xi, 435 pp. Includes bibliography.

ISBN: 0-826-5117-59   LC: 76-138985

Beringer and Alexander analyzed every roll call of the Constitutional convention and both houses of the two Confederate Congresses. They wanted to find out whether there is a relationship among a member's former party affiliation, position on secession, number of slaves owned, value of estate, average number of slaves, control of the home district by Confederate forces, and voting position on such important issues as conscription, impressment, suspension of habeas corpus, and economic and fiscal problems. The sixty-two tables and numerous appendix tables set out the results. This study of the Confederate Congress revealed that a member's position on secession and whether a member's district lay behind enemy lines were the best indicators of his voting behavior. On a more general level the findings showed some of the basic flaws in the Southern system of politics—no party in power and no structure to Confederate politics, so "individualism and localism were allowed to undermine the thrust for nationalism."

> *Reviewed in:*   AHR   79 (June 74) 869
>
>   CHO   9 (Nov. 72) 1195
>
>   JAH   60 (June 73) 139

242   Ballard, Michael B. *A Long Shadow: Jefferson Davis and the Final Days of the Confederacy.* Jackson, Miss.: University Press of Mississippi, 1986. 200 pp. : ill., photographs. Includes bibliography.

ISBN: 0-878-0529-5-X   LC: 86-5650

This interpretive study of Jefferson Davis in relation to the retreat of the Confederate government focuses on his dignified response to policy problems, the retreat of the administration, and the final dissolution of the government. Ballard devotes most of the book to the period of time between April 2 and May, when the government evacuated Richmond. He presents evidence for the influence of Davis and the retreat on later Southern and American history. Davis's continued faith in the Confederacy, even after the cabinet and generals had lost hope, reinforced his efforts to get money for future operations from Europe. Ballard thoughtfully handles the historical controversies surrounding the final days and the dispersal of government funds and archives.

> *Reviewed in:*   JSO   54 (Feb. 88) 125–126

243   Baum, Dale. *The Civil War Party System: The Case of Massachusetts, 1848–1876.* Chapel Hill: University of North Carolina Press, 1984. 289 pp. : ill., tables. Includes bibliography.

ISBN: 0-8078-1588-8   LC: 83-19687

Baum traces the rise and fall of radical Republicans through an analysis of voting behavior and extensive research into newspapers, manuscripts, and election returns. Baum argues, with an interpretation of the social and ideological bases of the party politics in this important northern state, that the Republican party gained its majority through a strong antislavery position, and that it was economics and not ethnicity that can explain the voting patterns in the war years. The party lines blurred after the war, when social issues replaced war-related concerns. There are numerous tables throughout the text, and for those who are statistically minded the appendix contains "Decomposition of Variance Analysis of Electoral Changes in Massachusetts Presidential, Congressional, and Gubernatorial Voting Returns, 1852–1896."

Reviewed in:	AHR	96 (Feb. 91) 263
	CWT	29 (March–April 90) 65
	JAH	77 (Dec. 90) 1032
	JSH	21 (Spring 91) 706–708
	JSO	57 (Feb. 91) 116–117

244 Bogue, Allan G. *The Congressman's Civil War.* New York: Cambridge University Press, 1989. xix, 189 pp. Includes index, bibliography, references, and appendix.

ISBN: 0-5213-5405-6/0-5213-5705-5(paper)   LC: 88-26001

Bogue examines the war from the perspective of the individual lawmaker, focusing on each man's personal objectives and institutional constraints. Each of the four chapters is concerned with a separate theme. Chapter 1 examines the careers of eighty-three representatives and senators who died while serving in Congress, and looks at the ways in which these men's careers related to the coming of the war. Chapter 2 looks at relations between Congress and the president, emphasizing patronage and Abraham Lincoln's role in setting a legislative agenda. In Chapter 3, Bogue explores congressional investigative functions and asserts that the committees of inquiry influenced the war effort. The final chapter examines the power structure of the House and concludes that no single individual or faction established a firm control over the various agendas under consideration. Bogue concludes that even though congressmen were concerned with vital national policy issues, they continued to be occupied with "patronage, personal power, and career advancements."

Reviewed in:	AHR	96 (Feb. 91) 263
	CWT	29 (March–April 90) 65
	JAH	77 (Dec. 90) 1032
	JSO	57 (Feb. 91) 116–117

245   Bogue, Allan G. *Earnest Men: Republicans of the Civil War Senate.* Ithaca, N.Y.: Cornell University Press, 1981. 369 pp. : ill., charts, graphs. Includes index and bibliographic references.

ISBN: 0-8014-1357-5   LC: 81-67176

In this quantitative study of the voting patterns of the Republican members of the United States Senate during the Civil War, Bogue uses sophisticated methods of scaling to study a significant number of roll-call votes on a variety of subjects. He takes issue with those who maintain that the Republicans were essentially unified. As a result of his investigations, Bogue concludes that there were significant intra-party differences within the Republican majority in the Senate during the Civil War and that these differences appeared most often in matters concerned with slavery, race relations, and the treatment of the South. In short, the differences among the various constituencies within the Republican Party were widespread and significant. This book is divided into two parts. The first, "Men, Context and Patterns," investigates the personal background of the senators under consideration, examines the character of the Senate's leadership corps, and investigates the institutional structure of the Senate. Bogue analyzes role-call vote patterns to distinguish between radical and moderate senators. In his analysis he considers living arrangements, seating, regionalism, and election results to account for differences in voting patterns. In the second part of the book, "The Substance of Disagreement," Bogue studies the debates in the Senate to determine the nature of the disagreements between the radicals and the moderates regarding, among other things, slavery and taxation. The text is supported with charts, figures, and tables.

Reviewed in:	AHR	88 (Feb. 83) 185–186
	CWH	28 (June 82) 180–181
	JAH	69 (Sept. 82) 457–458
	JSO	48 (Aug. 82) 433–434

246   *A Crisis of Republicanism: American Politics in the Civil War Era.* Edited by Lloyd E. Ambrosius. Lincoln: University of Nebraska Press, 1990. 140 pp. Includes index and references.

ISBN: 0-803-2102-64   LC: 89-38372

Covering the years from 1848 to 1868, this is a collection of essays by Thomas B. Alexander on the Free-Soil party of 1848, John Niven writing about Salmon P. Chase and the Republican conventions of 1856 and 1860, Phillip S. Paludan considering Abraham Lincoln and politics, Harold M. Hyman writing on Lincoln and antislavery, and Hans L. Trefousse comparing Lincoln and Andrew Johnson. The introduction is by Lloyd E. Ambrosius and the conclusion by Joel H. Silbey. At stake in this crisis, according to Ambrosius, were the fundamental values and characteristics of the United States. Many Republicans had adopted the tradition of Alexander Hamilton and favored a positive role for the federal government to promote economic development and preserve social order. Others, in the tradition of Thomas Jefferson, were distrustful of the government's power and favored states' rights.

Reviewed in: JAH   78 (Sept. 91) 679

JSO   58 (May 92) 351

247   DeRosa, Marshall L. *The Confederate Constitution of 1861: An Inquiry into American Constitutionalism.* Columbia, Mo.: University of Missouri Press, 1991.

ISBN: 0-8262-0812-6/0-8262-0806-1(paper)   LC: 91-23889

DeRosa places the Confederate constitution of 1861 into the context of American constitutional development since the late eighteenth century. He contends that the defense of state sovereignty lay at the heart of the Confederate constitution. DeRosa argues that the issue of slavery was not a significant factor in the process of shaping the constitution. He claims that the framers of the document sought to pattern it after the United States Constitution but also to reinforce more vigorously a centrifugal distribution of power between the states and the central government.

Reviewed in: CHO   29 (March 92) 1158

JAH   70 (Dec. 92) 1179

JSO   59 (May 93) 376

248   Escott, Paul D. *After Secession: Jefferson Davis and the Failure of Confederate Nationalism.* Baton Rouge, La.: Louisiana State University Press, 1978. xiv, 296 pp. Includes index.

ISBN: 0-807-1036-91   LC: 78-005726

For Escott, it was Jefferson Davis's call for an ideology of unity and nationalism that ignored slavery and emphasized the South's continuity that caused the failure of nationalism. The internal conflict in debate over the nature of the Confederacy was as crucial as military defeat. In Davis's attempt to build the spirit of Confederate nationalism, he failed to respond to the needs of the common people. It was the nonslaveholders and those not of the planter class, the ordinary citizens, who suffered greatly from inflation and shortages. Davis was insensitive to their needs and situations, and it was to them he needed to turn to build a policy that would ensure their loyalty. Escott also addresses the decline of nationalism in the Confederacy in its consideration of slavery and, ultimately, the purpose of the Confederacy. It climaxed with Davis's bold proposal to arm and emancipate the slaves. This portrayal of Davis is said to reflect the earlier scholarship of Frank L. Owsley and its emphasis on the common people. Confederate society and how it affected Confederate unity is traced through cabinet meetings and popular newspapers. Without the unity of nationalism, the Confederacy would seem not to have been able to sustain itself.

> *Reviewed in:*   AHR   84 (Dec. 79) 1480
>
> CHO   16 (June 79) 590
>
> JAH   66 (March 80) 940
>
> JSO   45 (Aug. 79) 443

249   Field, Phyllis F. *The Politics of Race in New York: The Struggle for Black Suffrage in the Civil War Era.* Ithaca, N.Y.: Cornell University Press, 1982. 264 pp. : ill. Includes bibliography.

ISBN: 0-8014-1408-3   LC: 81-070717

Analyzing New York's referendums on equal suffrage in 1846, 1860, and 1869, Field concludes that the outcome and issues were less tied to the issue of suffrage on its own than to other state and national issues of the day. Field studies the politics of race in the context of popular attitudes and political feelings in a state where there was considerable wealth, a large involvement by the people in politics, and a link between race and immigrants. Republicans joined the blacks' campaign to press for equal suffrage; Democrats pitted black labor against the increasing immigrant population. Using numerous statistical tables throughout, Field includes a "Scalogram of Black Suffrage Votes at the 1846 Constitutional Convention"; the percentages of voting prosuffrage by counties in 1846, 1860, and 1869; and information to support the research that, although black suffrage was finally realized, white New Yorkers apparently accepted it only out of inertia.

> *Reviewed in:*   AHR   88 (June 83) 755–756
>
> CWH   29 (March 83) 93–94

HRN   11 (March 83) 116
JAH   69 (March 83) 973–974
JSO   49 (May 83) 305–306

250 Foner, Eric. *Politics and Ideology in the Age of the Civil War.*
New York: Oxford University Press, 1980. 250 pp. Includes
index and references.

ISBN: 0-195-0278-17   LC: 80-013024

Known for his interpretation of the origins of the Civil War,
Foner has compiled previously published essays that reiterate the
theme of his book *Free Soil, Free Labor, Free Men,* all appropriately
preceded by a survey of American historiography of the 1970s. Foner
faults those historians for divorcing nineteenth-century social history
from politics and ideology, making it his aim to "reintegrate" political,
intellectual, and social history. The essays are offered under three
categories: "The Origins of the Civil War," "Ambiguities of Slavery,"
and "Land and Labor after the Civil War."

Reviewed in: CHO   18 (Feb. 81) 87

HRN   9 (Feb. 81) 87

JSO   47 (Feb. 81) 150

RAH   9 (June 81) 179

251 *Lincoln the War President: The Gettysburg Lectures.* Edited by
Gabor S. Boritt. New York: Oxford University Press, 1992. xxix,
242 pp. : ill. Includes references.

ISBN: 0-19-507891-8   LC: 92-19696

These traditional and distinguished analyses of Abraham Lin-
coln were all presented as lectures on the anniversary of Lincoln's
Gettysburg Address. The essays included are "The Shadow of a Com-
ing War," by Robert B. Bruce; "Lincoln and the Strategy of Uncondi-
tional Surrender," by James M. McPherson; "The Emancipation
Moment," by David Brion Davis; "One among Many: The United
States and National Unification," by Carl N. Degler; "One Alone? The
United States and National Self-Determination," by Kenneth M.
Stampp; "War and the Constitution: Abraham Lincoln and Franklin
D. Roosevelt," by Arthur M. Schlesinger, Jr.; and "War Opponent and
War President," by Gabor S. Boritt. In the introductory chapter that
summarizes the essays that follow, Boritt indicates that two main
themes appear, one is the need to understand the importance of Afri-

can American freedom in order to understand Lincoln, and the other is the artfulness of war.

> *Reviewed in:*   JSO   60 (May 94) 4124

252 Nelson, Larry E. *Bullets, Ballots, and Rhetoric: Confederate Policy for the United States Presidential Contest of 1864.* Tuscaloosa, Ala.: University of Alabama Press, 1980. 235 pp. Includes bibliography.

ISBN: 0-8717-3003-76 LC: 79-27869

This narrow study of the political arena within the Confederate States in 1864 treats the Jefferson Davis administration, other groups within the Confederacy, their differing expectations on the opportunity to influence the presidential and congressional elections in the North, and the extent of their commitment to independence. The lack of consensus within the Davis administration and lack of confidence in Davis himself made for many missed opportunities in the political sphere.

> *Reviewed in:*   AHR   87 (Feb. 82) 260
>
> HRN   9 (April 81) 134
>
> HIS   44 (Feb. 82) 279
>
> JAH   68 (Sept. 81) 393
>
> JSO   47 (Aug. 81) 456

253 Rawley, James A. *The Politics of Union: Northern Politics during the Civil War.* Hinsdale, Ill.: Dryden Press, 1974. vi, 202 pp. Includes index and bibliography.

ISBN: 0-03-083987-4 LC: 73-2095

Rawley presents a valuable, general overview that discusses all of the major issues raised by the war—emancipation, finance, sectionalism, slavery and racism, morale, factionalism, and Democratic opposition. He believes that the central importance of Union politics during the war was the maintenance of Northern unity without stifling democratic institutions. Although he includes brief references to Confederate politics for comparative purposes, Rawley's primary focus is an examination of the ideological aspects of Northern politics.

> *Reviewed in:*   AHR   83 (June 78) 810
>
> CHO   15 (Oct. 78) 1124
>
> HRN   6 (April 78) 117
>
> LIJ   103 (Feb. 15, 78) 460

254 Silbey, Joel. *A Respectable Minority: The Democratic Party in the Civil War Era.* New York: W. W. Norton, 1977. xviii, 267 pp. : ill., tables. Includes index, bibliography, and references.

ISBN: 0-393-05648-1/0-393-09087-6(paper)   LC: 77-24048

This is an institutional and behavioral study of how the American political system functioned in the nineteenth century. Silbey examines the Democratic party during the war years and demonstrates that after an initial period of uncertainty and bitterness about Republicans' attempts to equate any antiadministration stance with disloyalty, the Democrats were able to close ranks and function as an opposition party for the rest of the war. The focus of this study is on the Democratic party's strategy rather than on its day-to-day activities.

Reviewed in: AHR   83 (June 78) 810

JAH   65 (Dec. 78) 785

JSO   44 (Aug. 78) 469

Prisoners and Prisons

255 Bryant, William O. *Cahaba Prison and the Sultana Disaster.* Tuscaloosa, Ala.: University of Alabama Press, 1990. 180 pp. Includes index and bibliography.

ISBN: 0-8173-0468-1   LC: 89-33833

Cahaba Prison was unlike the notorious Andersonville Prison. The five thousand prisoners of war in Cahaba endured much of the familiar persecution men in other prisons also endured. The camp commander of Cahaba was apparently fair and humane, however, and the prison had some links with the nearby community in the form of a mother and daughter who supplied the inmates with food, books, and medicine. To put the camp in historical context, Bryant provides background material on other Civil War prisons, the town of Cahaba, and Captain Henderson and Lieutenant Colonel Jones, who shared command of the camp. The vivid account of the lives of the men who survived the ordeal of imprisonment becomes all the more tragic with the account of Union authorities, in their haste to return the prisoners to their homes, packing thousands of men aboard the steamboat *Sultana* only to see them perish in the Mississippi when the boilers explode. The disaster was long obscured by the collapse of the Confederacy and the assassination of Lincoln, but with the recent discovery of the site of the disaster, the memory of the event can now be preserved.

Reviewed in: GHQ   75 (Fall 91) 645–646

JAH   78 (June 91) 338

JSO   57 (Nov. 91) 750–751

JMH   53 (Feb. 91) 59–60

LAH   32 (Spring 91) 222–223

256 Cavada, Frederic Fernandez. *Libby Life: Experiences of a Prisoner of War in Richmond, Virginia, 1863–64.* Lanham, Va.: University Press of America, 1985. 221 pp. : ill., photographs. Includes appendix.

ISBN: 8-8191-4166-1   LC: 84-25719

Before the war Cuban-born Cavada was educated in Philadelphia. He had worked as a surveyor, civil engineer, and a topographer on the Isthmus of Panama. When the war broke out, he was commissioned a captain in the Twenty-third Pennsylvania Volunteers of the Army of the Potomac. As a captain and as a major he served in the cavalry and distinguished himself in the battle of Chantilly. As a lieutenant colonel he fought under General George B. McClellan at South Mountain and Harper's Ferry. Cavada was captured at Gettysburg and interned at Libby Prison in Richmond. He recorded his prison experiences on the margins of newspapers and on other scraps of paper that he smuggled out when he was released under a prisoner-exchange program in 1864. Cavada requested that the proceeds of the book go to the widows and orphans of his fellow prisoners. This book provides valuable insights into what Cavada described as the "vital society" that developed among the inmates and that included prayer meetings, lyceums, and collective escape attempts.

Reviewed in: HRN   14 (Sept. 85) 7

257 Domschcke, Bernhard. *Twenty Months in Captivity: Memoirs of a Union Officer in Confederate Prisons.* Translated and edited by Frederic Trautmann. Rutherford, N.J.: Fairleigh Dickinson University Press, 1987. 175 pp. Includes index, bibliography, references, and appendix.

ISBN: 0-8386-3286-6   LC: 85-46015

An ardent opponent of slavery, the German-born Domschcke edited several German-language newspapers in Milwaukee before volunteering to fight for the Union cause. He served as a captain in the all-German Twenty-sixth Wisconsin Volunteers before being taken prisoner at Gettysburg. Domschcke's memoir begins with his capture and his removal to Libby Prison, a facility for Union officers, in Richmond. Most of this account concerns Libby, although he also reports on conditions in Danville, Macon, Savannah, Charleston, and Columbia. During Domschcke's time in captivity, Confederate treatment of Union prisoners became harsher, and Trautmann emphasizes the effect on the prisoners of increasing bureaucratization and the South's determination to win at any price. Domschcke was a keen observer and capable reporter. His memoir is one of the most thorough, balanced, and authoritative accounts of conditions in federal prisons. The appendix presents another German officer's account of the great tunnel escape from Libby and a report of another officer's short confinement on Richmond's Belle Island.

> *Reviewed in:*   JMH   53 (Oct. 89) 442–443
>
> JSO   55 (May 89) 336–337

258 *Fiction Distorting Fact: The Prison Life, Annotated by Jefferson Davis.* Edited by Edward K. Eckert. Macon, Ga.: Mercer University Press, 1987. lxxi, 168 pp. Includes index and bibliography.

ISBN: 0-865-5420-15   LC: 86-23746

Jefferson Davis was captured by Union troops in May 1865 and spent the next two years imprisoned in Fort Monroe, Virginia. In 1866 *Prison Life of Jefferson Davis* was published. This memoir, which tells of Davis's first six months in captivity, was purported to have been written by his personal physician at Fort Monroe, John Craven. In contrast to the cold and aloof man who managed to alienate most of the people he came into contact with while he was the president of the Confederate States of America, the Davis of Craven's memoir is a romantic folk hero, the embodiment of the Lost Cause. When Davis read the book, he acknowledged that it was "fiction distorting fact," but he never publicly denied the accuracy of what had been written for fear that such a denial would have diminished him in the public's estimation. His only comments about the book were the annotations he made in the margins of his copy of *Prison Life*. Davis's annotated copy is reproduced in this book. Eckert has added a lengthy introduction in which he demonstrates that the memoir was not written by Craven but that it is a work of fiction written by a contemporary writer, Charles G. Halpine, for personal and political gain. The introduction also includes what Eckert considers a more "objective description" of Davis's imprisonment, based on his letters. There is an appendix, which is an account of Davis's first fifteen months in prison, by General Nelson A. Miles, commandant of Fort Monroe.

> *Reviewed in:*   CHO   25 (Jan. 88) 824
>
> JAH   75 (Sept. 88) 623–624

259   Potter, Jerry D. *The* Sultana *Tragedy: America's Greatest Maritime Disaster*. Gretna, La.: Pelican Publishing Co., 1992. xii, 300 pp. : ill., photographs. Includes index, bibliography, references, and appendix.

ISBN: 0-88289-861-2   LC: 91-29521

This is the first comprehensive study of the sinking of the steamboat *Sultana*, which exploded near Memphis at 2:00 A.M. on the morning of April 27, 1865. At the end of the war, Union survivors of the Andersonville and Cahaba prison camps were collected at Vicksburg to await transportation home to Ohio, Illinois, and Indiana. Using eyewitness accounts and the official investigations that were conducted following the incident, Potter reconstructs the tragedy that came about as a result of military corruption and incompetence combined with civilian greed. For illegal personal gain and despite the fact that they had been warned that the vessel's boilers were defective, four Union staff officers at Vicksburg crowded more than 2,400 men on board the *Sultana*, which had a passenger capacity of 376. More than 1,800 of the passengers, more than were to die on the *Titanic*, lost their lives when the boilers exploded. Although censured for neglect and poor judgment, the officers responsible escaped punishment. The appendix is a list of the passengers, both civilians and soldiers, and of the crew on board the *Sultana*.

> *Reviewed in:*   JSO   59 (Aug. 93) 565

Race and Slavery

260 Berry, Mary Frances. *Military Necessity and Civil Rights Policy: Black Citizenship and the Constitution, 1861–1864.* Port Washington, N.Y.: Kennikat Press, 1977. x, 132 pp. Includes index, bibliography, and references.

ISBN: 0-8046-91665   LC: 76-53822

This study examines the pre–Civil War background of the relationship between eligibility for citizenship rights and military policy concerning the service of blacks. The author makes the point that conscription of all races helped to define blacks as citizens. Berry contends that when the War Department and majority in Congress concluded that the use of black soldiers was absolutely essential to the defeat of the Confederacy, the national government abolished slavery and granted citizenship. Berry includes a discussion of the thirteenth, fourteenth, and fifteenth amendments.

> *Reviewed in:*   CHO   14 (Nov. 77) 478
>
> JAH   65 (Sept. 78) 478
>
> LIJ   102 (July 77) 1492

261 *The Black Military Experience.* Edited by Ira Berlin. Cambridge: Cambridge University Press, 1982. xxxv, 852 pp. : ill. Includes index and references.

ISBN: 0-521-22984-7   LC: 82-4446

These extraordinary documents are part of one of the most important documentary projects in United States social history, the series is called Freedom: A Documentary History of Emancipation, 1861–1867, Selected from the Holdings of the National Archives of the United States. Searching through twenty-two National Archives records groups, the editors chose from more than forty thousand documents those they felt were the most relevant to tracing the transition from slavery to freedom. Divided into six parts, this unprecedented collection of manuscripts documents the struggles of the black soldiers in the 1860s: their enlistment and the collapse of chattel bondage, the structure of military life and its limits, the life on and off duty, and their lives in postwar America. The documents were written by slaves and masters, blacks and whites. There are letters and testimonies, military dispatches, and regimental resolutions. Interpretative essays are provided by the editors. The enlistment of black soldiers into the Union ranks allowed them to join in the fight for freedom and turned their great numbers into a Northern advantage. The Union did recognize the value of the black soldiers, but these volunteers did not find the glory they had anticipated. Black soldiers were often not permitted to serve on equal terms with, or to have pay and rank equal to that of white soldiers. Military service shaped the lives of African American soldiers and their families for years to come. The documents are annotated, providing additional historical information.

Reviewed in:	JSH	20 (Spring 87) 568
	JSO	50 (Feb. 84) 135
	NYR	31 (March 1, 84) 37
	NYT	88 (Feb. 13, 83) 9
	RAH	12 (March 84) 31

262 Cimprich, John. *Slavery's End in Tennessee, 1861–1865.* Tuscaloosa, Ala.: University of Alabama Press, 1985. 191 pp. : ill., maps, tables. Includes index, bibliography, and references.

ISBN: 0-817-30257-3   LC: 84-16200

This brief but useful study tells the story of the demise of slavery in Tennessee, an atypical Southern state. Tennessee may be considered atypical because it had strong Unionist sympathies and for most of the war was occupied in large part by Union forces. Cimprich analyzes the roles and interactions of slaves, masters, Unionists, Confederates, Northern reformers, Southern Unionists, and free blacks. One noteworthy aspect of Cimprich's analysis is his effort to demonstrate the centrality of the black population's own efforts to achieve freedom by practicing noncooperation with their masters and participating as soldiers in the Union Army. He demonstrates the ways in which disloyal slaves exploited the disruptions caused by the war to seek privileges enjoyed by whites and eventually turned these privileges for some blacks into rights for all. Cimprich also includes a discussion of Andrew Johnson's role and motivations in regard to the abolition of slavery both as military governor of his home state and as vice-presidential candidate. The text is supplemented by a number of helpful charts and tables.

Reviewed in:

AHR	91 (Dec. 86)	1273
CHO	23 (June 86)	1594
JAH	73 (Sept. 86)	480
JSO	54 (Aug. 88)	508–509

263 Cox, LaWanda C. Fenlason. *Lincoln and Black Freedom: A Study in Presidential Leadership.* Columbia, S.C.: University of South Carolina Press, 1981. xiii, 254 pp. Includes index, bibliography, and references.

ISBN: 0-8724-9400-4   LC: 81-3350

In this revisionist view of the Republicans of the Civil War era, Cox puts forth three important suggestions. The first is that moral principle, not expediency, was behind Abraham Lincoln's opposition to slavery and his commitment to emancipate all slaves. The second suggestion advances the idea that, as evidenced in his wartime policies, Lincoln's concept of emancipation evolved from the relatively narrow idea of freedom from bondage toward the broader idea of equal citizenship. Cox's third proposition is perhaps her most speculative. She states that if Lincoln had lived, he would have worked with Congress to bring about a less radical postwar foundation for black rights throughout the South. In addition to her discussion of what she believes were Lincoln's liberal radical views and his skillful leadership in regard to equal citizenship rights for former slaves, Cox presents a detailed analysis of the wartime reconstruction program carried out in occupied Louisiana. She maintains that in contrast to Andrew Johnson's confrontational relationship with Congress, the Louisiana example indicates that Lincoln's policy of combining force and consent offered the "best hope for a solid and lasting achievement of racial justice."

Reviewed in:

AHR	88 (April 83)	473
CHO	19 (April 82)	1128
HIS	44 (Aug. 82)	574
JAH	69 (Dec. 82)	707
JSO	48 (Aug. 82)	430
RAH	11 (March 83)	20

Virginia slave family and their ramshackle house

264 *Destruction of Slavery.* Edited by Ira Berlin. Cambridge: Cambridge University Press, 1985. xxxviii, 852 pp. : ill. Includes index and references.

ISBN: 0-52122-979-0   LC: 85-6680

This is the first volume in a multivolume documentary history produced by the Freedmen and Southern Society Project. It focuses on the social, economic, and political contexts surrounding emancipation. The book is arranged into nine chapters according to geographic regions in the South. The introduction provides an overview, and each chapter begins with an essay detailing the differences and similarities of the emancipation process in the area under consideration. These essays are followed by a selection of documents from collections at the National Archives pertaining to the Civil War. The materials in this volume emphasize the role of the slaves themselves in bringing about the end of slavery.

Reviewed in:	AHR	92 (Feb. 87) 211–212
	JAH	73 (Sept. 86) 479–480
	JSH	21 (Summer 87) 805–807
	JSO	53 (May 87) 338–340

265   Durden, Robert Franklin. *The Gray and the Black: The Confederate Debate on Emancipation*. Baton Rouge, La.: Louisiana State University Press, 1972. 305 pp. Includes references.

ISBN: 0-8071-0244-X   LC: 72-079330

Beginning with a parallel comparison of the preamble and parts of Articles I, IV, and VI of the constitutions of the United States and the Confederate States, Durden has collected documents, letters, and journalistic reports of Jefferson Davis's proposal to the Confederate Congress to initiate a program of emancipation in order to recruit black soldiers for the Confederacy. Included is the text of the act "to increase the efficiency of the Army by the employment of free Negroes and slaves in certain capacities," approved by Davis on February 17, 1864. Durden has tried to let the Confederates speak for themselves through his selection of documents. The dilemma facing Davis and Robert E. Lee, who were pushing for emancipation of the slaves, was the need to forsake the institution of slavery in order to achieve an independent Southern nation. The debate that ensued and is evidenced by Durden's extensive sources lasted over a year; it is this compilation of documents that makes this work one of the largest resources on the background of Southern thinking about slavery and the fate of the Confederacy.

Reviewed in:	AHR	79 (Oct. 74) 1267–1268
	CWT	13 (Aug. 74) 49
	HIS	36 (Feb. 74) 343
	HRN	1 (April 73) 122–123

266   Fields, Barbara Jeanne. *Slavery and Freedom on the Middle Ground: Maryland during the Nineteenth Century*. New Haven, Conn.: Yale University Press, 1985. xv, 268 pp. : ill., map, tables. Includes index, references, and appendix.

ISBN: 0-300-02340-5   LC: 84-20949

According to Fields, the institution of slavery in the state of Maryland possessed a unique "character" because of the intermingling of free and slave labor. The black population in the state was almost evenly divided between slave and free, and because of this many historians considered the state an example of "moderation and mediation." Fields does not agree with this analysis. She claims that this middle position "concealed as intense and immoderate a drama as any enacted in the deep South" and that a high level of competition existed between slave and free labor within the state. This book is about slavery and freedom in one state, what they meant, and how the meanings changed. In addition to an analysis of Maryland demographics before, during, and after the war—and a discussion of the decline of slavery in the urban South in the years just before the war—using Baltimore as a focus, Fields also examines the slave trade in Maryland and the ways in which it disrupted family life. There were many small farms across the state, and slave families were often divided among several owners.

Reviewed in: AHR   91 (April 86) 464

CHO   23 (Sept. 85) 190

HRN   13 (July–Aug. 85) 464

JAH   72 (March 86) 956

JSO   52 (May 86) 311

RAH   14 (June 86) 216

267 Fogel, Robert William. *Without Consent or Contract: The Rise and Fall of American Slavery.* New York: W. W. Norton, 1989. 539 pp.: ill., graphs, maps, tables. Includes index and bibliography.

ISBN: 0-393-01887-3   LC: 88-23839

This is a nontechnical summary and interpretation of the findings of a twenty-four-year study of various aspects of the slave system. Fogel examines the interrelationship of economic, cultural, ideological, and political aspects of slavery. This integrated approach combines cliometric analysis and narrative history in an attempt to place the institution of slavery in a historical context. The work includes a synthesis of British and American antislavery movements. Three companion volumes are available for those interested in the technical foundations of the study: *Without Consent or Contract: The Rise and Fall of American Slavery,* Volume 1: *Evidence and Methods—Technical Papers; Without Consent or Contract: The Rise and Fall of American Slavery,* Volume 2: *Markets and Production—Technical Papers; Without Consent or Contract: The Rise and Fall of American Slavery,* Volume 3: *Conditions of Slave Life and the Transition to Freedom.*

Reviewed in: CHO   27 (April 90) 1381

JAH   77 (March 91) 1355–1356

JEH   50 (Sept. 90) 699

JSO   58 (Aug. 92) 491

RAH   18 (June 90) 190

268 Genovese, Eugene D. *Roll, Jordan, Roll: The World the Slaves Made.* New York: Pantheon Books, 1974. xxii, 823 pp. Includes references.

ISBN: 039-44913-19   LC: 74-4760

The culmination of twenty years of research on African American slavery, *Roll, Jordan, Roll* is a detailed description of the slave experience in America. One can feel the texture of the plantation life through Genovese's use not only of traditional sources such as plantation records and diaries but, more importantly, through slave narratives, autobiographies, and WPA interviews. Much effort is made by Genovese to discount the stereotypical view that different types of slavery supported different responses to the institution. He found that the life and treatment of a slave differed little between small and large farms. He tried to find that conditions were similar in all parts of the South and that the outlooks of slaves and free blacks, field hands or house slaves, were similar. Thus, he argues that accommodation and resistance to white rule were not in opposition to each other but, rather, that both were means of survival. Genovese also incorporates a lengthy portrayal of black religion, and argues that the African American experience can neither be seen strictly as a separate national experience nor simply as an "ethnically distinct" component of one. The argument continues that the "black nation," while enriching American culture as a whole, laid the foundations for a separate black national culture that has always been American, despite its African origins. *Roll, Jordan, Roll,* according to Genovese, is not so much the story of the immorality of bringing black people to white America in chains, and bringing up new generations in slavery, but more that of the black struggle to survive spiritually and physically under such adversity.

Reviewed in:	AHR	81 (Feb. 76) 209
	HRN	3 (July 75) 191
	JAH	62 (June 75) 130
	JSO	41 (May 75) 240

269 Gerber, David A. *Black Ohio and the Color Line, 1860–1915.* Urbana, Ill.: University of Illinois Press, 1976. xii, 500 pp. : ill., map, tables. Includes index, bibliography, and references.

ISBN: 0-252-00534-1   LC: 76-27285

Gerber analyzes the evolution of African American citizenship in the North by examining race relations in Ohio, a large, demographically complex Northern state. Using obscure black newspapers, he provides a detailed analysis of blacks who lived primarily in Ohio's small towns and farming communities. In addition to analyzing black-white relations, he presents new perspectives on class and color relations among blacks and provides an in-depth review of the nature and activities of a number of black institutions and voluntary associations. He also examines how the old elite and the new middle class reacted to the rapidly changing ideological currents sweeping across the country. Gerber surveys instances of discrimination in schools and public accommodations. He examines black occupations, class structure, and social organizations. According to Gerber, the 1860s saw the beginning of a period of improvement in the civil status of blacks, aided by the growing liberal sentiment of many whites who also realized the importance of the black vote in state and national elections.

Reviewed in: AHR   82 (Oct. 77) 1079–1080

CWH   23 (Sept. 77) 273–274

HRN   5 (April 77) 126

JSO   43 (Nov. 77) 622–623

270 Gerteis, Louis S. *From Contraband to Freedman: Federal Policy toward Southern Blacks, 1861–1865.* Westport, Conn.: Greenwood Press, 1973. xii, 255 pp. : ill., table. Includes index, bibliography, references, and appendix.

ISBN: 0-8371-6372-2   LC: 72-801

Gerteis presents a well-written contribution to the understanding of a national policy toward blacks in the South during the Civil War. He contends that the changes that took place were not revolutionary, because federal officials took care to ensure that radical social reconstruction did not occur. Gerteis discusses what he believes were the two major objectives of federal policy toward Southern blacks—the mobilization of black laborers and soldiers, and the prevention of violent change to the society and economy of the South. He produces substantial evidence to bolster his contention that capitalism and radical subordination were sustained in the South as a result of federal policy. According to Gerteis, decisions made during the war concerning the treatment, organization, and employment of Southern blacks shaped postwar policies toward freedmen.

Reviewed in: AHR   80 (April 75) 509

CHO   10 (Feb. 74) 1929

JAH   61 (Sept. 74) 491

JSO   40 (May 74) 319

271 Glatthaar, Joseph T. *Forged in Battle: The Civil War Alliance of Black Soldiers and White Officers.* New York: Free Press, 1990. 370 pp. 16 pages of plates. Includes bibliography.

ISBN: 0-0291-1815-8   LC: 89-011620

This is the story of the United States Colored Troops on the Civil War battlefields and the white men who served as their commissioned officers. The military service of these 180 thousand men, 80 percent of whom who had been slaves in the South, resulted from the Union Army policy of confiscating former slaves, the need for military support services, and the need for real employment of these newly freed men. Glatthaar supplements the earlier work of Dudley Taylor Cornish's *The Sable Arm: Black Troops in the Union Army, 1861–1865* with considerable data. An important portion of the book demonstrates that, despite the record of heroism of these men and the hope for equality, as symbolized by the organization of the United States Colored Troops, the fact of racism never disappeared. The appendixes include statistical samples, Congressional Medal of Honor winners in the United States Colored Troops, and a list of black officers in the Union Army.

> *Reviewed in:*   AHR   96 (Feb. 91) 263–264
>
> GHQ   74 (Summer 90) 330–332
>
> HIS   53 (Winter 91) 365–366
>
> JAH   77 (Dec. 90) 1035
>
> JSO   57 (Nov. 91) 749–750
>
> NCH   67 (July 90) 377–378

272 Levine, Bruce C. *Half Slave and Half Free: The Roots of Civil War.* New York: Hill and Wang, 1992. x, 292 pp. Includes index and bibliography.

ISBN: 0-3745-2309-6   LC: 91-10245

Levine examines antebellum political history in light of the broader economic, social, cultural, and ideological developments that shaped the lives of the American people. His focus is on the ordinary man—how he was mobilized for war and what sacrifices he made. Levine discusses what he identifies as the American paradox: the reality that, in a nation that celebrated liberty and equality, slavery was tolerated. He maintains that the sectional conflict was based on the divergent ways in which the North and the South organized their labor systems, a difference that affected all aspects of regional life. In the second half of the book, which examines the sectional crisis, Levine demonstrates how the different social systems that developed contributed to a reformulation of politics. He views the Civil War as a second American revolution between the slaveholding and free-labor communities.

Reviewed in: AHR   98 (April 93) 563
                HRN   21 (Spring 93) 106
                JAH   80 (June 93) 275
                JSO   59 (Aug. 93) 550

273 Litwack, Leon F. *Been in the Storm So Long: The Aftermath of Slavery.* New York: Alfred A. Knopf, 1979. xvi, 651 pp. Includes index and bibliography.

ISBN: 0-3945-0099-7   LC: 78-24311

Winner of the 1980 Pulitzer Prize for History, *Been in the Storm So Long* takes its title from a nineteenth-century spiritual and traces the history of the black slaves during the Civil War years and from 1867 through the early days of freedom. This transition from slavery to freedom, the emancipation of African Americans is documented through slave narratives, personal records, and secondary sources. The response to both slavery and emancipation was as varied as the individuals themselves. Southern dependence upon black labor was underscored by secession. The interdependency of the races was becoming clearer as the country headed into conflict. With the emergence of black freedom, hidden or disguised prejudices surfaced. Litwack perceives many dimensions to the collapse of slavery, the most profound being the four million black men and women who had known nothing but enslavement. Many were generations removed from the African experience, although Africa still entered into their religion, their music, and their culture. In 1860, as Litwack writes, they were as "American" in most other ways as their masters. This book seeks to examine how these men and women helped shaped their future in freedom. The Southern white reaction to emancipation was clearly evident in newspapers and diaries and journals. The impressions of former slaves are as abundant but are more difficult to retrieve. Newly freed slaves told their stories to reporters, teachers, and Union soldiers. During the New Deal, the Federal Writers Project conducted interviews with more than two thousand ex-slaves; Litwack consults all of these sources.

Litwack felt that the measure of the significance of emancipation was not in the material rewards it delivered but in the ways in which the newly freed men moved to reorder their lives. The enthusiasm that freedom engendered did not immediately destroy the old ways. The experience of slavery and sudden freedom could not be shared with other Americans; neither was white America completely ready to rearrange its values to accommodate equal rights. The former slaves had to find their own resources.

Reviewed in:	HRN	8 (Oct. 79) 3
	JSH	20 (Spring 87) 566
	JSO	46 (Feb. 80) 122

274 Mohr, Clarence L. *On the Threshold of Freedom: Masters and Slaves in Civil War Georgia.* Athens: University of Georgia Press, 1986. xxi, 397 pp. : ill. Includes index and bibliography.

ISBN: 0-8203-0793-9   LC: 85-5796

Mohr traces the changing patterns of race relations in the South in the years before 1865 and legal emancipation. He has included statistical tables on black flight in Georgia, blacks in the United States Colored Infantry, black laborers on fortifications, and black employment in Confederate arsenals and railroads. Mohr uses the state of Georgia, deep in the Confederate South, to produce a biracial composite of attitudes toward the approach of black freedom. He puts together an analysis of the state's blacks as industrial workers whose new responsibilities and opportunities eroded the slave world and prepared them for eventual freedom and independence. Culminating with the bitter debate on Jefferson Davis's authorization to enlist slaves as soldiers, Mohr uses letters, newspapers, and church archives to contribute to the understanding of black history during the Civil War.

Reviewed in:	HRN	14 (May 86) 132
	JAH	73 (March 87) 1041–1042
	JEH	46 (Dec. 86) 1065
	JSO	53 (Feb. 87) 115

275 Ransom, Roger L. *Conflict and Compromise: The Political Economy of Slavery, Emancipation, and the American Civil War.* New York: Cambridge University Press, 1989. xv, 317 pp. : ill., maps, tables, graphs. Includes index, bibliography, and references.

ISBN: 0-521-31167-51/0-521-32343-6(paper)   LC: 88-36741

According to Ransom, the root of the conflict that resulted in the American Civil War was "The Great Contradiction"—the presence and acceptance of slavery and racism in the land of freedom. He believes that it was the economic aspects of slavery that made political compromise increasingly difficult and finally impossible. Ransom contends that the moral and political impasse that developed over the spread of slavery short-circuited the American political system, which had been designed by the Founding Fathers to accommodate diversity and seek compromise. Ransom also includes an examination of the ways in which Northern capitalists of all types seized the numerous opportunities provided by the war to shape the postwar economic environment.

Reviewed in: AHR 96 (April 91) 609–610

       CWH 37 (Sept. 91) 284–286

       JEH 50 (Dec. 90) 982–984

       JSO 57 (Aug. 91) 519–521

276 Roark, James L. *Masters without Slaves: Southern Planters in the Civil War and Reconstruction.* New York: W. W. Norton, 1977. xii, 273 pp. Includes index, bibliography, and references.

ISBN: 0-393-05562-0 LC: 76-47689

Writing from the perspective of the slave owner, Roark is concerned with the impact of secession, war, defeat, emancipation, and Reconstruction on the behavior and beliefs of the Southern planter class. Using letters, diaries, and notebooks, Roark presents a well-researched and well-written account that examines the planters' responses to events such as attacks by poor whites on the wartime privileges of the rich and Confederate government policies that closed cotton markets and commandeered slaves. Roark contends that the Civil War marked not only the economic and political transition between the old South and the new but also the end of the social order that defined the Southern agricultural elite.

Reviewed in: AHR 83 (April 78) 529

       CWT 16 (Dec. 77) 50

       HRN 6 (Oct. 77) 4–5

       JSO 44 (Feb. 78) 131–132

       LAH 19 (Fall 78) 471–472

       WVH 39 (Fall 77) 82–84

277 *Slaves No More: Three Essays on Emancipation and the Civil War.* Edited by Ira Berlin. Cambridge: Cambridge University Press, 1992. xx, 243 pp. : ill. Includes index and references.

ISBN: 0-5214-3102-6   LC: 92-18299

This work brings together the introductory essays from the first three volumes of the multivolume work Freedom, a Documentary History of Emancipation. The three volumes are *The Destruction of Slavery, 1861–1865; The Wartime Genesis of Free Labor, 1861–1865;* and *The Black Military Experience, 1861–1867.* This single volume is a thoroughly annotated presentation, with a guide to further research, which presents the author's vision of the most "cataclysmic transformation" in United States history: the emancipation of more than one-third of the Southern population. In the first essay credit is given to those white Americans who helped end slavery but, more importantly, to the central role African Americans had in attaining their own emancipation. The second essay concentrates on the North's theory of free, meaningful contract labor that emerged in the Union-occupied regions in the South. The third essay presents the accomplishments of the African Americans in the military and their mistreatment by their white commanders and former masters.

Reviewed in: NCH   70 (July 93) 349–350

278 Venet, Wendy Hamand. *Neither Ballots nor Bullets: Women Abolitionists and the Civil War.* Charlottesville, Va.: University Press of Virginia, 1991. xii, 210 pp. : ill., photographs, table. Includes index, bibliography, and references.

ISBN: 0-8139-1342-X   LC: 91-12421

Although much has been written about the prewar activities of women abolitionists, little has been documented regarding their efforts during the war to win public support for the abolition of slavery and to petition Congress for constitutional emancipation. Venet provides a detailed discussion of women abolitionists during the war years, arguing that although these women focused their energy on the abolition of slavery, they used the issues generated by the conflict to promote the cause of women's rights. Elizabeth Cady Stanton, Susan B. Anthony, Harriet Beecher Stowe, and Julia Howe are among the women whose activities are examined. Venet discusses, in addition to other things, the women's prewar activities, their emphasis on emancipation when the war broke out, their influence on British public opinion, and the efforts of their wartime activism on the postwar feminist movement. She offers new insights into the extent of these women's political activism during the war through their participation in the Woman's National Loyal League. Although they had limited impact on the Abraham Lincoln administration, the prominence they achieved as political activists reduced popular resistance to female public speakers and opened paths for postwar feminist speakers. Focusing on black rights, feminist women reminded other women that their work for black emancipation would prepare them to work for women's rights after the war. When these women realized that they were unable to combine their cause with that of the black slaves, they broke with the abolitionists and Republican parties to form the National Woman Suffrage Association. Venet examines how the rift in the Loyal League influenced the feminist movement positively by impelling women to put their own cause into the spotlight.

Reviewed in: JAH   79 (Dec. 92) 1169

                JSO   59 (May 93) 390

                LIJ   116 (Nov. 1, 91) 117

279   *The Wartime Genesis of Free Labor.* Edited by Ira Berlin. Cambridge: Cambridge University Press, 1990. xxxviii, 937 pp.

ISBN: 0-521-4174-22   LC: 92-030974

This is the third volume in Freedom, a Documentary History of Emancipation, a multivolume documentary history produced by the Freedmen and Southern Society Project. It focuses on the emergence of a free system of labor for blacks in the lower South—southern Louisiana, the low country, and the Mississippi Valley. Explanatory essays that discuss the locales under consideration place the accompanying documents in perspective. The documents have been selected from collections pertaining to the Civil War at the National Archives.

Reviewed in: JEH   52 (Sept. 92) 725

280   *Witness for Freedom: African American Voices on Race, Slavery, and Emancipation.* Edited by Peter C. Ripley. Chapel Hill, N.C.: University of North Carolina Press, 1991. xxiv, 306 pp. : ill. Includes index, bibliography, chronology, and glossary.

ISBN: 0-8078-2072-5/0-8078-4404-7(paper)   LC: 92-21591

Ripley presents a collection of eighty-nine documents that guides the reader through the history of black abolitionism in the United States. The selection is taken from the materials collected for the Black

Abolitionist Papers Project, which compiled a collection of almost fourteen thousand documents related to the involvement of African Americans in the movement to end slavery in the United States. The documents describe the rise of the colonizations movement, immediatism, and the emergence of distinct black and white antislavery perspectives. One chapter discusses black women abolitionists, another discusses the impact of the Emancipation Proclamation, and one examines the meaning of Reconstruction.

Reviewed in: CHO   30 (June 93) 1697
                NYR   40 (Nov. 4, 93) 6

Reconstruction

281 Benedict, Michael Les. *A Compromise of Principle: Congressional Republicans and Reconstruction, 1863–1869*. New York: W. W. Norton, 1974. 493 pp. : ill., photographs, lists, charts, graphs. Includes index, bibliography, references, and appendixes.

ISBN: 0-393-05524-8   LC: 74-10645

Benedict consolidates and amplifies the revisionist writings of the 1960s in this legislative history of Reconstruction. His focus is the struggle within the Republican Party between the "radical Radicals" and the "not-so-radical Radicals." Benedict argues that the differences between the factions within the Republican Party had more to do with differing perceptions of what was politically attainable than with any conflict of principle. The text is supplemented with seventy pages of charts, lists, appendixes, and a statistical analysis of roll-call votes, which help define, generally, who the radicals, moderates, and conservatives were individually. The effort of the Republican party, in the context of Reconstruction, was to grant black suffrage soon after the

war and to establish legal and political equality for the newly freed
slaves.

| Reviewed in: | HRN | 3 (May–June 75) 162 |
| | JAH | 62 (Sept. 75) 404–405 |

282 Dawson, Joseph G. *Army Generals and Reconstruction: Louisiana, 1862–1877.* Baton Rouge, La.: Louisiana State University Press, 1982. 294 pp. Includes index and bibliography.

ISBN: 0-8071-0896-0   LC: 81-11735

Reconstruction lasted longest in the state of Louisiana; never nonpolitical and never really neutral, political forces could even be influenced by the inactivity of the Union commanders. The commanders, serving under orders of three presidents, were a diverse group. According to Dawson, some were radicals and strongly favored the Republican causes, some were Democrats or opponents of Radical Reconstruction, and some did try to carry out the national policy as fairly as possible. The job was a difficult one; the commanders were to rule in all matters of government: finance, education, and justice. Society and Southern government were in chaos, millions of ex-slaves were uncertain of their new rights, thousands of ex-soldiers were returning to their homes, and the Army had no experience with military government. The commanders could not smash the Louisiana area rebellion of 1866–1876. They could not or would not stop the subordination of the black citizens of Louisiana, and they could not make the Army's police action effective. Dawson discusses Washington's inability to enforce the civil rights laws and chronicles the activities of the commanders of the Lost Cause. Several appendixes add information: "Departmental Changes Pertaining to Louisiana during Reconstruction, 1862–1877," "Reconstruction Commanders of Louisiana, 1862–1877," and "Approximate Troop Totals in Louisiana during Reconstruction, 1865–1877." Dawson presents the reader with analysis of the Army's responsibilities, accomplishments, and failures from the fall of New Orleans to Union troops through the collapse of Packard's Republican government in 1877.

Reviewed in:	AHR	88 (Feb. 83) 186–187
	CWH	28 (Dec. 82) 351–352
	JAH	69 (March 83) 979–980
	NCH	60 (Jan. 83) 109–110
	VMH	9 (April 83) 226–228

283   Foner, Eric. *Freedom's Lawmakers: A Directory of Black Office-holders during Reconstruction.* New York: Oxford University Press, 1993. xlvi, 290 pp.

ISBN: 0-19-507406-8   LC: 92-031777

This volume presents information on almost fifteen hundred blacks who held political office in the South during the Reconstruction period. It includes entries for officeholders on national, state, and local levels. The biographical entries are arranged alphabetically. They include information on whether the officeholder had been free or a slave during the antebellum period; his occupation, education, office or offices held; and the value of his property. A brief bibliography accompanies each essay. Four indexes are included: state, birth status, occupation, and offices held during the Reconstruction period.

Reviewed in: CHO   31 (Sept. 93) 80

JSO   59 (Aug. 93) 599

284   Harris, William C. *The Day of the Carpetbagger: Republican Reconstruction in Mississippi.* Baton Rouge, La.: Louisiana State University Press, 1979. xiv, 760 pp. : ill., photographs, map. Includes index, bibliography, and references.

ISBN: 0-8071-0366-7   LC: 78-18779

Harris presents a comprehensive history of Mississippi beginning with the Congressional Reconstruction Acts of 1867 until the state's readmission to the Union in 1876. He provides new insights into the three-year period of military rule, the organization and growth of the Mississippi Republican Party, the elections of 1868 and 1869, and the activities of the Klu Klux Klan. Considerable attention is devoted to the dynamics of Republican party politics. Harris claims that the state's Republicans believed that social welfare and the provision of basic services were local matters and that federal government-sponsored programs should be kept to a minimum. He demonstrates that Republican-imposed taxes were higher than the planters and farmers could afford and that this contributed to the state's prolonged agricultural depression. Using public documents, private manuscripts, and contemporary newspapers, Harris presents the first published account of the administration of the moderate carpetbagger Ridgley C. Powers, whose term as governor has been largely ignored by other historians.

Reviewed in: HRN   8 (Nov.–Dec. 79) 27

NCH   57 (Winter 80) 108–109

RAH   8 (March 80) 69–73

285 McCrary, Peyton. *Abraham Lincoln and Reconstruction: The Louisiana Experiment*. Princeton, N.J.: Princeton University Press, 1978. xv, 423 pp. : ill., tables. Includes index, bibliography, references, and appendixes.

ISBN: 0-691-04660-3   LC: 78-51181

McCrary presents a comprehensive account of the social and political upheavals in Louisiana as the state became the testing ground for Abraham Lincoln's approach to reconstruction. He sketches the political structure of antebellum society, tracing the secession movement and the Union capture of New Orleans. There is also a detailed discussion of the reestablishment of a federal government in the South. McCrary discusses the moderate Republican regime set up by Lincoln and contrasts it with the reactionary government established in 1865 under Andrew Johnson and the Democratic party. In addition, the author explores the social evolution of the Freedmen's Bureau and the growing participation of blacks in the Louisiana Republican movement. McCrary finds that Nathaniel P. Banks, less open to the idea of black suffrage than Lincoln, was the real force behind the gradualist approach in Louisiana. Lincoln's approach, and probably the more realistic one in that the country was in the throes of a war, was more radical. McCrary asserts that only a forceful demonstration by the victorious occupation forces could produce a stable postwar order. The text is supplemented by two appendixes. One presents a regression analysis of electoral behavior in antebellum Louisiana, 1840–1861. The second appendix is an examination of the occupational background of the delegates to the Louisiana Constitutional Convention of 1864.

Reviewed in:	AHR	84 (Oct. 78) 1161–1162
	CWH	25 (June 79) 181–183
	HRN	7 (Sept. 79) 212–213
	JAH	66 (Dec. 79) 662–663
	JSO	45 (Nov. 79) 613–614
	RAH	8 (March 80) 57–62

286 Sawrey, Robert D. *Dubious Victory: The Reconstruction Debate in Ohio*. Lexington, Ky.: The University Press of Kentucky, 1992. 194 pp. : ill., photographs, map, tables. Includes index, bibliography, and references.

ISBN: 0-8131-1776-3   LC: 91-40414

Sawrey identifies Ohio as a representative Northern state and examines the post–Civil War attitudes of politically active Ohioans in an effort to determine what they sought in a reconstruction policy. He uses contemporary newspapers, manuscripts, diaries, and legislative debates to present a comprehensive picture of Northern attitudes on two critical issues of the reconstruction process: terms of readmission and the fate of former slaves. Sawrey contends that Ohioans who voted Republican did so in the belief that a Republican government could guarantee freedmen protection under the law. Ohio's Republican leaders viewed freedmen as loyal Republican voters who would sustain the party in its efforts to challenge Southern planters on the national level. They believed that the war had been caused by the "planter conspiracy" and sought to ensure peace by controlling the planters. This strategy compelled them to advocate basic rights for former slaves.

Reviewed in: HRN   22 (Spring 94) 106
                  RAH   22 (March 94) 824

287 Summers, Mark Wahlgren. *The Era of Good Stealings.* New York: Oxford University Press, 1993. xiv, 390 pp. : ill. Includes index and references.

ISBN: 0-19-507503-X   LC: 92-7604

Summers is concerned with the growth of corruption in the postwar years and its consequences. He claims that any actual corruption has less important consequences than did the corruption "issue." He identifies three reasons why the enormities of corruption after the war were not so significant as they have been portrayed in popular lore. First, Summers maintains that the postwar years were no more corrupt than the 1850s, the decade preceding the conflict. Second, many scandals turned out to be nothing more than instances of negligence, incompetence, or extravagance. And finally, with certain exceptions, corruption was scattered rather than systematic. According to Summers, the great reforms did not occur in spite of the corruption but in large part because of it. The very forces that impelled the corruption were the ones that defined and limited the character of reform. The boss, the organized lobby, the swindling contractors, all owed their rise to the fact that small, limited government with popularly elected officials could no longer perform all the tasks that were expected of it—either efficiently or even competently. For Summers, the issue of corruption changed politics. It helped destroy the national commitment to blacks in the South and the Republican governments they put into power. It restricted the popular meaning of reform to narrow change in public administration.

> *Reviewed in:*   CHO   30 (July 93) 1834
> JAS   28 (Aug. 94) 311
> JEH   54 (March 94) 220
> JSO   60 (Aug. 94) 597

288   Trefouse, Hans L. *Historical Dictionary of Reconstruction.* Westport, Conn.: Greenwood Press, 1991. xii, 284 pp. Includes index and bibliography.

ISBN: 0-313-25862-7   LC: 91-10419

The preface to this dictionary surveys changes in Reconstruction historiography since the middle of the twentieth century. The entries are concerned with significant people, legislation, court cases, groups, issues, and terms related to the time period between 1862 and 1896. Economic, military, political, and social events are examined and placed within the larger context of Reconstruction history. Entries are cross-referenced and include a short bibliography. There is a chronology of events for the years 1862–1896.

> *Reviewed in:*   CHO   29 (Jan. 92) 728
> JSO   59 (May 93) 391
> LIJ   116 (Sept. 1, 91) 186

Regimental Histories

289   Anders, Leslie. *The Twenty-first Missouri: From Home Guard to Union Regiment.* Westport, Conn.: Greenwood Press, 1975. 298 pp. : ill., map. Includes index and bibliography.

ISBN: 0-8371-7962-9   LC: 75-6482

The regiment was the basic administrative and combat unit during the Civil War. This history of the Twenty-first Missouri mirrors the social and political realities of the community from which the volunteers came. Anders offers an especially useful description of the operations of the ad hoc Unionist homeguard companies that suppressed secessionist bands in northeast Missouri during 1861. The Twenty-first Missouri was formed in December 1861 by the merger of two of these battle-experienced home guard units—the First and Second Northeast Missouri Volunteers. The Twenty-first was the first Union regiment fully engaged at Shiloh, and its members went on to fight at Corinth, Tupelo, Nashville, and Mobile. Anders has written more than just a combat history. He integrates the personal accounts of soldiers with discussions of regimental administration and an analysis of Missouri and national politics. There is also a chapter on the lives of veterans who returned to civilian life.

Reviewed in: HRN   4 (Jan. 76) 57
               JAH   63 (Sept. 76) 423
               JSO   42 (Aug. 76) 434

290   Bergeron, Arthur W., Jr. *Guide to Louisiana Confederate Military Units, 1861–1865.* Baton Rouge, La.: Louisiana State University Press, 1989. viii, 229 pp. Includes index, bibliography, and appendixes.

ISBN: 0-8071-1149-60 LC: 88-29214

Men of Company E, 4th US Colored Troops in the defense of Washington

183

This is a guide to all of the 111 artillery, cavalry, and infantry units that Louisiana sent to the Army of the Confederate States of America. References to Louisiana troops in the Official Records of the War are incomplete and inaccurate following the surrender of Vicksburg. To compile this study, Bergeron used the official records as well as records in the National Archives and Record Group 109 of the War Department collection of Confederate records, which include service records of Confederate soldiers who served in organizations from Louisiana. This book includes a capsule history and list of the field officers and company commanders of each Louisiana regiment, battalion, and independent company. There is a summary of each unit's movements and engagements as well as a bibliography of sources for that unit. Militia, home-guard, reserve-corps, and irregular units are not included because insufficient information exists regarding them and few of them saw active service. The appendixes include lists of independent infantry and cavalry companies and of several Louisiana companies that served in battalions from other states.

Reviewed in: JAH   (March 91) 1482

291   Burton, William L. *Melting Pot Soldiers: The Union's Ethnic Regiments*. Ames, Iowa: Iowa State University Press, 1988. 282 pp. : ill., photographs. Includes bibliography.

ISBN: 0-81381-115-5   LC: 87-3299

Researched through military records of the Northern Army, this study of predominantly European immigrant participation in the Civil War demonstrates the loyalty to the country of the immigrant groups, the recruiting and involvement of the Irish and Germans in politics and the military, and the quest by these ethnic groups for assimilation into America.

Reviewed in: AHR   94 (June 89) 850
CWH   34 (Dec. 88) 359–360
JAH   75 (Dec. 88) 958–959
JSO   55 (Aug. 89) 497–498

292   Daniel, Larry J. *Cannoneers in Gray: The Field Artillery of the Army of Tennessee, 1861–1865*. Tuscaloosa, Ala.: University of Alabama Press, 1984. xii, 234 pp. : ill. Includes index, bibliography, references, and appendix.

ISBN: 0-8173-0203-4   LC: 83-17899

The author claims that the artillery corps of the Army of Tennessee serves as a microcosm of the entire Army of Tennessee, highlighting the problems that pervaded it. He believes that the corps lived under the shadow of the Army of Northern Virginia. Daniel calls the artillery the neglected branch of the Army of Tennessee and asserts that the generals in question never fully understood the importance of the artillery's supportive role. He also claims that although the leaders of the artillery were knowledgeable, they lacked the necessary experience and creativity that would have enabled them to make a more substantial contribution to the Army's operations. Daniel has relied on an extensive range of archival and secondary sources to present a balanced, authoritative study. The text is supplemented with an appendix that presents organizational tables for the Army of Tennessee during various battles.

Reviewed in: AHR   91 (Feb. 86) 188

HRN   13 (Jan. 85) 64

JAH   72 (Sept. 85) 419

JSO   51 (Nov. 85) 633

293   Gaines, W. Craig. *The Confederate Cherokees: John Drew's Regiment of Mounted Rifles*. Baton Rouge, La.: Louisiana State University Press, 1989. 178 pp.

ISBN: 0-8071-1488-X   LC: 88-031358

At the beginning of the war, the Cherokee nation signed a treaty with the Confederate government. Subsequently, two units of Cherokee were recruited. This book tells the story of one Confederate regiment, Colonel John Drew's First Arkansas Cherokee Mounted Rifles. Gaines relates details of the organization of the regiment as well as the campaigns the regiment was involved in. He also examines the internal politics of the Cherokee that eventually contributed to the demise of the regiment, which was the only one in the Confederate Army to have almost its entire membership desert into Union service. The appendixes include the names of the men who enlisted in the regiment.

Reviewed in: AHR   48 (Winter 89) 365–366

CWH   36 (June 90) 190–191

GHQ   74 (Spring 90) 176–178

HRN   19 (Winter 91) 56

JAH   77 (Sept. 90) 677–678

JSO   57 (Feb. 91) 115–116

294   Hale, Douglas. *The Third Texas Cavalry in the Civil War.*
      Norman, Okla.: University of Oklahoma Press, 1993. xvii, 347
      pp. : ill., photographs, maps, tables. Includes index, bibliogra-
      phy, and references.

      ISBN: 0-8061-2462-8   LC: 92-54153

      The men of the Third Texas Cavalry served under some of the
most notable and controversial commanders of the war: Sterling Price,
Earl Van Dorn, Nathan B. Forrest, and John Bell Hood. Hale is interested in the ways in which regional cultures shaped men's reactions
to the war. He explores the civilian background of the troops of the
Third Texas Cavalry to provide a socioeconomic profile of those who
served in the unit. Hale concludes that the men in the Third Texas
were representative of the generation of young Southerners who went
to war in 1861. He relates the daily life of the common soldier in the
unit, focusing on a variety of aspects, including camp life, battles, disease, and desertion. The text is supplemented with tables that record
the casualties and losses of the regiment in the years 1861–1865; the
original command as of August 31, 1861; and the original members
(Company Rolls) as of August 31, 1861. There are also maps that detail the unit's marches and campaigns in the years 1861–1865 as well
as its participation in the Atlanta Campaign.

> *Reviewed in:*   AHR   99 (April 91) 660
>
>   CHO   31 (Sept. 93) 202
>
>   JSH   60 (Aug. 94) 590

295   Moe, Richard. *The Last Full Measure: The Life and Death of the
      First Minnesota Volunteers.* New York: Henry Holt, 1993. xvii,
      345 pp. : ill., photographs, maps. Includes index, bibliography,
      and references.

      ISBN: 0-8050-2309-7   LC: 92-32687

      Moe has written an account of the First Minnesota Volunteer
Infantry Regiment, which served from the First Battle of Bull Run until
Gettysburg, where the regiment's casualties were estimated at 82 percent. The regiment was composed primarily of frontiersmen, farmers,
and small-town residents. Moe relies on the letters, diaries, and personal narratives of the men, as well as on contemporary newspaper
accounts, to present a graphic picture of the horrors and suffering
endured by the members of a unit that was usually on the front line.
One of the broad themes that Moe examines is the nature of leadership. He finds that all members of the First Minnesota Volunteers,

both officers and enlisted men, assumed leadership responsibility at one time or another.

Reviewed in: CHO   31 (Oct. 93) 355

LIJ   118 (March 1, 93) 92

NYT   (May 30, 93) 14

296 Rowell, John W. *Yankee Artillerymen: Through the Civil War with Eli Lilly's Indiana Battery.* Knoxville, Tenn.: University of Tennessee Press, 1975. xvi, 320 pp. : ill., photographs, maps. Includes index, bibliography, and appendixes.

ISBN: 0-87049-171-7   LC: 75-5918

Rowell describes the experiences of the men of the Eigthteenth Indiana Light Artillery Battery, using their journals and diaries as well as official reports, correspondence from the official records, manuscripts, and contemporary newspaper accounts. The most frequently quoted source is the 360-page journal of Bugler Henry Campbell, which included newspaper clippings and maps. Campbell and his fellow soldiers discuss a variety of topics in their letters and journals, including religion, slavery, and politics. This artillery battery was recruited by Eli Lilly in the summer of 1862, and it performed a vital role in both the battle of Chicamauga and in the Atlanta campaign. During its existence the battery marched approximately six thousand miles and travelled an additional one thousand miles by rail. The text is supplemented with a number of useful maps. There are three appendixes, which present a list of the battery's commissioned officers, the roster of the volunteer enlisted men of 1862, and the 1864 roster of recruits.

Reviewed in: CHO   12 (Feb. 76) 1624

JAH   63 (Sept. 76) 425

297 Starr, Stephen Z. *Jennison's Jayhawkers: A Civil War Cavalry Regiment and Its Commander.* Baton Rouge, La.: Louisiana State University Press, 1974. xvi, 405 pp. ill. Includes bibliography.

ISBN: 0-8071-0218-0   LC: 72-094152

Regimental histories of the Civil War often blend scholarship and anecdotes and are not necessarily based on firsthand recollections but on collections of personal documents. The Seventh Kansas Cavalry was not typical of the Union Army. It was a collection of Kansas border warriors and reinforcements of antislavery recruits from other states, particularly Illinois. Unabashedly patriotic, the men and their commanders felt justified in their guerilla-warfare tactics of burning out and killing civilians. It was an abolitionist regiment whose history lies more in the bitter and tangled conflicts of the Missouri-Kansas border than in its combat duties. Starr gives prominence in this work to an eccentric and largely overlooked unit.

> *Reviewed in:*   AHR   80 (Dec. 75) 1396–1397
> CHO   11 (Oct. 74) 1209
> JAH   62 (June 75) 136
> JSO   40 (Nov. 74) 667
> VQR   48 (Spring 72) 58

298   Swinfen, D. B. *Ruggles' Regiment: The 122nd New York Volunteers and the American Civil War.* Hanover, N.H.: University Press of New England, 1982. xv, 159 pp. : ill. Includes index and references.

ISBN: 0-8745-1230-1   LC: 81-069940

This regimental history differs from others that served as memory books for the veterans who wrote them in that Swinfen has incorporated in it a collection of twenty-two drawings done after the Civil War by one of its participants: Private William E. Ruggles. The highly stylized drawings depict the regiment in action. In the remainder of the volume, Swinfen summarizes the unit's war career, including a topical treatment of the soldiers' life in the regiment and an essay on how the drawings came to be produced. Also included is a regimental roster and a casualty list.

> *Reviewed in:*   CWT   22 (March 83) 6
> HRN   11 (Feb. 83) 86–87

299   Weinert, Richard P. Jr. *The Confederate Regular Army.* Shippensburg, Pa.: White Mane Publishing Co., 1991. vi, 135 pp. : ill., photographs, maps. Includes index, bibliography, and appendixes.

ISBN: 0-942597-21-4   LC: 91-2216

Previous studies have claimed that the Confederate regular army existed only on paper and that those few officers who held regular commissions served "alongside and indistinguishably" from the officers of the Provisional Army. Weinert identifies 1,650 men who were attached to the regular army, and of this number 850 were officers and cadets. His study is arranged in two sections. The first provides the legislative framework and records the efforts to organize the regular army. The second section follows the campaigns of Confederate regular army units. Weinert concedes that the Confederate regular army proved to be of "virtually no tactical significance" during the war. One appendix lists the officers who held commissions in the regular army and their ranks.

> *Reviewed in:*   JAH   79 (June 92) 281

300 Wert, Jeffrey D. *Mosby's Rangers.* New York: Simon and Schuster, 1990. 384 pp. : ill., photographs, maps. Includes index, bibliography, references, and appendix.

ISBN: 0-671-67360-2   LC: 90-37917

John Singleton Mosby opposed secession, but when the war began he reluctantly enlisted in a militia company that became part of the First Virginia Cavalry. After Mosby's exceptional scouting abilities came to the attention of Colonel J. E. B. "Jeb" Stuart, the Confederate military leadership authorized Mosby to organize the Forty-third Battalion of the Virginia Cavalry. In January 1863 Mosby and fifteen men began their independent operation in northern Virginia, attacking Union supply lines and camps, and providing intelligence reports to Stuart and Robert E. Lee. Over the next twenty-eight months, Mosby and his men, who were also known as Mosby's Partisan Rangers, remained unvanquished; all Union counter-operations were unsuccessful. By the end of the war, more than nineteen hundred men belonged to Mosby's battalion. Using published and unpublished sources, Wert presents a careful and insightful study of the organization, membership, mode of operations, and exploits of Mosby's Rangers.

> *Reviewed in:*   HIS   54 (Spring 92) 577
> JAH   78 (Dec. 91) 1092
> JSO   58 (May 92) 357
> LIJ   115 (Oct. 15, 90) 96

301 Wilkinson, Warren. *Mother, May You Never See the Sights I Have Seen: The Fifty-seventh Massachusetts Veteran Volunteers.* New York: Harper & Row, 1990. 665 pp. : ill. Includes bibliography.

ISBN: 0-0601-6257-0   LC: 89-045507

The Fifty-seventh Massachusetts Veteran Volunteers Regiment was recruited late in the war; the regiment was made up of veterans and young men, farmers, and laborers. They served only for a year, but their involvement in so many battles gave them the dubious distinction of the unit sustaining one of the highest percentages of casualties suffered by any regiment. The diaries and letters detail the life in camp waiting for action; it is the men's own story of war, of boredom, and of racial and ethnic fighting. Wilkinson has provided rosters and descriptive lists of the officers and soldiers who made up the various companies in this regiment. These biographical sketches were prepared from original descriptive lists of the regiments, morning reports, pension files, and other primary-source material.

> 103. Wilcox, Charles H., private. Res: New Marlboro, MA. Credit: unknown. Born: Massachusetts. Age: 18. No description available. Occup: laborer. Enlisted March 15, 1864; mustered April 6, 1864. Never in combat. Absent sick in an army general hospital from on or before May 6, 1864, until between March 25 and April 30, 1865. Issued one forage cap, one sack coat (unlined), one pair of trousers, one pair of drawers. . . . Issued a new .58 cal. Springfield rifle and new leather equipment May 16, 1865. Mustered out with the regiment at Delaney house, Washington, DC, July 30, 1865. . . . (p. 476)

The work also includes battle statistics, demographics by company, table of organization, general orders, and medical advice in the form of the text of a pamphlet, "Take Care of Your Health."

Reviewed in: AHR   96 (April 91) 610–611
                        GHQ   76 (Winter 90) 740–741
                        JAH   78 (June 91) 340–341

Religious Aspects

302 *"God Ordained This War": Sermons of the Sectional Crisis, 1830–1865.* Edited by David Cheseborough. Columbia, S.C: University of South Carolina Press, 1991. x, 360 pp. Includes index, bibliography, and references.

ISBN: 0-87249-753-4   LC: 91-6865

This volume examines how preachers contributed to the war spirit that turned Americans against each other. It contains thirteen sermons—six from Northern white pulpits, six from Southern white pulpits, and one by a Northern black preacher. Each sermon is introduced with a brief synopsis of the issues involved and a biographical essay about the preacher.

Reviewed in: CWH   29 (March 83) 88–89

FHQ   62 (Oct. 83) 218–219

GHQ   67 (Summer 83) 254–256

JAH   70 (June 83) 164–165

JSO   49 (Aug. 83) 465–466

LAH   24 (Winter 83) 101–102

303   Howard, Victor R. *Religion and the Radical Republican Movement, 1860–1870.* Lexington, Ky.: University Press of Kentucky, 1990. x, 297 pp. Includes index and bibliographical references.

ISBN: 0-8131-1702-X   LC: 89-49233

This is an examination of the growing influence of the evangelical and liberal churches and the extent to which they set the moral tone in the North. The influence exerted through these radical church groups was mainly on the radical Republicans. Although a minority in the North, their hostility toward slavery helped to keep the party of Lincoln from deemphasizing the issues affecting the freedmen. They were not entirely successful but pressed their views through the pulpits, the press, and Congress in an effort to transform American society into one of total racial equality. According to Howard, many saw emancipation as the first essential step in saving the Union.

Reviewed in: AHR   96 (Oct. 91) 1305

CHO   28 (Dec. 90) 693

HIS   53 (Summer 91) 827

JAH   78 (Sept. 91) 676

JSO   58 (Feb. 92) 144

304   Moorhead, James H. *American Apocalypse: Yankee Protestants and the Civil War, 1860–1869.* New Haven, Conn.: Yale University Press, 1978. xiv, 278 pp. Includes index and bibliography.

ISBN: 0-3000-2152-6   LC: 77-014360

Moorhead's study of Yankee Protestants during the Civil War was a winner of the Frank S. and Elizabeth D. Brewer Prize from the American Society of Church History. Based on a review of the popular religious press and pamphlet sermons, Moorhead's findings are that the four major northern Protestant churches—Baptist, Congregationalist, Methodist and Presbyterian—viewed the North as a redeemer nation compatible with the religious vision of the millennium. Moorhead shows how the churches spoke of "providential destiny in the context of contemporary problems" and focuses attention on their prewar millennial thought, their vision of the Civil War as a holy crusade. However, the unity and conformity desired by these northern Protestants could not sustain itself against the radical changes, including the emancipation of the slaves, in nineteenth-century American society.

Reviewed in: AHR   84 (April 79) 558

JAH   65 (March 79) 1127

VQR   54 (Autumn 78) 148

305   Nelson, Jacquelyn. *Indiana Quakers Confront the Civil War.* Indianapolis, Ind.: Indiana Historical Society, 1991. xvii, 303 pp. Includes index, bibliography, references, and appendixes.

ISBN: 0-8719-5064-2   LC: 91-8983

This study challenges the generally accepted treatment of Civil War Quakers as undeviating pacifists. It focuses on a number of Indiana Quakers who temporarily abandoned Quaker antiwar dogma. Nelson concludes that a significant number of Indiana Quakers risked "disownment" by their sect and either enlisted in the Union Army or engaged in activities that directly supported the war effort. This study begins with a general discussion of the growth and development of the Society of Friends in the United States and an examination of those Quakers who remained true to the peace testimony. Other chapters examine the contributions of those Quakers who performed military service believing that the war was a "righteous crusade to end slavery." There is also a discussion of those who remained on the homefront, marshaling their activities to support the war effort. Nelson points out that many Quaker women sent supplies to the army, ministered to the sick and imprisoned, or worked for the Sanitary Commission. Five appendixes supply additional information. One contains the names and short biographies of Quakers who enrolled in the army, and another lists the names of soldiers buried in Indiana Quaker cemeteries.

Reviewed in:	CHO	29 (Feb. 92) 955
	JAH	79 (June 92) 279

306 Shattuck, Gardiner H., Jr. *A Shield and a Hiding Place: The Religious Life of the Civil War Armies.* Macon, Ga.: Mercer University Press, 1987. x, 161 pp. : ill., photographs. Includes index, bibliography, and references.

ISBN: 0-8655-5427-32 LC: 87-11157

Shattuck maintains that the fundamentally different views of the relationship between faith and society held by the North and the South affected the outcome of the Civil War. In this book he is primarily concerned with manifestations of these differences within the military forces of the two regions. According to Shattuck, Northern evangelicals emphasized a faith that would bring about the redemption of all society. The destruction of the Confederacy was viewed as the will of God and the Union Army a divine instrument whose purpose was to accomplish this end. Because they emphasized religion's relation to society, Northern churches were quickly organized to support the war effort. On the other hand, Southern clergymen preached a more personal faith, stressing the sovereignty of God and the independence of the church from the state. The transformation and redemption of the individual was the central focus; in fact, this may be why many churches lost financial support and members during the war. The author also discusses the role and status of the clergy in the two armies as well as the impact that revivalism had on the troops. He maintains that revivals tended to boost the morale of Northern soldiers, giving them encouragement to forge ahead. Their Southern counterparts did not experience this same sense of purpose; for them, these encounters tended to perpetuate the idea that they were righteous sufferers engaged in the Lost Cause.

Reviewed in:	AHR	94 (Feb. 89) 220
	FHQ	67 (Oct. 89) 217–218
	GHQ	72 (Summer 88) 374–376
	JAH	75 (Sept. 88) 621–622
	JSO	55 (Feb. 89) 126–127
	NCH	65 (April 88) 238–239

Secession

307 Barney, William. *The Secessionist Impulse: Alabama and Mississippi in 1860*. Princeton, N.J.: Princeton University Press, 1974. xv, 371 pp. Includes bibliography.

ISBN: 0-6910-4622-0   LC: 73-016769

In trying to understand the secessionist movement, Barney analyzes party leadership and voting behavior in Alabama and Mississippi around the presidential election in 1860. It became clear after the breakup of the National Democratic party at Charleston in April of 1860 that the Breckinridge Democrats—largely young, new landowners and slaveholders—were the force behind the secessionist movement. They were threatened by the high slave prices and the scarcity of fertile land, and, having grown up viewing the North as a threatening force, saw the Union as an obstacle to their ambitions. They viewed congressional protection of slavery and the right to expand slave territory in the West as in their best interests and as protection of their future. Using both published and unpublished census returns, Barney's study contributes to an understanding of what was happening in 1860 to the South as a whole. Politically and economically, Mississippi and Alabama were the empires of the cotton aristocracy. If secession were to happen, it would have to begin here. Numerous tables on party membership by age, wealth, and slaveholdings, as well as maps of county secessionist and presidential votes, are included.

Reviewed in: AHR   80 (Dec. 85) 1395–1396
CWH   20 (Sept. 74) 276–277
GHQ   59 (Sept. 75) 171–173
HIS   37 (May 75) 518–519
RAH   3 (June 75) 221–228

308 Walther, Eric H. *The Fire-Eaters*. Baton Rouge, La.: Louisiana State University Press, 1992. xviii, 333 pp.

ISBN: 0-8071-1775-7/0-8071-1731-5(paper)   LC: 91-38321

According to Walther, little has been written about the "fire-eaters," the persistent advocates of Southern independence and the South's most fervent "apostles" of secession. He has found commonalities beyond their advocacy of secession, however, that link these men in this collective biography: Nathaniel Beverley Tucker, William Lowndes Yancey, John Anthony Quitman, Robert Barnwell Rhett, Laurence M. Kiett, Louis T. Wigfall, James D. B. De Bow, Edmund Ruffin, and William Porcher Miles. Walther has sought out and found the forces that shaped the secessionist movement: all were concerned about the growing power of the federal government, the loss of states' rights, the belief that slavery was essential to maintain the republic, and the view that ideal government could be successful only in a seceded South. All retained their individuality, however, and cannot be considered as a unit.

Secession rosette
and badge

Reviewed in:	CHO	30 (Jan. 93) 874
	LIJ	117 (July 92) 104
	NYT	(Sept. 20, 92) 464

Social Aspects

309   Bernstein, Iver. *The New York City Draft Riots: Their Significance in American Society and Politics in the Age of the Civil War.* New York: Oxford University Press, 1990. ix, 363 pp. Includes index and bibliography.

ISBN: 0-1950-5006-1   LC: 89-2858

To Bernstein, who examines the economic and political history of New York City between 1850 and 1872, the draft riots of 1863 are the center point in the city's struggles. They laid bare the undercurrents of the social and political life of the city. This work is based on the author's doctoral dissertation, which was awarded the George Washington Eggleston Prize by Yale University in 1985. The work identifies the participants, causes, and consequences of the riots. It was the complexity of political and social relationships, the Irish and German workers, the Wall Street businessmen, and the workings of City Hall—all in the context of the Civil War atmosphere—that contributed to the bloodshed and death of more than one hundred people in July 1863. The riot mattered in terms of both the life of the city and the context of the war. What began as a demonstration against the draft escalated into loyalty issues against the federal government, which in time of war was felt to be treasonous. Bernstein sees the riot as expanding into an assault against local institutions and Lincoln's Republican Party, and into a bloody race riot. The stage for riots was set by the interpretation of the Conscription Act as biased against the poor; this view magnified white fears. The riots gave sudden exposure to controversial questions—such as the authority of the federal government over local affairs and the future beyond the Emancipation Proclamation—that New Yorkers would have preferred to ignore. Numerous appendixes are attached to explain uptown social geography, occupations of the Anti-Draft Committee members, the decline in black population. Others include a list of signers of various petitions, maps that pinpoint attacks on brothels, and the location of racial murders during the riot.

Reviewed in:	AHR	96 (Dec. 91) 1614–1615
	CWH	36 (Dec. 90) 365–368
	GHQ	75 (Spring 91) 169–171
	HRN	19 (Fall 90) 6
	JAH	77 (Dec. 90) 973–974
	RAH	18 (Dec. 90) 493–499

310   Bremner, Robert Hamlett. *The Public Good: Philanthropy and Welfare in the Civil War Era.* New York: Alfred A. Knopf, 1980. xviii, 234 pp. : ill. Includes index and references.

ISBN: 0-39451-123-9   LC: 80-7623

Part of a series on the impact of the Civil War, this work by Bremner interprets the history of public welfare and private philanthropy for the 1850s through the 1880s. Nearly one-third of the book is concerned with the Civil War years. Bremner touches upon the effects of the United States Sanitary Commission, state and local groups, and the Freedman's Bureau, in their attempts to help Northern soldiers and needy blacks. In the South, however, little help was available, because resources were stretched to the limit. While wartime prosperity in the North helped to establish nonmilitary charities, the New York City draft riots laid open the reality of poverty and squalor in the city. According to Bremner, the war lent such stature to private philanthropy that groups actually competed for recognition of leadership in the public support of their projects. Higher education was an important ideal for these private charities, which were funded in large part by the wealthy. They shared the philosophy of self-help for the poor, offering charitable assistance as a ladder. Using contemporary sources, the author examines the methods of providing relief to the poor and the influence the war had on public and private giving, the need for ongoing relief, and the efforts to meet the material, educational, and spiritual needs of former slaves.

> *Reviewed in:*   AHR   86 (June 81) 653–654
> CWH   29 (June 81) 175–176
> CWT   20 (June 81) 8
> HIS   44 (Feb. 82) 278–279
> JAH   68 (Sept. 81) 394–395
> RAH   9 (Sept. 81) 377–381

311 *Divided Houses: Gender and the Civil War.* Edited by Catherine Clinton and Nina Silber. New York: Oxford University Press, 1992. xvii, 418 pp. Includes index and references.

ISBN: 0-19-507407-6   LC: 91-47143

This unique analysis of the Civil War from the perspective of Northern and Southern women's history and social history—women and children, husbands and wives—brings together eighteen articles by both new and established scholars. The essays are divided into sections: "Men at War," "Women at War," "The Southern Homefront," "The Northern Homefront," and "The War Comes Home." Considered in the work are two fundamental questions that historians have asked: Would the republic survive the division? and Would a nation founded on equal rights continue as the largest slaveholding country in the world? The Civil War touched the lives of the entire population, male and female. Political tensions in antebellum America became gender issues. Through the war years, the concept of family life was dismantled and transformed to meet the requirements of war. With the majority of Southern men engaged in the conflict, it became necessary for Southern women to play vital but untraditional roles in the economic and social aspects of the war. The essays deal with women and gender, racial and familial attitudes, change in gender roles and attitudes, and the interaction of race and class—all of which would form the beginnings of a new society.

> *Reviewed in:*   LIJ   117 (Sept. 15, 92) 74
>
> PUW   239 (Sept. 14, 92) 120

312   Foster, Gaines M. *Ghosts of the Confederacy: Defeat, the Lost Cause, and the Emergence of the New South, 1865 to 1913.* New York: Oxford University Press, 1987. x, 306 pp. : ill., photographs, tables. Includes index, bibliography, and appendixes.

ISBN: 0-19-504213-1   LC: 86-11420

Foster examines what the legacy of defeat meant to white Southerners after the war and concludes that most whites were realistic concerning the demise of the Confederacy and were not interested in sentimentalizing the "Old South." He discusses how the growth of industrialization and the displacements that it engendered, during the late nineteenth-century, aroused in many middle-class whites a desire to memorialize the Confederacy. Foster traces the beginnings of a movement, led by members of the prewar social elite during the 1870s, to revitalize the idea of the Confederacy as an antidote to postwar changes. The following decade witnessed the growth of societies such as the United Confederate Veterans and the Sons and Daughters of the Confederacy. Those involved in these groups participated in parades and attended unveiling ceremonies of monuments honoring Confederate war heroes. Foster maintains that these ceremonies emphasized the traditional values of hard work, personal loyalty, and the importance of the contributions of the common man in the effort to build a stable society. At the same time, these Lost Cause celebrations tended to validate the emerging conservative ethics of the "New South," which stressed social deference, business values, and white male supremacy. There are three appendixes. One lists Confederate monuments erected in the South between 1865 and 1912. The two others present the occupational structure of selected groups of veterans and their sons.

> *Reviewed in:*   AHR   93 (June 88) 776
>
> CHO   25 (Oct. 87) 371
>
> HRN   15 (May 87) 134

JSO   54 (Aug. 88) 509

RAH   16 (Sept. 88) 403

313 Hess, Earl J. *Liberty, Virtue, and Progress: Northerners and Their War for the Union.* New York: New York University Press, 1988. 154 pp. Includes bibliography.

ISBN: 0-8147-3451-0   LC: 88-1620

It is Hess's contention that emotion and ideology, the idealistic attitude toward American democracy, sustained Northerners, giving them a sense of purpose and a belief in the need to preserve the Union. He focuses on the values of the citizenry—and the value it placed on American identity, individualism, and self-government—that supported them through the war even after defeats and setbacks.

Reviewed in: AHR   95 (June 90) 911–912

CHO   26 (Feb. 89) 996

GHQ   73 (Spring 89) 141–142

JAH   76 (Sept. 89) 608–609

JSO   56 (Feb. 90) 125–126

314 Jimerson, Randall C. *The Private Civil War: Popular Thought during the Sectional Conflict.* Baton Rouge, La.: Louisiana State University Press, 1988. 270 pp. Includes index and bibliography.

ISBN: 0-8071-1454-5   LC: 88-11765

In the tradition of Bell I. Wiley, Jimerson draws on letters and diaries to study popular attitudes in both the North and the South. These grass-root opinions cover a great diversity of states, social classes, and military ranks; many of the letters were originally intended to be read by the participants after the war, or to break the monotony of camp life, or to add personal observations and feeling to the daily newspaper reports with which their families would be familiar. Jimerson explores four main themes: what the war meant to the writers and their reasons for fighting; the changing role of, and racial attitudes toward, African Americans in society; each side's seeing the other as the ideological enemy, and internal divisions in class and region. The letters and Jimerson's scholarship present several of the larger concepts of the Civil War in more-human dimensions than a straightforward account might.

Reviewed in: AHR   95 (June 90) 912

CWH   35 (Dec. 89) 339–340

FHQ   68 (April 90) 497–498
GHQ   73 (Fall 89) 654–656
JAH   76 (March 90) 1270–1272
JSO   56 (May 90) 361–362

315 Klement, Frank L. *Dark Lanterns: Secret Political Societies, Conspiracies, and Treason Trials in the Civil War.* Baton Rouge, La.: Louisiana State University Press, 1984. 263 pp. : ill. Includes bibliography.

ISBN: 0-8071-1174-0   LC: 84-834

Klement argues, in this revisionist book, that the secret societies that existed during the Civil War were founded by Democrats in order to defend their political and civil rights in their opposition to the Lincoln administration. The treasonable reputations of the societies were, at least in part, result of political exaggerations by Republicans (including inflated boasts of membership, near-treason rhetoric by opponents of the administration, and the conspiracies rumors that abounded). Klement recounts the actual histories of the societies, shows how they were sensationalized in newspaper and magazine exposés, and explores the treason trials.

Reviewed in: AHR   90 (Oct. 85) 1017
              CHO   22 (April 85) 1218
              JAH   72 (Dec. 85) 692
              JSO   51 (Nov. 85) 632
              RAH   13 (June 85) 217

316 Marszalek, John F. *Sherman's Other War: The General and the Civil War Press.* New York: Free Press, 1981. x, 230 pp. Includes index and bibliography.

ISBN: 0-8787-0203-2   LC: 81-9483

During the Civil War, military commanders such as General William Tecumseh Sherman decided on an ad hoc basis how to balance the demands of reporters for information with the military's need for tight security. Sherman believed that the rights of the press must be subordinated to the military effort, and he waged a continuing battle with reporters over the meaning of "freedom of the press." On occasion, he threatened to hang correspondents, banished many from his army, and finally court-marshalled *New York Herald* reporter Thomas

W. Knox. Sherman's antipress activities were so blatant that he became the constant target of reporters' retaliation. During the critical Atlanta campaign he imposed tight security measures. However, as Marszalek points out, Sherman did not attempt to censor the press when its criticism of the war effort agreed with his own views. Sherman blamed his early military failures on the press and eventually convinced himself that there was a direct relationship between press censorship and military victory. Using manuscript and newspaper sources, Marszalek presents a detailed account of General Sherman's monomania about the press. The introduction to this book provides a useful discussion on the First Amendment in wartime. As the author points out, Sherman's war within a war "exemplified the problems inherent in the universal problem of freedom of the press within a democracy at war."

> *Reviewed in:* AHR   87 (Dec. 82) 1466
> CWH   29 (March 83) 76–78
> HRN   10 (Sept. 82) 252–253
> JAH   69 (Dec. 82) 706–707
> JSO   48 (Nov. 82) 586–587
> HIS   45 (Aug. 83) 588–589

317 Mitchell, Reid. *The Vacant Chair: The Northern Soldier Leaves Home.* New York: Oxford University Press, 1993. xiv, 201 pp. : ill., photographs. Includes index and references.

ISBN: 0-19-507893-4   LC: 92-36921

Mitchell examines the ways in which "domestic imagery"—images of home and family—shaped how Northern soldiers experienced the war. He maintains that the concepts of home and family were central to both Northern culture and the ways in which Northerners integrated the experience of war into their lives. In Mitchell's view, the image of the vacant chair at the family table symbolized the family's belief that the soldier would ultimately return to the family and home and that this belief gave meaning to his absence.

> *Reviewed in:* CHO   31 (Jan. 94) 858
> NYR   41 (April 7, 94) 36

318 Rable, George. *Civil Wars: Women and the Crisis of Southern Nationalism.* Urbana, Ill.: University of Illinois Press, 1989. xv, 391 pp. : ill., tables. Includes index, bibliography, and references.

ISBN: 0-252-015975   LC: 88-23242

This is a wide-ranging study of the complex reactions of Southern women to the stress of war. Rable examines how the war under-
mined women's social identity as well as their views of the world and
themselves. The discussion is limited to an examination of white women
from the planter, yeoman, and poor white classes. The focus of Rable's
thoroughly researched study is the war years, but he also briefly treats
the antebellum and Reconstruction periods. For the most part, Rable's
findings indicate that Southern women exerted a conservative influence over society during this period. He concludes that Southern
women were reluctant to question the racial, class, and sexual mores
of their society, and that despite the challenges and opportunities presented by the conflict, these women continued to accept conventional
stereotypes. An important contribution of Rable's study is that it reveals the disintegrating effects of the war on civilian morale. The author
claims that Southern women's disillusionment contributed to the collapse of Southern nationalism and ultimately to the loss of the will to
fight.

Reviewed in: AHR   96 (April 91) 610

HRN   18 (Spring 90) 104

JSO   57 (Feb. 91) 119

HIS   53 (Winter 91) 377

RAH   18 (Sept. 90) 343

319 Silber, Nina. *The Romance of Reunion: Northerners and the
South, 1865–1900.* Chapel Hill, N.C.: University of North
Carolina Press, 1993. xii, 257 pp. : ill. Includes index, bibliog-
raphy, and references.

ISBN: 0-8078-2116-0   LC: 93-18626

This is a study of the conciliatory culture that blossomed in the
United States in the late nineteenth century. The author emphasizes the
metaphors and cultural images of reconciliation, as well as the Northern image of the South, within the context of the political, social, and
economic transformations that swept through American society in the
years following Appomattox. According to Silber, Northern anger
against the South was transformed into feelings of pity and respect; the
hostile clamor of sectionalism became the sentimental rhetoric of
reunion. She contends that Northern culture created a notion of reconciliation that romanticized and feminized Southern society. In the end,
Silber believes that the South "won the peace" with the assistance of
anxious Northerners eager to embrace the myths of the Lost Cause.

Reviewed in: CHO   31 (April 94) 1356
                NYT   (Feb. 3, 94) 29

320   Simpson, Lewis P. *Mind and the American Civil War.* Baton
      Rouge, La.: Louisiana State University Press, 1989. xiv, 110 pp.
      Includes index.

ISBN: 0-8071-1555-X   LC: 89-30159

This volume presents the 1988 Walter Lynwood Fleming Lectures in Southern History. Simpson contends that the South's secession
and New England's commitment to the Union are representative of the
particular view of what the Union meant for different sections of the
country. He centers his analysis of the war around Ralph Waldo Emerson. Emerson's allegiance to America as "the idea of emancipation"
reflected New England's ever-deepening estrangement from slaveholders as well as from a constitution that sanctioned slavery. Simpson
maintains that Emerson's concept of unionism was taken up by many
as a vehicle for the cultural conquest of the South. In the end the war
produced a modern nation that absorbed New England, the South,
and the West into a single, integrated entity.

Reviewed in: HRN   19 (Winter 91) 52
                JAH   77 (Dec. 90) 1029
                JSO   58 (May 92) 359–360
                NYR   37 (March 15, 90) 39
                RAH   20 (March 92) 65

AUTHOR AND EDITOR INDEX

References are to entry numbers.

SUBJECT INDEX

References are to entry numbers.

Abbott, Henry Livermore, 202
Abolitionists, 065, 162, 267, 278, 280
Admirals, 060
African Americans, 004, 055, 124,
 125, 136, 205, 208, 224, 249,
 260, 262, 263, 266, 269, 270,
 271, 273, 280, 283
Alabama, 009, 024, 107, 159, 255,
 307
Alabama (Confederate cruiser), 064,
 128
Alexander, Edward Porter, 192
Amazon River, 102
American Red Cross, 173
Anderson, Edward C., 201
Andersonville Prison, 054, 058
Antietam, battle of (1862), 038, 040
Antislavery movements, 055, 065,
 120, 162, 267, 280
Apalachicola River (Florida), 190
Appalachia, 117
Appomattox, 159
Arizona, 216
Arkansas, 111, 216, 293
Arkansas Cherokee Mounted Rifles,
 1st, 293
Army—Confederate States of
 America, 019, 047, 049, 053,
 054, 056, 067, 070, 077, 078,
 080, 082, 087, 090, 091, 092,
 094, 096, 105, 108, 138, 141,
 151, 160, 177, 178, 179, 181,
 183, 184, 192, 197, 216, 217,
 292, 293, 306
Army Corps of Engineers—
 Confederate States of America,
 228

Army of Northern Virginia, 181
Army of Tennessee, 075, 175, 181,
 292
Army of the Potomac, 074, 081, 093,
 110, 194,
Army—United States of America,
 019, 074, 079, 081, 088, 090,
 091, 092, 093, 108, 138, 140,
 151, 160, 177, 178, 179, 184,
 195, 209, 217, 226, 295, 296,
 298, 301, 306
Art, 001, 002, 003, 004, 138, 236
Artillery, 074, 292, 296
Assassination of Lincoln, 005, 006,
 007, 159, 168
Atlanta Campaign (1864), 010, 033,
 218, 228
Atlases, 135, 137
Averell, William Woods, 193

Barton, Clara, 173
Battle Pieces and Aspects of the War,
 169
Battlefields, 011, 035
Beauregard, Pierre, 031, 039, 175,
 192
Bellard, Alfred, 194
Belmont (Missouri) battle of (1861),
 027
Bermuda Hundred Peninsula
 (Virginia), 039
Blockades, 009, 024, 064, 122, 189,
 191
Booth, John Wilkes, 005, 007, 168
Boston, Massachusetts, 120
Booth, Edwin, 168

Ethics, 180
Ethnic relations, 164, 291
Ewell, Richard Stoddert, 080
Executions, 185
Expatriates, 102

Fiction, historical, 167
Fingal, 201
Florida, 036, 190
Foreign public opinion, 126, 127,
    131, 133, 134
Foreign relations, 095, 127, 128, 129,
    130, 131, 132, 133, 134, 201
Fort Henry, battle of (1862), 012
Fort Jackson (Louisiana), seige of
    (1862), 221
Fort Monroe (Virginia), 258
Forts, 012, 110, 221, 258
Fredericksburg (Virginia), battle of,
    194
Freedmen, 124, 125, 261, 264, 270

Gantz, Jacob, 223
Geer, Allan Morgan, 203
Gender, 311
Generals—Confederate States of
    America, 049, 053, 054, 070,
    071, 073, 077, 078, 080, 085,
    087, 089, 090, 094, 101, 103,
    106
Generals—United States of America,
    074, 076, 079, 081, 213
Georgia, 014, 033, 067, 086, 107,
    123, 159, 274
German Americans, 257
Gettysburg Address, 146, 161
Gettysburg, battle of (1863), 022,
    037, 146, 161, 233
Gettysburg, Pennsylvania, 161
Gooding, James Henry, 204
Gordon, John Brown, 067
Governors, 086
Grant, Julia Dent, 207
Grant, Ulysses Simpson, 027, 030,
    048, 076, 207
Grayson, George Washington, 069
Great Britain, 127, 128, 131, 132,
    133
Guerilla warfare, 018, 117

Habeas corpus, 119
Hamlet, 168
Hampton Roads, battle of (1862),
    017, 102
Hancock, Winfield Scott, 072
Hawks, Esther Hill, 208
Health, aspects of, 172, 174
Heyward, Pauline DeCaradeuc, 210
Historiography, 085, 117, 163, 164,
    165, 166
Homer, Winslow, 004
Hood, John Bell, 077, 175
Hotchkiss, Jedediah, 214
Hunt, Henry Jackson, 074

Illinois, 203
Illinois Volunteer Infantry Regiment,
    Twentieth, 203
Immigrants, 257, 291
Indiana, 090, 296, 305
Indiana Light Artillery Battery,
    Eighteenth, 296
Infantry, 097, 187, 194, 195, 198,
    202, 204, 222, 226, 257, 289,
    295, 298, 301
Iowa, 118, 223
Iowa Cavalry Regiment, Fourth, 223
Irish, 200
Iroquois Indians, 187
Izucar de Matamoros, Mexico, 122

Jackson, Thomas ("Stonewall"), 028,
    047, 056, 092, 101, 214
Jennison, Charles Rainsford, 297
Jayhawkers, 297
Jewish officers, 229
Johnson, Andrew, 281
Johnston, Joseph Eggleston, 033,
    073, 094, 175, 192
Jones, Joseph, 058
Journalists, 316
Julius Caesar, 168

Kansas, 297
Kansas Cavalry Regiment, Seventh,
    297
Kell, John McIntosh, 064
Kentucky, 090, 112

New York Volunteer Infantry
Regiment, One Hundred
Twenty-third, 198
New York Volunteer Infantry
Regiment, One Hundred
Twenty-second, 298
North Anna River (Virginia), battle
of, 048
North Carolina, 117, 159
Nuns, 172
Nurses, 172, 173

Oakes, Ziba B., 196
Ocean Pond, battle of, 036
Ohio, 090, 269, 286
Olmsted, Frederick Law, 174
Olustee, battle of (1864), 036
Oratory, 161
Osborn, Thomas War, 218
Overland Campaign (1864), 048

Pacifists, 305
Pea Ridge, battle of (1862), 042
Peace, 159
Pemberton, John Clifford, 053
Peninsular campaign (1862), 039,
194
Pennsylvania, 037, 161
Peru, 102
Petersburg, siege of (1864–1865),
043
Pettigrew, James Johnston, 106
Photographers, 145, 234
Photography—historiography, 231,
232, 233, 234, 235, 237, 238
Physicians, 058, 208, 211
Pillow, Gideon, 027
Pioneer Corps, 228
Plantation life, 154, 274, 276
Poetry, 003, 169
Political parties, 243, 244, 245, 246
Politics and government, 005, 067,
076, 086, 095, 100, 111, 118,
136, 142, 143, 145, 149, 150,
152, 155, 157, 158, 241, 242,
243, 244, 245, 246, 247, 248,
249, 250, 251, 252, 253, 254,
269, 281, 284, 285, 287, 288,
303, 307, 313

Polk, Leonidas, 027
Port Hudson, Siege of (1863), 026
Portraits, 002
Presidential election of 1864, 252
Presidents—biography, 063, 066,
068, 076, 084
Prisoners and prison, 117, 225, 255,
256, 257, 258, 259
Protestant churches, 304
Provost Guard, 183
Psychological aspects of war, 019
Public opinion, 006, 127, 286, 314,
319
Public welfare, 310

Quakers, 305

Race relations, 164, 249, 263, 266,
271, 272,
Railroads, 073
Reconstruction, 004, 055, 086, 109,
115, 116, 124, 125, 150, 156,
164, 263, 273, 276, 281, 282,
283, 284, 285, 286, 287, 288,
303, 319
Red Cross. See American Red Cross
Religious aspects, 162, 172, 302,
303, 304, 305, 306
Republican party, 245, 281
Richards, Almarin Cooley, 007
Richmond (Virginia), siege of, 242
Ruggles, William E., 298
Russell, Lord John, 133
Russell, Sir William Howard, 219

Sea Islands (South Carolina), 208
Seabury, Caroline, 220
Secession, 248, 302, 307, 308
Secret societies, 057, 315
Sectionalism, 153, 164, 165, 302,
319
Sermons, 302
Seward, William Henry, 095, 131
Sex roles, 311
Sexual behavior, 147
Seymour, William J., 221
Shakespeare, William, 168
Shaw, Robert Gould, 222

TITLE INDEX

References are to entry numbers.

Domenica Barbuto holds a Ph.D. in history from the State University of New York at Stony Brook and a master's in library science from C. W. Post College. She is currently an associate professor in the reference department at the Joan and Donald E. Axinn Library, Hofstra (N.Y.) University, where she is responsible for business-related reference services.

Martha Kreisel holds an M.A. in library science from the University of Chicago and an M.A. in humanities from the State University of New York at Buffalo. She is currently an assistant professor in the reference department at Axinn Library, Hofstra (N.Y.) University. She was previously a reference librarian for the Nassau (N.Y.) and Westchester (N.Y.) library systems, and art librarian at the State University College at Buffalo and at the Memphis Public Library and Information Center.

WITHDRAWN

ABI-2258